THE FIRST ADMINISTRATION

OF

THOMAS JEFFERSON

1801—1805

HISTORY OF THE UNITED STATES.

BY

HENRY ADAMS.

HISTORY

OF THE

UNITED STATES OF AMERICA

DURING THE FIRST ADMINISTRATION OF

THOMAS JEFFERSON

By HENRY ADAMS

Vol. II.

ANTIQUARIAN PRESS LTD.
New York
1962

First Published
1891-1896
by
Charles Scribner's Sons

———

Reprinted 1962
by
Antiquarian Press, Ltd.
New York, N.Y.

Edition Limited to 750 Sets

Library of Congress Catalog Card Number: 61-8054

Printed in the U.S.A.
———
NOBLE OFFSET PRINTERS, INC.
NEW YORK 3, N.Y.

CONTENTS OF VOL. II.

HISTORY OF THE UNITED STATES.

CHAPTER I.

CONGRESS expired; Monroe set sail March 8, 1803; Washington relapsed into silence; and the President and his Cabinet waited alone in the empty village, triumphing for the moment over their difficulties. Although a French prefect was actually in New Orleans, and the delivery of Louisiana to Bonaparte might from day to day be expected, not an additional soldier stood on the banks of the Mississippi, and the States of Kentucky and Tennessee were as quiet as though their flat-boats still floated down to New Orleans. A month passed before Madison or Jefferson again moved. Then the President asked his Cabinet [1] what Monroe should do in case France, as he expressed it, "refused our rights." He proposed an alliance with England, and suggested three inducements which might be offered to Great Britain : "1. Not to make a separate peace. 2. To let her

[1] Cabinet Memoranda of Mr. Jefferson, April 8, 1803; Jefferson MSS.

take Louisiana. 3. Commercial privileges." The
Cabinet unanimously rejected the second and third
concessions, but Dearborn and Lincoln were alone in
opposing the first ; and a majority agreed to instruct
Monroe and Livingston, " as soon as they find that
no arrangements can be made with France, to use all
possible procrastination with them, and in the mean
time enter into conferences with the British government, through their ambassador at Paris, to fix principles of alliance, and leave us in peace till Congress
meets ; and prevent war till next spring."

Madison wrote the instructions. If the French government, he said,[1] should meditate hostilities against
the United States, or force a war by closing the
Mississippi, the two envoys were to invite England to
an alliance, and were to negotiate a treaty stipulating
that neither party should make peace or truce without
consent of the other. Should France deny the right
of deposit without disputing the navigation, the envoys
were to make no positive engagement, but should let
Congress decide between immediate war or further
procrastination.

At no time in Talleyrand's negotiations had the
idea of war against the United States been suggested.
Of his intentions in this respect alone he had given
positive assurances.[2] Above all things both he and
the First Consul feared a war with the United States.

[1] Madison to Livingston and Monroe, April 18 and 20, 1803;
State Papers, ii. 555.

[2] Livingston to Madison, Nov. 11, 1802; State Papers, ii. 526.

They had nothing to gain by it. Madison's instructions therefore rested on an idea which had no
foundation, and which in face of the latest news
from Europe was not worth considering; yet even if
intended only for use at home, the instructions were
startling enough to warrant Virginians in doubting
their authenticity. The late Administration, British
in feeling as it was supposed to be, had never thought
an alliance with England necessary even during actual
hostilities with France, and had not hesitated to risk
the chances of independent action. Had either of
Jefferson's predecessors instructed American ministers abroad, in case of war with France, to bind
the United States to make no peace without England's consent, the consequence would have been an
impeachment of the President, or direct steps by
Virginia, Kentucky, and North Carolina, as in 1798,
tending to a dissolution of the Union. Such an
alliance, offensive and defensive, with England contradicted every principle established by President
Washington in power or professed by Jefferson in
opposition. If it was not finesse, it was an act such
as the Republicans of 1798 would have charged as
a crime.

While Madison was writing these instructions, he
was interrupted by the Marquis of Casa Yrujo,[1] who
came in triumph to say that his Government had sent
out a brigantine especially to tell the President that
the right of deposit would be restored and contin-

[1] State Papers, ii. 556.

ued till another agreement or equivalent place could be fixed upon.[1] Yrujo was instructed to thank the President for his friendly, prudent, and moderate conduct during the excitement. He sent to New Orleans the positive order of King Charles IV. to the Intendant Morales, that the right of deposit should be immediately restored ; the western people were told that their produce might go down the river as before, and thus the last vestige of anxiety was removed. In face of this action by Godoy, and of the war evidently at hand between France and England, the success of the peace policy was assured. These events in some degree explained the extraordinary nature of the new instructions of April, 1803.

Monroe was then already at Paris. In order to make clear the situation in which he found himself, the sequence of events in Europe needs to be understood.

Bonaparte's expedition to Louisiana was to have sailed at the end of September, 1802.[2] A general of division, three generals of brigade, five battalions of infantry, two companies of artillery, sixteen pieces of cannon, and three thousand muskets were to be collected at Dunkirk for shipment ; but as fast as regiments could be named they were consumed by the fiery furnace of St. Domingo. Nevertheless, all

[1] Yrujo to Madison, Notes of April 19 and 20, 1803; MSS. State Department Archives.

[2] Bonaparte to Decrès, 6 Fructidor, An x. (Aug. 24, 1802); Correspondance, viii. 4.

the orders and arrangements were gradually made. Victor was to command the forces in Louisiana; Laussat was to be prefect, charged with the civil administration. Both received elaborate written instructions; and although Victor could not sail without ships or troops, Laussat was sent on his way.

These instructions, which were never published, had extreme value for the decision of disputes which were to perturb American politics for the next twenty years. Although Victor was forced to wait in Holland for the expedition he commanded, a copy of his instructions was given to Laussat, and served to regulate his conduct as long as he remained in office. Decrès, the Minister of Marine, was the author of this paper, which unfolded the purpose that had guided France in recovering, and was to control her in administering, this vast possession. Nothing could be simpler, clearer, or more consistent with French policy than this document, which embodied so large a part of Talleyrand's political system.

The instructions began, as was natural, by a careful definition of the new province. After reciting the terms of the retrocession according to the Third Article of Berthier's Treaty, Decrès fixed the boundaries of the territory which Victor, on the part of the French republic, was to receive from the Marquis of Somoruelos, the Captain-General of Cuba.[1]

[1] Instructions secrètes pour le Capitaine-Général de la Louisiane, approuvées par le Premier Consul le 5 Frimaire, An xi. (Nov. 26, 1802); Archives de la Marine, MSS.

" The extent of Louisiana," he said, " is well determined on the south by the Gulf of Mexico. But bounded
on the west by the river called Rio Bravo from its mouth
to about the 30° parallel, the line of demarcation stops
after reaching this point, and there seems never to have
been any agreement in regard to this part of the frontier. The farther we go northward, the more undecided
is the boundary. This part of America contains little
more than uninhabited forests or Indian tribes, and the
necessity of fixing a boundary has never yet been felt
there. There also exists none between Louisiana and
Canada."

In this state of things the captain-general would
have to relieve the most remote Spanish garrisons,
in order to establish possession ; in other respects he
would be guided only by political and military interests. The western and northern boundary was of less
consequence than the little strip which separated New
Orleans from Mobile ; and to this point the instructions specially called Victor's attention. Quoting the
treaty of 1763 between Spain, Great Britain, and
France, when Florida was to become a British possession, Decrès fixed its terms as still binding upon all
the interested parties.

" ' It is agreed,' " said the seventh article of this treaty,
" ' that in future the boundaries between the States of
his Most Christian Majesty and those of his Britannic
Majesty shall be irrevocably fixed by a line drawn down
the middle of the Mississippi River from its source to the
River Iberville, and from there by a line down the middle

of that river and of the lakes Maurepas and Pontchartrain to the sea. New Orleans and the island on which it stands shall belong to France.' Such is still to-day the eastern limit of Louisiana. All to the east and north of this limit makes part of the United States or of West Florida."

Nothing could be clearer. Louisiana stretched from the Iberville to the Rio Bravo; West Florida from the Iberville to the Appalachicola. The retrocession of Louisiana by Spain to France could restore only what France had ceded to Spain in 1762. West Florida had nothing to do with the cession of 1762 or the retrocession of 1800, and being Spanish by a wholly different title could not even be brought in question by the First Consul, much as he wanted Baton Rouge, Mobile, and Pensacola. Victor's orders were emphatic : —

" There is therefore no obscurity as to our boundary on this side any more than as to that of our allies ; and although Florida belongs to Spain, Spain's right of property in this quarter will have as much interest for the Captain-General of Louisiana as though Florida were a French possession."

After thus establishing the boundary, as far as possible, in every direction, the minister treated at some length of the English claim to navigation on the Mississippi, and at last reached the general subject of the relation between Louisiana and the world about it, — the subject in which Jefferson would have found acute interest : —

"The system of this, as of all our other colonies, should be to concentrate its commerce in the national commerce; it should have in particular the aim of establishing its relations with our Antilles, so as to take the place, in these colonies, of the American commerce for all the objects whose import and export is permitted to them. The captain-general should especially abstain from every innovation favorable to strangers, who should be restricted to such communications as are absolutely indispensable to the prosperity of Louisiana and to such as are explicitly determined by the treaties."

Commercial relations with the Spanish colonies were to be encouraged and extended as much as possible, while the utmost caution was to be observed toward the United States: —

"From what has been said of Louisiana and the adjacent States, it is clear that the republic of France, being master of both banks at the mouth of the Mississippi, holds the key to its navigation. This navigation is nevertheless a matter of the highest importance for the western States of the Federal Government. . . . This is enough to show with what jealousy the Federal Government will see us take possession of Louisiana. Whatever may be the events which this new part of the continent has to expect, the arrival of the French forces should be marked there by the expression of sentiments of great benevolence for these new neighbors."

Expression of benevolent sentiments was a pleasing duty; but it was not to interfere with practical measures, both defensive and offensive: —

THE COAST OF
WEST FLORIDA
AND
LOUISIANA

(From Jeffery's American Atlas. London, 1800.)

"The greatest circumspection will be required in directing the colonial administration. A little local experience will soon enable you to discern the sentiments of the western provinces of the Federal Government. It will be well to maintain sources of intelligence in that country, whose numerous, warlike, and sober population may present you a redoubtable enemy. The inhabitants of Kentucky especially should fix the attention of the captain-general. . . . He must also fortify himself against them by alliance with the Indian nations scattered to the east of the river. The Chibackas, Choctaws, Alabamas, Creeks, etc., are represented as being entirely devoted to us. . . . He will not forget that the French government wishes peace ; but that if war takes place, Louisiana will certainly become the theatre of hostilities. . . . The intention of the First Consul is to raise Louisiana to a degree of strength which will allow him in time of war to abandon it to its own resources without anxiety ; so that enemies may be forced to the greatest sacrifices merely in attempting to attack it."

In these instructions not a word could be found which clashed with Jefferson's pacific views ; and partly for that reason they were more dangerous to the United States than if they had ordered Victor to seize American property on the Mississippi and occupy Natchez with his three thousand men. Victor was instructed, in effect, to tamper with every adventurer from Pittsburg to Natchez; buy up every Indian tribe in the Georgia and Northwestern Territory ; fortify every bluff on the western bank from St. Louis to New Orleans ; and in a few years create a series

of French settlements which would realize Madison's
"sound policy" of discouraging the United States
from colonizing the west bank.

Fortified by these instructions, the Citizen Laussat
set sail Jan. 12, 1803, and in due time arrived at New
Orleans. Victor labored in Holland to put his ships
and supplies in a condition to follow. As Laussat
sailed, another step was taken by the French government. General Bernadotte, a very distinguished republican officer, brother-in-law of Joseph Bonaparte,
was appointed minister at Washington.[1] The First
Consul had his own reasons for wishing to remove
Bernadotte, as he meant to remove Moreau; and
Washington was a place of indirect banishment for a
kinsman whose character was to be feared. Bernadotte's instructions [2] were signed by Talleyrand Jan.
14, 1803, the day after Monroe was confirmed as
special envoy to France by the Senate at Washington,
and while Laussat was still on the French coast. Although Bonaparte had been obliged to withdraw a
part of Victor's force, he still intended that the expedition should start at once with two thousand men; [3]
and its departure was to be so timed that Bernadotte
should reach Washington as Victor and his troops
reached New Orleans. Their instructions were on one

[1] Livingston to Madison, Feb. 18, 1803; State Papers, ii. 533.

[2] Talleyrand to Bernadotte, 24 Nivôse, An xi. (Jan. 14, 1803);
Archives des Aff. Étr., MSS.

[3] Correspondance, viii. 145; Bonaparte to Decrès, 28 Frimaire,
An xi. (Dec. 19, 1802).

point identical. News of the closure of the Mississippi by Morales had reached Paris, and had already caused an official protest by Livingston, when Talleyrand drew up the instructions to Bernadotte : —

" Louisiana being soon to pass into our hands, with all the rights which have belonged to Spain, we can only with pleasure see that a special circumstance has obliged the Spanish Administration to declare formally [*constater*] its right to grant or to refuse at will to the Americans the privilege of a commercial *entrepôt* at New Orleans ; the difficulty of maintaining this position will be less for us than that of establishing it. . . . Yet in any discussion that may arise on this subject, and in every discussion you may have to sustain, the First Consul wishes you to be informed of his most positive and pronounced desire to live in good understanding with the American government, to cultivate and to improve for the advantage of American commerce the relations of friendship which unite the two peoples. No one in Europe wishes the prosperity of that people more than he. In accrediting you to its Government he has given it a peculiar mark of his good disposition ; he doubts not that you will make every effort to bind closer the ties which exist between the two nations. In consequence of the firm intention which the First Consul has shown on this subject, I must recommend you to take every care to avoid whatever might alter our relations with that nation and its Government. The agents of the French republic in the United States should forbid themselves whatever might even remotely lead to a rupture. In ordinary communication, every step should show the benevolent disposition and mutual friendship which animate the chiefs and all the members of the two Governments; and when any unforeseen difficulty rises which may in any degree whatever compromise their good understanding, the simplest and most effectual means of preventing all danger is to refer its solution to the inquiry and direct judgment of the two Governments."

Talleyrand's language was more elaborate, but not clearer, than that which Bonaparte himself used to Victor.[1]

"I have no need to tell you," the First Consul wrote, "with what impatience the Government will wait for news from you in order to settle its ideas in regard to the pretensions of the United States and their usurpations over the Spaniards. What the Government may think proper to do must not be judged in advance until you have rendered an account of the state of things. Every time you perceive that the United States are raising pretensions, answer that no one has an idea of this at Paris (*que l'on n'a aucune idée de cela à Paris*); but that you have written, and that you are expecting orders."

These were the ideas held by the government of France at the moment when Jefferson nominated Monroe as a special envoy to buy New Orleans and West Florida. Jefferson's hopes of his success were small; and Livingston, although on the spot and eager to try the experiment, could only write:[2] "Do not absolutely despair." Whatever chance existed of ob-

[1] Correspondance, viii. 146; Bonaparte to Victor, 25 Frimaire, An xi. (Dec. 16, 1802).
[2] Livingston to Madison, Dec. 20, 1802; State Papers, ii. 528.

taining New Orleans seemed to lie in the possibility
that Addington's peaceful administration in England
might be driven into some act contrary to its vital
interests ; and even this chance was worth little, for
so long as Bonaparte wanted peace, he could always
keep it. England was thoroughly weary of war ; and
proved it by patiently looking on while Bonaparte,
during the year, committed one arbitrary act after
another, which at any previous time would have been
followed by an instant withdrawal of the British
minister from Paris.

On the other hand, the world could see that Bonaparte was already tired of peace; his *rôle* of beneficent
shopkeeper disgusted him, and a new war in Europe
was only a question of months. In such a case the
blow might fall on the east bank of the Rhine, on
Spain, or on England. Yet Bonaparte was in any
case bound to keep Louisiana, or return it to Spain.
Florida was not his to sell. The chance that Jefferson
could buy either of these countries, even in case of
a European war, seemed so small as hardly to be
worth considering ; but it existed, because Bonaparte
was not a man like other men, and his action could
never be calculated in advance.

The news that Leclerc was dead, that his army
was annihilated, St. Domingo ruined, and the negroes
more than ever beyond control, reached Paris and
was printed in the "Moniteur" Jan. 7, 1803, in the
same active week when Bernadotte, Laussat, and
Victor were ordered from France to America, and

Monroe was ordered from America to France.   Of all
the events of the time, Leclerc's death was the most
decisive.   The colonial system of France centred in
St. Domingo.   Without that island the system had
hands, feet, and even a head, but no body.   Of what
use was Louisiana, when France had clearly lost the
main colony which Louisiana was meant to feed and
fortify ?   The new ruler of France was not unused to
failure.   More than once he had suddenly given up
his dearest plans and deserted his oldest companions
when their success was hopeless.   He had abandoned
Paoli and Corsica with as little compunction as afterward he abandoned the army and the officers whom
he led to Egypt.   Obstinate in pursuing any object
which led to his own advancement, he was quick to
see the moment when pursuit became useless ; and
the difficulties that rose in his path toward colonial
empire were quite as great as those which had driven
him to abandon Corsica and Egypt.   Not only had
the island of St. Domingo been ruined by the war,
its plantations destroyed, its labor paralyzed, and its
population reduced to barbarism, so that the task of
restoring its commercial value had become extremely
difficult ; but other and greater objections existed to
a renewal of the struggle.   The army dreaded service
in St. Domingo, where certain death awaited every
soldier ; the expense was frightful ; a year of war
had consumed fifty thousand men and money in vast
amounts, with no other result than to prove that at
least as many men and as much money would be

still needed before any return could be expected for
so lavish an expenditure. In Europe war could be
made to support war ; in St. Domingo peace alone
could but slowly repair some part of this frightful
waste.

Leclerc was succeeded at St. Domingo by General
Rochambeau, a son of the Comte de Rochambeau,
who twenty years before had commanded the French
corps which enabled Washington to capture Corn-
wallis at Yorktown. A brave officer, but known to
be little fit for administration, Rochambeau was incompetent for the task that fell on him. Leclerc
had warned the Government that in case of his
own retirement he had no officer fit to replace
him, — least of all Rochambeau, who was next in
rank. Rochambeau wrote to inform the First Consul that thirty-five thousand men must be sent to
save the island.[1] Without a new commander-in-chief
of the highest ability, a new army was useless ;
and meanwhile Rochambeau was certain to waste the
few thousand acclimated soldiers who should form
its nucleus.

The First Consul found himself in a difficult and
even dangerous situation. Probably the colonial
scheme had never suited his tastes, and perhaps he
had waited only until he should be firm in power in
order to throw off the tutelage of Talleyrand ; but
the moment had arrived when his tastes coincided

[1] Rochambeau to Decrès, 16 Frimaire, An xi. (Dec. 7, 1802):
Archives de la Marine, MSS.

with policy. A second failure at St. Domingo would destroy his own credit, and disgust both the army and the public. Abandonment of the island was equally hazardous; for it required the abandonment of French traditions and a confession of failure. Retirement from St. Domingo was impossible, except under cover of some new enterprise; and as Europe stood, no other enterprise remained for France to undertake which would not lead her armies across the Rhine or the Pyrenees. For this undertaking Bonaparte was not yet ready; but even had he been so, it would have offered no excuse for abandoning the colonies. The ocean would still have been open, and St. Domingo within easy reach.

Only one resource remained. Bonaparte told no one his plans; but he was not a man to hesitate when decision was needed. From the day when news of Leclerc's death arrived, during the first week of January, 1803, the First Consul brooded over the means of abandoning St. Domingo without appearing to desert intentionally a policy dear to France. Talleyrand and Decrès were allowed to go on as before; they gave instructions to Bernadotte, and hurried the preparations of Victor, whom the ice and snow of Holland and the slowness of the workmen held motionless; they prepared a reinforcement of fifteen thousand men for Rochambeau, and Bonaparte gave all the necessary orders for hastening the departure of both expeditions. As late as February 5, he wrote to Decrès that fifteen thousand men had been, or were

about to be, sent to St. Domingo, and that fifteen
thousand more must be ready to sail by the middle of
August.[1] Yet his policy of abandoning the colonial
system had been already decided; for on January 30
the " Moniteur " produced Sebastiani's famous Report
on the military condition of the East, — a publication which could have no other object than to alarm
England.[2]

Livingston was quick to see the change of policy;
but although he understood as much as was known
to any one, he could not count with certainty on the
result.[3] Not even Joseph and Lucien knew what was
in their brother's mind. Talleyrand seems to have
been elaborately deceived; even as late as February
19 he was allowed to instruct General Beurnonville,
the French ambassador at Madrid, to express " the
warm satisfaction which the last acts of sovereignty
exercised by the King of Spain in Louisiana have
given to the First Consul." [4] The last act of sovereignty exercised by Spain in Louisiana had been
the closure of the Mississippi. Before Beurnonville
could obey this order, Godoy, hastening to anticipate possible interference from France, promised
Pinckney, February 28, that the *entrepôt* should be

[1] Correspondance, viii. 201; Bonaparte to Decrès, 16 Pluviôse,
An xi. (Feb. 5, 1803).

[2] Lucien Bonaparte et ses Mémoires, Th. Jung, ii. 165, *n.*;
Lanfrey's Napoleon, ii. 495.

[3] Livingston to Madison, Feb. 18, 1803; State Papers, ii. 533.

[4] Beurnonville to Talleyrand, 15 Ventôse, An xi. (March 6,
1803); Archives des Aff. Étr., MSS.

restored. King Charles's order of restitution bore
date March 1, 1803 ; Beurnonville's note, urging the
King to sustain Morales, bore date March 4, and
March 10 Don Pedro Cevallos replied to Talleyrand's
congratulation in a tone so evasive as to show that
Godoy was again deceiving the First Consul.[1] Cevallos did not say that the right of deposit had ten
days before been restored ; he contented himself with
mentioning the reasons alleged by Morales for his
act, adding at the close the empty assurance that
" in every way his Majesty prizes highly the applause
of the French government." In January, only a
few weeks before, Godoy had told Beurnonville, with
unconcealed satisfaction, that Bonaparte should not
have Florida, — although without Florida the town
of New Orleans was supposed to be of little value.
In February he snatched away what he could of
New Orleans by replacing the Americans in all their
privileges there.

Livingston plied the French officials with arguments and memorials ; but he might have spared himself the trouble, for Bonaparte's policy was already
fixed. The First Consul acted with the rapidity which
marked all his great measures. England at once took
Sebastiani's Report as a warning, and began to arm.
February 20 Bonaparte sent to the Corps Législatif
his Annual Report, or Message, which spoke of Great
Britain in language that could not be disregarded ;

[1] Cevallos to Beurnonville, March 10, 1803; Archives des Aff.
Étr., MSS.

finally, March 12, Livingston saw a melodramatic spectacle which transfixed him with surprise and excitement.[1] The scene was at Madame Bonaparte's drawing-room; the actors were Bonaparte and Lord Whitworth, the British ambassador. "I find, my Lord, your nation want war again!" said the First Consul. "No, sir," replied Whitworth; "we are very desirous of peace." "*I must either have Malta or war!*" rejoined Bonaparte. Livingston received these words from Lord Whitworth himself on the spot; and returning at once to his cabinet, wrote to warn Madison. Within a few days the alarm spread through Europe, and the affairs of St. Domingo were forgotten.

Bonaparte loved long-prepared transformation-scenes. Such a scene he was preparing, and the early days of April, 1803, found the actors eagerly waiting it. All the struggles and passions of the last two years were crowded into the explosion of April. At St. Domingo, horror followed fast on horror. Rochambeau, shut in Port au Prince, — drunken, reckless, surrounded by worthless men and by women more abandoned still, wallowing in the dregs of the former English occupation and of a half-civilized negro empire, — waged as he best could a guerilla war, hanging, shooting, drowning, burning all the negroes he could catch; hunting them with fifteen hundred bloodhounds bought in Jamaica for something more than one hundred dollars each;

[1] Livingston to Madison, March 12, 1803; State Papers, ii. 547.

wasting money, squandering men; while Dessalines
and Christophe massacred every white being within
their reach. To complete Bonaparte's work, from
which he wished to turn the world's attention, high
among the Jura Mountains, where the ice and snow
had not yet relaxed their grip upon the desolate
little Fortress and its sunless casemate, in which
for months nothing but Toussaint's cough had been
heard, Commander Amiot wrote a brief military
Report to the Minister of Marine:[1] "On the 17th
[April 7], at half-past eleven o'clock of the morning, on taking him his food, I found him dead, seated
on his chair near his fire." According to Tavernier,
doctor of medicine and *chirurgien* of Pontarlier, who
performed the autopsy, pleuro-pneumonia was the
cause of Toussaint's death.

Toussaint never knew that St. Domingo had successfully resisted the whole power of France, and
that had he been truer to himself and his color he
might have worn the crown that became the play-
thing of Christophe and Dessalines; but even when
shivering in the frosts of the Jura, his last moments
would have glowed with gratified revenge, had he
known that at the same instant Bonaparte was turn-
ing into a path which the negroes of St. Domingo
had driven him to take, and which was to lead him
to parallel at St. Helena the fate of Toussaint himself
at the Château de Joux. In these days of passion,

[1] Amiot to Decrès, 19 Germinal, An xi. (April 9, 1803); Archives de la Marine, MSS.

men had little time for thought; and the last subject
on which Bonaparte thereafter cared to fix his mind
was the fate of Toussaint and Leclerc. That the
" miserable negro," as Bonaparte called him, should
have been forgotten so soon was not surprising; but
the prejudice of race alone blinded the American
people to the debt they owed to the desperate courage of five hundred thousand Haytian negroes who
would not be enslaved.

If this debt was due chiefly to the negroes, it was
also in a degree due to Godoy and to Spain. In the
new shifting of scenes, Godoy suddenly found himself, like Toussaint eighteen months before, face to
face with Bonaparte bent on revenge. No one knew
better than Godoy the dangers that hung over him
and his country. Aware of his perils, he tried, as
in 1795, to conciliate the United States by a course
offensive to France. Not only did he restore the
entrepôt at New Orleans, but he also admitted the
claims for damages sustained by American citizens
from Spanish subjects in the late war, and through
Don Pedro Cevallos negotiated with Pinckney a convention which provided for a settlement of these
claims.[1] Although he refused to recognize in this convention the spoliations made by Frenchmen within
Spanish jurisdiction, and insisted that these were in
their nature claims against France which Spain was
not morally bound to admit, he consented to insert
an article copied from the expunged Article II. of

[1] Claims Convention, Aug. 11, 1802; State Papers, ii. 476.

the treaty of Morfontaine, reserving to the United
States the right to press these demands at a future
time.

So well pleased was Jefferson with the conduct of
Spain and the Spanish ministers, that not a complaint
was made of ill treatment; and even the conduct of
Morales did not shake the President's faith in the
friendliness of King Charles. No doubt he mistook
the motives of this friendliness, for Spain had no
other object than to protect her colonies and commerce on the Gulf of Mexico, and hoped to prevent
attack by conciliation ; while Madison imagined that
Spain might be induced by money to part with her
colonies and admit the United States to the Gulf.
In this hope he instructed Pinckney,[1] in case he
should find that Louisiana had not been retroceded
to France, to offer a guaranty of Spanish territory
west of the Mississippi as part of the consideration
for New Orleans and the Floridas. The offer was
made with a degree of cordiality very unlike the similar offer to France, and was pressed by Pinckney so
zealously that at last Cevallos evaded his earnestness
by a civil equivocation.

" The system adopted by his Majesty," said he,[2] " not
to dispossess himself of any portion of his States, de-
prives him of the pleasure of assenting to the cessions
which the United States wish to obtain by purchase. . . .

[1] Madison to Pinckney, May 11, 1802 ; State Papers, ii.
517.

[2] Cevallos to Pinckney, May 4, 1803; State Papers, ii. 557.

The United States can address themselves to the French
government to negotiate the acquisition of territories
which may suit their interest."

Cevallos knew that Bonaparte had bound himself
formally never to alienate Louisiana, and in referring
Pinckney to France he supposed himself safe. Pinckney, on the other hand, prided himself on having
helped to prevent France from gaining Florida as
well as Louisiana, and was anxious to secure West
Florida for his own credit ; while he had no idea
that Louisiana could be obtained at all.

Yet nearly a week before this note was written
Louisiana had become American property. So completely was Godoy deceived, that when April arrived
and he saw Spain again about to be dragged into
unknown perils, he never divined that he was to be
struck in America ; his anxieties rose from fear that
Spain might be dragged into a new war in Europe, in
subservience to France. He could expect to escape
such a war only by a quarrel with Napoleon, and he
knew that a war with Napoleon was a desperate
resource.

In London statesmanship had an easier game, and
played it at first simply and coolly. Rufus King
watched it with anxious eyes. He wished to escape
from the duty of expressing a diplomatic policy which
he might not approve, to a Government which had
other and heavier tasks than that of listening to his
advice or warnings. The British Ministry behaved
well to America ; for their advices from Thornton led

them to hope that the United States would, if properly supported, seize Louisiana and accept war with Bonaparte. " If you can obtain Louisiana, — well ! " said Addington to Rufus King;[1] "if not, we ought to prevent its going into the hands of France."

[1] Rufus King to Madison, April 2, 1803; State Papers, ii. 551.

CHAPTER II.

MONROE arrived in sight of the French coast April 7, 1803; but while he was still on the ocean, Bonaparte without reference to him or his mission, opened his mind to Talleyrand in regard to ceding Louisiana to the United States. The First Consul a few days afterward repeated to his Finance Minister, Barbé Marbois,[1] a part of the conversation with Talleyrand; and his words implied that Talleyrand opposed Bonaparte's scheme, less because it sacrificed Louisiana than because its true object was not a war with England, but conquest of Germany. "He alone knows my intentions," said Bonaparte to Marbois. "If I attended to his advice, France would confine her ambition to the left bank of the Rhine, and would make war only to protect the weak States and to prevent any dismemberment of her possessions; but he also admits that the cession of Louisiana is not a dismemberment of France." In reality, the cession of Louisiana meant the overthrow of Talleyrand's influence and the failure of those hopes which had led to the coalition of the 18th Brumaire.

[1] History of Louisiana, Barbé Marbois, p. 277.

Easter Sunday, April 10, 1803, arrived, and Monroe was leaving Havre for Paris, when Bonaparte, after the religious ceremonies of the day at St. Cloud, called to him two of his ministers, of whom Barbé Marbois was one.[1] He wished to explain his intention of selling Louisiana to the United States; and he did so in his peculiar way. He began by expressing the fear that England would seize Louisiana as her first act of war. " I think of ceding it to the United States. I can scarcely say that I cede it to them, for it is not yet in our possession. If, however, I leave the least time to our enemies, I shall only transmit an empty title to those republicans whose friendship I seek. They ask of me only one town in Louisiana; but I already consider the colony as entirely lost; and it appears to me that in the hands of this growing Power it will be more useful to the policy, and even to the commerce, of France than if I should attempt to keep it."

To this appeal the two ministers replied by giving two opposite opinions. Marbois favored the cession, as the First Consul probably expected him to do; for Marbois was a republican who had learned republicanism in the United States, and whose attachment to that country was secured by marriage to an American wife. His colleague, with equal decision, opposed the scheme. Their arguments were waste of breath. The First Consul said no more, and dismissed them; but the next morning, Monday, April 11, at daybreak,

[1] History of Louisiana, Barbé Marbois, p. 263.

summoning Marbois, he made a short oration of the
kind for which he was so famous : [1] —

" Irresolution and deliberation are no longer in season ;
I renounce Louisiana. It is not only New Orleans that
I cede ; it is the whole colony, without reserve. I know
the price of what I abandon. I have proved the importance I attach to this province, since my first diplomatic
act with Spain had the object of recovering it. I renounce it with the greatest regret ; to attempt obstinately
to retain it would be folly. I direct you to negotiate
the affair. Have an interview this very day with Mr.
Livingston."

The order so peremptorily given was instantly carried out ; but not by Marbois. Talleyrand, in an interview a few hours afterward, startled Livingston
with the new offer.[2]

" M. Talleyrand asked me this day, when pressing the
subject, whether we wished to have the whole of Louisiana. I told him no ; that our wishes extended only to
New Orleans and the Floridas ; that the policy of France,
however, should dictate (as I had shown in an official
note) to give us the country above the River Arkansas,
in order to place a barrier between them and Canada.
He said that if they gave New Orleans the rest would be
of little value, and that he would wish to know ' what we
would give for the whole.' I told him it was a subject
I had not thought of, but that I supposed we should not
object to twenty millions [francs], provided our citizens

[1] Marbois's Louisiana, p. 274.
[2] Livingston to Madison, April 11, 1803 ; State Papers, ii.
552.

were paid. He told me that this was too low an offer, and that he would be glad if I would reflect upon it and tell him to-morrow. I told him that as Mr. Monroe would be in town in two days, I would delay my further offer until I had the pleasure of introducing him. He added that he did not speak from authority, but that the idea had struck him."

The suddenness of Bonaparte's change disconcerted Livingston. For months he had wearied the First Consul with written and verbal arguments, remonstrances, threats, — all intended to prove that there was nothing grasping or ambitious in the American character; that France should invite the Americans to protect Louisiana from the Canadians ; that the United States cared nothing for Louisiana, but wanted only West Florida and New Orleans, — "barren sands and sunken marshes," he said; "a small town built of wood ; . . . about seven thousand souls ; " a territory important to the United States because it contained "the mouths of some of their rivers," but a mere drain of resources to France.[1] To this rhapsody, repeated day after day for weeks and months, Talleyrand had listened with his imperturbable silence, the stillness of a sceptical mind into which such professions fell meaningless ; until he suddenly looked into Livingston's face and asked : " What will you give for the whole ? " Naturally Livingston for a moment lost countenance.

[1] Livingston to Talleyrand, Jan. 10, 1803; Livingston to Bonaparte, Feb. 27, 1803; State Papers, ii. 531, 539.

The next day, Tuesday, April 12, Livingston, partly recovered from his surprise, hung about Talleyrand persistently, for his chance of reaping alone the fruit of his labors vanished with every minute that passed. Monroe had reached St. Germain late Monday night, and at one o'clock Tuesday afternoon descended from his postchaise at the door of his Paris hotel.[1] From the moment of his arrival he was sure to seize public attention at home and abroad. Livingston used the interval to make one more effort with Talleyrand :[2] —

" He then thought proper to declare that his proposition was only personal, but still requested me to make an offer; and upon my declining to do so, as I expected Mr. Monroe the next day, he shrugged up his shoulders and changed the conversation. Not willing, however, to lose sight of it, I told him I had been long endeavoring to bring him to some point, but unfortunately without effect; and with that view had written him a note which contained that request. . . . He told me he would answer my note, but that he must do it evasively, because Louisiana was not theirs. I smiled at this assertion, and told him that I had seen the treaty recognizing it. . . . He still persisted that they had it in contemplation to obtain it, but had it not."

An hour or two afterward came a note from Monroe announcing that he would wait upon Livingston in

[1] Memoir of James Monroe, 1828; Colonel Mercer's Journal, p. 55.

[2] Livingston to Madison, April 13, 1803 ; State Papers, ii. 552.

the evening. The two American ministers passed
the next day together,[1] examining papers and preparing to act whenever Monroe could be officially
presented. They entertained a party at dinner that
afternoon in Livingston's apartments, and while sitting at table Livingston saw Barbé Marbois strolling
in the garden outside. Livingston sent to invite
Marbois to join the party at table. While coffee was
served, Marbois came in and entered into conversation with Livingston, who began at once to tell him
of Talleyrand's "extraordinary conduct." Marbois
hinted that he knew something of the matter, and
that Livingston had better come to his house as
soon as the dinner company departed. The moment
Monroe took leave, Livingston acted on Marbois's
hint, and in a midnight conversation the bargain
was practically made. Marbois told a story, largely
of his own invention, in regard to the First Consul's
conduct on Easter Sunday, three days before. Bonaparte mentioned fifty million francs as his price for
Louisiana ; but as Marbois reported the offer to
Livingston, Bonaparte said : "Well! you have charge
of the Treasury. Let them give you one hundred
millions of francs, and pay their own claims, and
take the whole country." The American claims were
estimated at about twenty-five millions, and therefore
Marbois's price amounted to at least one hundred and
twenty-five million francs.

[1] Livingston to Madison, April 13, 1803; State Papers, ii. 552,
544.

Yet twenty-four or twenty-five million dollars for the whole west bank of the Mississippi, from the Lake of the Woods to the Gulf of Mexico, and indefinitely westward, was not an extortionate price, especially since New Orleans was thrown into the bargain, and indirect political advantages which could not be valued at less than the cost of a war, whatever it might be.   Five million dollars were to be paid in America to American citizens, so that less than twenty millions would come to France. Livingston could hardly have been blamed for closing with Marbois on the spot, especially as his instructions warranted him in offering ten millions for New Orleans and the Floridas alone ; but Livingston still professed that he did not want the west bank.   " I told him that the United States were anxious to preserve peace with France ; that for that reason they wished to remove them to the west side of the Mississippi ; that we would be perfectly satisfied with New Orleans and the Floridas, and had no disposition to extend across the river ; that of course we would not give any great sum for the purchase. . . . He then pressed me to name the sum."   After a little more fencing, Marbois dropped at once from one hundred millions to sixty, with estimated claims to the amount of twenty millions more.   " I told him that it was vain to ask anything that was so greatly beyond our means ; that true policy would dictate to the First Consul not to press such a demand ; that he must know it would render the present government unpopular." The conversation closed by Livingston's departure at midnight with a final protest : " I told him that I would consult Mr. Monroe, but that neither he nor I could accede to his ideas on the subject." Then he went home ; and sitting down to his desk wrote a long despatch to Madison, to record that without Monroe's help he had won Louisiana. The letter closed with some reflections : —

" As to the quantum, I have yet made up no opinion. The field open to us is infinitely larger than our instructions contemplated, the revenue increasing, and the land more than adequate to sink the capital, should we even go the sum proposed by Marbois, — nay, I persuade myself that the whole sum may be raised by the sale of the territory west of the Mississippi, with the right of sovereignty, to some Power in Europe whose vicinity we should not fear. I speak now without reflection and without having seen Mr. Monroe, as it was midnight when I left the Treasury Office, and it is now near three o'clock. It is so very important that you should be apprised that a negotiation is actually opened, even before Mr. Monroe has been presented, in order to calm the tumult which the news of war will renew, that I have lost no time in communicating it. We shall do all we can to cheapen the purchase ; but my present sentiment is that we shall buy."

A week was next passed in haggling over the price.[1] Livingston did his utmost to beat Marbois down, but without success. Meanwhile he ran some risk of

[1] Livingston to Madison, April 17, 1803 ; State Papers, ii. 554.

losing everything ; for when Bonaparte offered a favor suitors did well to waste no time in acceptance.
A slight weight might have turned the scale; a divul-
gence of the secret, a protest from Spain, a moment
of irritation at Jefferson's coquetry with England or
at the vaporings of the American press, a sudden per-
ception of the disgust which every true Frenchman
was sure sooner or later to feel at this squandering
of French territory and enterprise, — any remonstrance
that should stir the First Consul's pride or startle his
fear of posterity, might have cut short the thread of
negotiation.   Livingston did not know the secrets of
the Tuileries, or he would not have passed time in
cheapening the price of his purchase.   The voice of
opposition was silenced in the French people, but
was still so high in Bonaparte's family as to make the
Louisiana scheme an occasion for scenes so violent as
to sound like the prelude to a tragedy.

One evening when Talma was to appear in a new
rôle, Lucien Bonaparte, coming home to dress for the
theatre, found his brother Joseph waiting for him.[1]
" Here you are at last ! " cried Joseph ; " I was afraid
you might not come.   This is no time for theatre-
going ; I have news for you that will give you no
fancy for amusement.   The General wants to sell
Louisiana."

Lucien, proud of having made the treaty which
secured the retrocession, was for a moment thunder-
struck ; then recovering confidence, he said, " Come,

[1] Lucien Bonaparte et ses Mémoires, Th. Jung, ii. 121–192.

now! if he were capable of wishing it, the Chambers would never consent."

" So he means to do without their consent," replied Joseph. " This is what he answered me, when I said to him, like you, that the Chambers would not consent. What is more, he added that this sale would supply him the first funds for the war. Do you know that I am beginning to think he is much too fond of war?"

History is not often able to penetrate the private lives of famous men, and catch their words as they were uttered. Although Lucien Bonaparte's veracity was not greatly superior to that of his brother Napoleon, his story agreed with the known facts. If his imagination here and there filled in the gaps of memory, — if he was embittered and angry when he wrote, and hated his brother Napoleon with Corsican passion, these circumstances did not discredit his story, for he would certainly have told the truth against his brother under no other conditions. The story was not libellous, but Napoleonic; it told nothing new of the First Consul's character, but it was honorable to Joseph, who proposed to Lucien that they should go together and prevent their brother from committing a fault which would rouse the indignation of France, and endanger his own safety as well as theirs.

The next morning Lucien went to the Tuileries; by his brother's order he was admitted, and found Napoleon in his bath, the water of which was opaque with mixture of *eau de Cologne.* They talked for some time on indifferent matters. Lucien was timid, and dared not speak until Joseph came. Then Napoleon announced his decision to sell Louisiana, and invited Lucien to say what he thought of it.

" I flatter myself," replied Lucien, " that the Chambers will not give their consent."

" You flatter yourself ! " repeated Napoleon in a tone of surprise ; then murmuring in a lower voice, " that is precious, in truth ! " (*c'est précieux, en vérité !*)

" And I too flatter myself, as I have already told the First Consul," cried Joseph.

" And what did I answer ? " said Napoleon warmly, glaring from his bath at the two men.

" That you would do without the Chambers."

" Precisely ! That is what I have taken the great liberty to tell Mr. Joseph, and what I now repeat to the Citizen Lucien, — begging him at the same time to give me his opinion about it, without taking into consideration his paternal tenderness for his diplomatic conquest." Then, not satisfied with irony, he continued in a tone of exasperating contempt : " And now, gentlemen, think of it what you will ; but both of you go into mourning about this affair, — you, Lucien, for the sale itself ; you, Joseph, because I shall do without the consent of any one whomsoever. Do you understand ? "

At this Joseph came close to the bath, and rejoined in a vehement tone : " And you will do well, my dear brother, not to expose your project to parliamentary discussion; for I declare to you that if necessary I will put myself first at the head of the opposition which will not fail to be made against you."

The First Consul burst into a peal of forced laughter, while Joseph, crimson with anger and almost stammering his words, went on: "Laugh, laugh, laugh, then! I will act up to my promise; and though I am not fond of mounting the tribune, this time you will see me there!"

Napoleon, half rising from the bath, rejoined in a serious tone: "You will have no need to lead the opposition, for I repeat that there will be no debate, for the reason that the project which has not the fortune to meet your approval, conceived by me, negotiated by me, shall be ratified and executed by me alone, do you comprehend? — by me, who laugh at your opposition!"

Hereupon Joseph wholly lost his self-control, and with flashing eyes shouted: "Good! I tell you, General, that you, I, and all of us, if you do what you threaten, may prepare ourselves soon to go and join the poor innocent devils whom you so legally, humanely, and especially with such justice, have transported to Sinnamary."

At this terrible rejoinder Napoleon half started up, crying out: "You are insolent! I ought —" then threw himself violently back in the bath with a force which sent a mass of perfumed water into Joseph's flushed face, drenching him and Lucien, who had the wit to quote, in a theatrical tone, the words which Virgil put into the mouth of Neptune reproving the waves, —

" *Quos ego . . .*"

Between the water and the wit the three Bonapartes recovered their tempers, while the valet who was present, overcome by fear, fainted and fell on the floor. Joseph went home to change his clothes, while Lucien remained to pass through another scene almost equally amusing. A long conversation followed after the First Consul's toilet was finished. Napoleon spoke of St. Domingo. "Do you want me to tell you the truth?" said he. "I am to-day more sorry than I like to confess for the expedition to St. Domingo. Our national glory will never come from our marine." He justified what he called, in jest at Lucien, his "Louisianicide," by the same reasons he gave to Marbois and Talleyrand, but especially by the necessity of providing funds for the war not yet declared. Lucien combated his arguments as Joseph had done, until at last he reached the same point. "If, like Joseph, I thought that this alienation of Louisiana without the assent of the Chambers might be fatal to me, — to me alone, — I would consent to run all risks in order to prove the devotion you doubt; but it is really too unconstitutional and —"

"Ah, indeed!" burst out Napoleon with another prolonged, forced laugh of derisive anger. "You lay it on handsomely! Unconstitutional is droll from you. Come now, let me alone! How have I hurt your Constitution? Answer!"

Lucien replied that the intent to alienate any portion whatever of territory belonging to the Republic without the consent of the Chambers was an unconstitutional project. " In a word, the Constitution — "

" Go about your business! " broke in the guardian of the Constitution and of the national territory. Then he quickly and vehemently went on : " Constitution! unconstitutional! republic! national sovereignty! — big words! great phrases! Do you think yourself still in the club of St. Maximin ? We are no longer there, mind that! Ah, it becomes you well, Sir Knight of the Constitution, to talk so to me! You had not the same respect for the Chambers on the 18th Brumaire! "

Nothing exasperated Lucien more than any allusion to the part he took in the *coup d'état* of the 18th Brumaire, when he betrayed the Chamber over which he presided. He commanded himself for the moment; but when Napoleon went on to say with still more contempt, " I laugh at you and your national representation," Lucien answered coldly, " I do not laugh at you, Citizen Consul, but I know well what I think about it."

" *Parbleu!* " said Napoleon, " I am curious to know what you think of me : say it, quick! "

" I think, Citizen Consul, that having given your oath to the Constitution of the 18th Brumaire into my own hands as President of the Council of Five Hundred, seeing you despise it thus, if I were not your brother I would be your enemy."

" My enemy ! ah, I would 'advise you ! My enemy ! That is a trifle strong ! " cried Napoleon, advancing as though to strike his younger brother. " You my enemy ! I would break you, look, like this box ! " And so saying he flung his snuff-box violently on the floor.

In these angry scenes both parties knew that Napoleon's bravado was not altogether honest. For once, Lucien was in earnest ; and had his brother left a few other men in France as determined as he and his friend Bernadotte, the First Consul would have defied public opinion less boldly. Joseph, too, although less obstinate than his brothers, was not easily managed. According to Lucien there were further scenes between them, at one of which Joseph burst into such violence that the First Consul took refuge in Josephine's room. These stories contained nothing incredible. The sale of Louisiana was the turning-point in Napoleon's career ; no true Frenchman forgave it. A second betrayal of France, it announced to his fellow conspirators that henceforward he alone was to profit by the treason of the 18th Brumaire.

Livingston and Monroe knew nothing of all this ; they even depended upon Joseph to help their negotiation. Monroe fell ill and could not act. Over the negotiation of the treaty has always hung a cloud of mystery such as belonged to no other measure of equal importance in American history. No official report showed that the commissioners ever met in formal conference ; no protocol of their proceedings, no account of their discussions; no date when their agreement was made, was left on record. Both the treaty itself and the avowals of Livingston gave evidence that at the end all parties acted in haste. If it were not for a private memorandum by Monroe, — not sent to the Government, but preserved among his private papers, — the course of negotiation could not be followed.

A fortnight passed after Monroe's arrival without advancing matters a step. This period of inaction seems to have been broken by the First Consul. April 23 he drew up a "*Projet* of a Secret Convention,"[1] which he gave to Marbois and which set forth that to prevent misunderstandings about the matters of discussion mentioned in Articles II. and V. of the Morfontaine treaty, and also to strengthen friendly relations, the French republic was to cede its rights over Louisiana ; and " in consequence of the said cession, Louisiana, its territory, and its proper dependencies shall become part of the American Union, and shall form successively one or more States on the terms of the Federal Constitution ; " in return the United States were to favor French commerce in Louisiana, and give it all the rights of American commerce, with perpetual *entrepôts* at six points on the Mississippi, and a corresponding perpetual right of navigation ; further, they were to assume all debts due to American citizens under the treaty of Morfontaine ; and, finally, were to pay a hundred million

[1] Correspondance, viii. 289.

francs to France. With this *projet* Marbois went by appointment, at two o'clock, April 27, to Monroe's lodgings, where the three gentlemen had an informal meeting, of which no other record is known to exist than Monroe's memoranda.[1] Monroe himself was too unwell to sit at the table, and reclined on a sofa throughout the discussion. Marbois produced Bonaparte's *projet*, and after admitting that it was hard and unreasonable, presented a substitute of his own which he thought the First Consul would accept.

Livingston tried to give precedence to the claims; he wanted to dispose of them first, in case the cession should fail; but after pressing the point as far as he could, he was overruled by Monroe, and Livingston took Marbois's project for consideration. The two American commissioners passed a day in working over it. Livingston drafted a claims convention, and it was drawn, as he thought, "with particular attention."[2] Monroe thought differently. "My colleague took Mr. Marbois's project with him, and brought me one, very loosely drawn, founded on it."[3] Monroe made a draft of his own which was certainly not creditable to his legal or diplomatic skill, and which began by adopting an oversight contained in Bonaparte's draft, according to which the cancelled Article

[1] Monroe's Memoranda, Monroe MSS., State Department Archives.

[2] Livingston to Madison, May 3, 1804; MSS. State Department Archives.

[3] Monroe's Memoranda, Monroe MSS., State Department Archives.

II. of the treaty of Morfontaine was made a foundation
of the new convention.[1]   " We called on Mr. Marbois
the 29th, and gave him our project, which was read
to him and discussed. We proposed to offer fifty
millions to France, and twenty millions on account
of her debt to the citizens of the United States,
making seventy in the whole." Marbois replied that
he would proceed only on the condition that eighty
millions were accepted as the price. Then at last
the American commissioners gave way; and with this
change Marbois took their *projet* for reference to the
First Consul the next morning.

The 30th of April was taken by Marbois for consultation with the First Consul. May 1 Monroe was
presented at the Tuileries, and dined there with
Livingston ; but Bonaparte said nothing of their
business, except that it should be settled. The same
evening the two envoys had a final discussion with
Marbois. " May 2, we actually signed the treaty and
convention for the sixty million francs to France, in
the French language ; but our copies in English not
being made out, we could not sign in our language.
They were however prepared, and signed in two or
three days afterward. The convention respecting
American claims took more time, and was not signed
till about the 8th or 9th." All these documents were
antedated to the 30th April.[2]

[1] Draft of Convention in Monroe's writing, Monroe MSS.,
State Department Archives.

[2] State Papers, ii. 507-509.

The first object of remark in this treaty was the absence of any attempt to define the property thus bought and sold. " Louisiana with the same extent that is now in the hands of Spain, and that it had when France possessed it, and such as it should be after the treaties subsequently entered into between Spain and other States," — these words, taken from Berthier's original treaty of retrocession, were convenient for France and Spain, whose governments might be supposed to know their own boundaries; but all that the United States government knew upon the subject was that Louisiana, as France possessed it, had included a part of Florida and the whole Ohio Valley as far as the Alleghany Mountains and Lake Erie. The American commissioners at first insisted upon defining the boundaries, and Marbois went to the First Consul with their request. He refused.[1] " If an obscurity did not already exist, it would perhaps be good policy to put one there." He intentionally concealed the boundary he had himself defined, a knowledge of which would have prevented a long and mortifying dispute. Livingston went to Talleyrand for the orders given by Spain to the Marquis of Somoruelo, by France to Victor and Laussat. " What are the eastern bounds of Louisiana ? " asked Livingston. " I do not know," replied Talleyrand ; " you must take it as we received it." " But what did you mean to take ? " urged Livingston. " I do not know," repeated Talleyrand. " Then you mean

[1] Marbois, Louisiana, pp. 283, 286.

that we shall construe it our own way?" "I can give you no direction. You have made a noble bargain for yourselves, and I suppose you will make the most of it," was the final reply of Talleyrand. Had Livingston known that Victor's instructions, which began by fixing the boundaries in question, were still in Talleyrand's desk, the answer would have been the same.

One point alone was fixed, — the Floridas were not included in the sale; this was conceded on both sides. In his first conversation with Marbois, Livingston made a condition that France should aid him in procuring these territories from Spain.[1] "I asked him, in case of purchase, whether they would stipulate that France would never possess the Floridas, and that she would aid us to procure them, and relinquish all right that she might have to them. He told me that she would go thus far." Several days later, Marbois repeated this assurance to Monroe, saying that the First Consul authorized him, besides offering Louisiana, "to engage his support of our claim to the Floridas with Spain."[2] Yet when the American commissioners tried to insert this pledge into the treaty, they failed. Bonaparte would give nothing but a verbal promise to use his good offices with Spain.

Besides the failure to dispose of these two points, which were in reality but one, the treaty contained a

[1] Livingston to Madison, April 13, 1803; State Papers, ii. 552.
[2] Monroe to Madison, April 19, 1803; State Department Archives.

positive provision, Article III., taken from Bonaparte's *projet*, with slight alteration, that "the inhabitants of the ceded territory shall be incorporated in the Union of the United States, and admitted as soon as possible, according to the principles of the Federal Constitution, to the enjoyment of all the rights, advantages, and immunities of citizens of the United States." On republican principles of the Virginian school, only the States themselves could by a new grant of power authorize such an incorporation. Article III. violated Madison's instructions, which forbade the promise.[1] "To incorporate the inhabitants of the hereby-ceded territory with the citizens of the United States," said these instructions, "being a provision which cannot now be made, it is to be expected, from the character and policy of the United States, that such incorporation will take place without unnecessary delay." The provision, which Madison said could not be made, was nevertheless made by Livingston and Monroe.

Embarrassing as these omissions or provisions were, they proved not so much that the treaty was carelessly drawn, as that the American negotiators were ready to stipulate whatever was needed for their purpose. Other portions of the treaty were not to be defended on that excuse. The price stipulated for Louisiana was sixty million francs, in the form of United States six-per-cent bonds, representing a capital of $11,250,000.

[1] Madison to Livingston and Monroe, March 2, 1803; State Papers, ii. 540.

Besides this sum of eleven and a quarter million dollars, the United States government was to assume and pay the debts due by France to American citizens, estimated at twenty million francs, or, at the same rate of exchange, $3,750,000, — making fifteen million dollars in all as the price to be paid. Livingston himself drew the claims convention with what he supposed to be particular attention; but it was modified by Monroe, and still further altered by Marbois. "The moment was critical; the question of peace or war was in the balance; and it was important to come to a conclusion before either scale preponderated. I considered the convention as a trifle compared with the other great object," avowed Livingston; "and as it had already delayed us many days, I was ready to take it under any form." [1]   The claims convention was not signed till nearly a week after the signature of the treaty of cession. The form in which Livingston took it showed that neither he nor Monroe could have given careful attention to the subject; for not only did the preamble declare that the parties were acting in compliance with Article II. of the treaty of Morfontaine, — an Article which had been formally struck out by the Senate, cancelled by Bonaparte, and the omission ratified by the Senate and President since Livingston's residence at Paris; not only did the claims specified fail to embrace all the cases provided for by the treaty of 1800, which

[1] Livingston to Madison, May 3, 1804; View of the Claims, etc., by a Citizen of Baltimore, p. 75.

this convention was framed to execute; not only were the specifications arbitrary, and even self-contradictory, — but the estimate of twenty million francs was far below the amount of the claims admitted in principle; no rule of apportionment was provided, and, worst of all, the right of final decision in every case was reserved to the French government. The meaning of this last provision might be guessed from the notorious corruption of Talleyrand and his band of confidential or secret agents.

Doubtless Livingston was right in securing his main object at any cost; but could he have given more time to his claims convention, he would perhaps have saved his own reputation and that of his successor from much stain, although he might have gained no more than he did for his Government. In the two conventions of 1800 and 1803 the United States obtained two objects of the utmost value, — by the first, a release from treaty obligations which, if carried out, required war with England; by the second, the whole west bank of the Mississippi River and the island of New Orleans, with all the incidental advantages attached. In return for these gains the United States government promised not to press the claims of its citizens against the French government beyond the amount of three million seven hundred and fifty thousand dollars, which was one fourth part of the price paid for Louisiana. The legitimate claims of American citizens against France amounted to many million dollars; in the result, certain favored

claimants received three million seven hundred and
fifty thousand dollars less their expenses, which reduced the sum about one half.

The impression of diplomatic oversight was deep-
ened by the scandals which grew out of the distribu-
tion of the three million seven hundred and fifty
thousand dollars which the favored claimants were
to receive. Livingston's diplomatic career was poisoned by quarrels over this money.[1] That the French
government acted with little concealment of venality
was no matter of surprise; but that Livingston should
be officially charged by his own associates with favor-
itism and corruption, — "imbecility of mind and a
childish vanity, mixed with a considerable portion of
duplicity," — injured the credit of his Government;
and the matter was not bettered when he threw back
similar charges on the Board of Commissioners, or
when at last General Armstrong, coming to succeed
him, was discredited by similar suspicions. Considering how small was the amount of money distributed,
the scandal and corruption surpassed any other experience of the national government.

Livingston's troubles did not end there. He could
afford to suffer some deduction from his triumph; for
he had achieved the greatest diplomatic success recorded in American history. Neither Franklin, Jay,
Gallatin, nor any other American diplomatist was so
fortunate as Livingston for the immensity of his results compared with the paucity of his means. Other

[1] View of the Claims, etc., by a Citizen of Baltimore.   1829.

treaties of immense consequence have been signed by
American representatives, — the treaty of alliance
with France; the treaty of peace with England which
recognized independence; the treaty of Ghent; the
treaty which ceded Florida; the Ashburton treaty;
the treaty of Guadeloupe Hidalgo, — but in none of
these did the United States government get so much
for so little. The annexation of Louisiana was an
event so portentous as to defy measurement; it gave
a new face to politics, and ranked in historical importance next to the Declaration of Independence
and the adoption of the Constitution, — events of
which it was the logical outcome; but as a matter
of diplomacy it was unparalleled, because it cost
almost nothing.

The scandalous failure of the claims convention
was a trifling drawback to the enjoyment of this
unique success; but the success was further embittered by the conviction that America would give the
honor to Monroe. Virginia was all-powerful. Livingston was unpopular, distrusted, not liked even by
Madison; while Monroe, for political reasons, had
been made a prominent figure. Public attention had
been artificially drawn upon his mission; and in consequence, Monroe's name grew great, so as almost
to overshadow that of Madison, while Livingston
heard few voices proclaiming his services to the
country. In a few weeks Livingston began to see
his laurels wither, and was forced to claim the credit
that he thought his due. Monroe treated him less

generously than he might have done, considering that
Monroe gained the political profit of the success.[1]
Acknowledging that his own share was next to nothing in the negotiation, he still encouraged the idea
that Livingston's influence had been equally null.
This view was doubtless correct, but if universally
applied in history, would deprive many great men of
their laurels.   Monroe's criticism helped only to di-
minish the political chances of a possible rival who
had no Virginia behind him to press his preferment
and cover his mistakes.

[1] Livingston to Madison, Nov. 15, 1803; State Papers, ii. 573.
Diary of John Quincy Adams, v. 433.   Memoir of James Monroe, 1828.

CHAPTER III.

WHEN Marbois took the treaty to the First Consul, Bonaparte listened to its provisions with lively interest; and on hearing that twenty millions were to be employed in paying claims, — a use of money which he much disliked, — he broke out: " Who authorized you to dispose of the money of the State ? I want to have these twenty millions paid into the Treasury. The claimants' rights cannot come before our own." [1] His own *projet* had required the Americans to assume these claims, — which was, in fact, the better plan. Marbois's alteration turned the claims into a French job. Perhaps Bonaparte was not averse to this; for when Marbois reminded him that he had himself fixed the price at fifty millions, whereas the treaty gave him sixty, and settled the claims besides, — " It is true," he said; " the negotiation leaves me nothing to wish. Sixty millions for an occupation that will not perhaps last a day ! I want France to have the good of this unexpected capital, and to employ it in works of use to her marine." On the spot he dictated a decree for the construction of five canals. This excellent use of the money seemed

[1] Marbois's Louisiana, pp. 311, 312.

inconsistent with Lucien's remark that it was wanted for war, — but the canals were never built or begun; and the sixty millions were spent, to the last centime, in preparations for an impracticable descent on England.

Yet money was not the inducement which caused Bonaparte to sell Louisiana to the United States. The Prince of Peace would at any time have given more money, and would perhaps have been willing, as he certainly was able, to pay it from his private means rather than allow the United States to own Louisiana. In other respects, the sale needed explanation, since it contradicted the First Consul's political theories and prejudices. He had but two rooted hatreds. The deeper and fiercer of these was directed against the republic, — the organized democracy, and what he called ideology, which Americans knew in practice as Jeffersonian theories; the second and steadier was his hatred of England as the chief barrier to his military omnipotence. The cession of Louisiana to the United States contradicted both these passions, making the ideologists supreme in the New World, and necessarily tending in the end to strengthen England in the Old. Bonaparte had been taught by Talleyrand that America and England, whatever might be their mutual jealousies, hatreds, or wars, were socially and economically one and indivisible. Barely ten years after the Revolutionary War had closed, and at a time when the wounds it made were still raw, Talleyrand remarked: "In every part of

America through which I have travelled, I have not found a single Englishman who did not feel himself to be an American ; not a single Frenchman who did not find himself a stranger." Bonaparte knew that England held the monopoly of American trade, and that America held the monopoly of democratic principles ; yet he did an act which was certain to extend British trade and fortify democratic principles.

This contradiction was due to no change in Bonaparte's opinions ; these remained what they were. At the moment when talking to Marbois about " those republicans whose friendship I seek," he was calculating on the chance that his gift would one day prove their ruin. " Perhaps it will also be objected to me," he said,[1] " that the Americans may in two or three centuries be found too powerful for Europe ; but my foresight does not embrace such remote fears. Besides, we may hereafter expect rivalries among the members of the Union. The confederations that are called perpetual last only till one of the contracting parties finds it to its interest to break them. . . . It is to prevent the danger to which the colossal power of England exposes us that I would provide a remedy." The colossal power of England depended on her navy, her colonies, and her manufactures. Bonaparte proposed to overthrow it by shattering beyond repair the colonial system of France and Spain ; and even this step was reasonable compared with what followed. He expected to check the power of England by giving

[1] Marbois's Louisiana, p. 276.

Louisiana to the United States, — a measure which opened a new world to English commerce and manufactures, and riveted England's grasp on the whole American continent, inviting her to do what she afterward did, — join hands with the United States in revolutionizing Mexico and South America in her own interests. As though to render these results certain, after extending this invitation to English commerce and American democracy, Bonaparte next invited a war with England, which was certain to drive from the ocean every ship belonging to France or Spain, — a war which left even the United States at England's mercy.

Every detail that could explain Bonaparte's motives becomes interesting in a matter so important to American history. Certain points were clear. Talleyrand's colonial and peace policy failed. Resting on the maintenance of order in Europe and the extension of French power in rivalry with the United States and England in America, it was a statesmanlike and honorable scheme, which claimed for the Latin races what Louis XIV. tried to gain for them; but it had the disadvantage of rousing hostility in the United States, and of throwing them into the arms of England. For this result Talleyrand was prepared. He knew that he could keep peace with England, and that the United States alone could not prevent him from carrying out his policy. Indeed, Madison in his conversation with Pichon invited such action, and Jefferson had no means of resisting it; but from

the moment when St. Domingo prevented the success
of the scheme, and Bonaparte gained an excuse for
following his own military instincts, the hostility of
the United States became troublesome.   President
Jefferson had chiefly reckoned on this possibility as
his hope of getting Louisiana ; and slight as the
chance seemed, he was right.

This was, in effect, the explanation which Talleyrand officially wrote to his colleague Decrès, communicating a copy of the treaty, and requesting him to
take the necessary measures for executing it.[1]

" The wish to spare the North American continent the
war with which it was threatened, to dispose of different
points in dispute between France and the United States
of America, and to remove all the new causes of misunderstanding which competition and neighborhood might
have produced between them ; the position of the French
colonies ; their want of men, cultivation, and assistance ;
in fine, the empire of circumstances, foresight of the future, and the intention to compensate by an advantageous
arrangement for the inevitable loss of a country which
war was going to put at the mercy of another nation, —
all these motives have determined the Government to pass
to the United States the rights it had acquired from Spain
over the sovereignty and property of Louisiana."

Talleyrand's words were always happily chosen,
whether to reveal or to conceal his thoughts.   This
display of reasons for an act which he probably
preferred to condemn, might explain some of the

[1] Talleyrand to Decrès, 4 Prairial, An xi. (May 24, 1803);
Archives des Aff. Étr., MSS.

First Consul's motives in .ceding Louisiana to the
United States; but it only confused another more per-
plexing question. Louisiana did not belong to France,
but to Spain. The retrocession had never been completed ; the territory was still possessed, garrisoned,
and administered by Don Carlos IV.; until actual delivery was made, Spain might yet require that the conditions of retrocession should be rigorously performed.
Her right in the present instance was complete, because she held as one of the conditions precedent to
the retrocession a solemn pledge from the First Consul never to alienate Louisiana. The sale of Louisiana
to the United States was trebly invalid : if it were
French property, Bonaparte could not constitutionally
alienate it without the consent of the Chambers ; if
it were Spanish property, he could not alienate it at
all ; if Spain had a right of reclamation, his sale was
worthless. In spite of all these objections the alienation took place ; and the motives which led the First
Consul to conciliate America by violating the Constitution of France were perhaps as simple as he represented them to be ; but no one explained what
motives led Bonaparte to break his word of honor
and betray the monarchy of Spain.

Bonaparte's evident inclination toward a new war
with England greatly distressed King Charles IV.
Treaty stipulations bound Spain either to take part
with France in the war, or to pay a heavy annual
subsidy ; and Spain was so weak that either alternative seemed fatal. The Prince of Peace would have

liked to join England or Austria in a coalition against
Bonaparte; but he knew that to this last desperate
measure King Charles would never assent until
Bonaparte's hand was actually on his crown; for no
one could reasonably doubt that within a year after
Spain should declare an unsuccessful war on France,
the whole picturesque Spanish court — not only Don
Carlos IV. himself and Queen Luisa, but also the
Prince of Peace, Don Pedro Cevallos, the Infant Don
Ferdinand, and the train of courtiers who thronged
La Granja and the Escorial — would be wandering
in exile or wearing out their lives in captivity. To
increase the complication, the young King of Etruria
died May 27, 1803, leaving an infant seated upon
the frail throne which was sure soon to disappear
at the bidding of some military order countersigned
by Berthier.

In the midst of such anxieties, Godoy heard a public rumor that Bonaparte had sold Louisiana to the
United States; and he felt it as the death-knell of
the Spanish empire. Between the energy of the
American democracy and the violence of Napoleon
whom no oath bound, Spain could hope for no
escape. From New Orleans to Vera Cruz was but a
step; from Bayonne to Cadiz a winter campaign of
some five or six hundred miles. Yet Godoy would
probably have risked everything, and would have
thrown Spain into England's hands, had he been
able to control the King and Queen, over whom Bonaparte exercised the influence of a master. On learn-

ing the sale of Louisiana, the Spanish government
used language almost equivalent to a rupture with
France. The Spanish minister at Paris was ordered
to remonstrate in the strongest terms against the step
which the First Consul had taken behind the back of
the King his ally.[1]

"This alienation," wrote the Chevalier d'Azara to
Talleyrand, "not only deranges from top to bottom the
whole colonial system of Spain, and even of Europe, but
is directly opposed to the compacts and formal stipulations agreed upon between France and Spain, and to the
terms of the cession in the treaty of Tuscany ; and the
King my master brought himself to give up the colony
only on condition that it should at no time, under no
pretext, and in no manner, be alienated or ceded to any
other Power."

Then, after reciting the words of Gouvion St.-Cyr's
pledge, the note continued : —

"It is impossible to conceive more frankness or loyalty
than the King has put into his conduct toward France
throughout this affair. His Majesty had therefore the
right to expect as much on the part of his ally, but un-
happily finds himself deceived in his hopes by the sale
of the said colony. Yet trusting always in the straight-
forwardness and justice of the First Consul, he has ordered me to make this representation, and to protest
against the alienation, hoping that it will be revoked, as
manifestly contrary to the treaties and to the most solemn
anterior promises."

[1] D'Azara to Talleyrand, June 6, 1803; Archives des Aff. Étr.,
MSS.

Not stopping there, the note also insisted that Tuscany should be evacuated by the French troops, who were not needed, and had become an intolerable burden, so that the country was reduced to the utmost misery. Next, King Charles demanded that Parma and Piacenza should be surrendered to the King of Etruria, to whom they belonged as the heir of the late Duke of Parma. Finally, the note closed with a complaint even more grave in substance than any of the rest: —

" The King my master could have wished also a little more friendly frankness in communicating the negotiations with England, and especially in regard to the dispositions of the Northern courts, guarantors of the treaty of Amiens; but as this affair belongs to negotiations of another kind, the undersigned abstains for the moment from entering into them, reserving the right to do so on a better occasion."

Beurnonville, the French minister at Madrid, tried to soothe or silence the complaints of Cevallos; but found himself only silenced in return. The views of the Spanish secretary were energetic, precise, and not to be met by argument.[1] " I have not been able to bring M. Cevallos to any moderate, conciliatory, or even calm expression," wrote Beurnonville to Talleyrand; " he has persistently shown himself inaccessible to all persuasion." The Prince of Peace was no more manageable than Cevallos: " While substituting

[1] Beurnonville to Talleyrand, 24 Prairial, An xi. (June 13, 1803); Archives des Aff. Étr., MSS.

a soft and pliant tone for the sharpest expressions,
and presenting under the appearance of regret what
had been advanced to me with the bitterness of reproach, the difference between the Prince's conduct
and that of M. Cevallos is one only in words." Both
of them said, what was quite true, that the United
States would not have objected to the continued possession of Louisiana by Spain, and that France had
greatly exaggerated the dispute about the *entrepôt.*

" The whole matter reduces itself to a blunder (*gau-
cherie*) of the Intendant," said Cevallos ; " it has been
finally explained to Mr. Jefferson, and friendship is restored.   On both sides there has been irritation, but not
a shadow of aggression ; and from the moment of coming
to an understanding, both parties see that they are at
bottom of one mind, and mutually very well disposed
toward each other.   Moreover, it is quite gratuitous to
assume that Louisiana is so easy to take in the event of
a war, either by the Americans or by the English.   The
first have only militia, — very considerable, it is true, but
few troops of the line ; while Louisiana, at least for the
moment, has ten thousand militia-men, and a body of
three thousand five hundred regular troops.   As for the
English, they cannot seriously have views on a province
which is impregnable to them ; and all things considered, it would be no great calamity if they should take
it.   The United States, having a much firmer hold on the
American continent, should they take a new enlargement,
would end by becoming formidable, and would one day
disturb the Spanish possessions.   As for the debts due
to Americans, Spain has still more claim to an arrangement of that kind ; and in any case the King, as Bona-

parte must know, would have gladly discharged all the debts contracted by France, and perhaps even a large instalment of the American claim, in order to recover an old domain of the crown. Finally, the intention which led the King to give his consent to the exchange of Louisiana was completely deceived. This intention had been to interpose a strong dyke between the Spanish colonies and the American possessions; now, on the contrary, the doors of Mexico are to stay open to them."

To these allegations, which Beurnonville called "insincere, weak, and ill-timed," Cevallos added a piece of evidence which, strangely enough, was altogether new to the French minister, and reduced him to confusion: it was Gouvion St.-Cyr's letter, pledging the First Consul never to alienate Louisiana.

When Beurnonville's despatch narrating these interviews reached Paris, it stung Bonaparte to the quick, and called from him one of the angry avowals with which he sometimes revealed a part of the motives that influenced his strange mind. Talleyrand wrote back to Beurnonville, June 22, a letter which bore the mark of the First Consul's hand.

"In one of my last letters," he began,[1] "I made known to you the motives which determined the Government to give up Louisiana to the United States. You will not conceal from the Court of Madrid that one of the causes which had most influence on this determination was discontent at learning that Spain, after having promised to sustain the measures taken by the Intendant of

[1] Talleyrand to Beurnonville, 3 Messidor, An xi. (June 22, 1803); Archives des Aff. Étr., MSS.

New Orleans, had nevertheless formally revoked them.
These measures would have tended to free the capital of
Louisiana from subjection to a right of deposit which was
becoming a source of bickerings between the Louisianians
and Americans. We should have afterward assigned to
the United States, in conformity to their treaty with Spain,
another place of deposit, less troublesome to the colony
and less injurious to its commerce ; but Spain put to flight
all these hopes by confirming the privileges of the Americans at New Orleans, — thus granting them definitively
local advantages which had been at first only temporary.
The French government, which had reason to count on
the contrary assurance given in this regard by that of
Spain, had a right to feel surprise at this determination ;
and seeing no way of reconciling it with the commercial
advantages of the colony and with a long peace between
the colony and its neighbors, took the only course which
actual circumstances and wise prevision could suggest."

These assertions contained no more truth than
those which Cevallos had answered. Spain had not
promised to sustain the Intendant, nor had she revoked the Intendant's measures after, but before, the
imagined promise ; she had not confirmed the American privileges at New Orleans, but had expressly reserved them for future treatment. On the other
hand, the restoration of the deposit was not only
reconcilable with peace between Louisiana and the
United States, but the whole world knew that the risk
of war rose from the threat of disturbing the right
of deposit. The idea that the colony had become
less valuable on this account was new. France had

begged for the colony with its American privileges, and meaning to risk the chances of American hostility ; but if these privileges were the cause of selling the colony to the Americans, and if, as Talleyrand implied, France could and would have held Louisiana if the right of deposit at New Orleans had been abolished and the Americans restricted to some other spot on the river-bank, fear of England was not, as had been previously alleged, the cause of the sale. Finally, if the act of Spain made the colony worthless, why was Spain deprived of the chance to buy it back ?

The answer was evident. The reason why Bonaparte did not keep his word to Don Carlos IV. was that he looked on Spain as his own property, and on himself as representing her sovereignty. The reasons for which he refused to Spain the chance to redeem the colony, were probably far more complicated. The only obvious explanation, assuming that he still remembered his pledge, was a wish to punish Spain.

After all these questions were asked, one problem still remained. Bonaparte had reasons for not returning the colony to Spain ; he had reasons, too, for giving it to the United States, — but why did he alienate the territory from France ? Fear of England was not the true cause. He had not to learn how to reconquer Louisiana on the Danube and the Po. At one time or another Great Britain had captured nearly all the French colonies in the New World, and had been forced not only to disgorge conquests, but to abandon possessions; until of the three great European Powers in America, England was weakest. Any attempt to regain old ascendency by conquering Louisiana would have thrown the United States into the hands of France; and had Bonaparte anticipated such an act, he should have helped it. That Great Britain should waste strength in conquering Louisiana in order to give it to the United States, was an idea not to be gravely argued. Jefferson might, indeed, be driven into an English alliance in order to take Louisiana by force from France or Spain; but this danger was slight in itself, and might have been removed by the simple measure of selling only the island of New Orleans, and by retaining the west bank, which Jefferson was ready to guarantee. This was the American plan; and the President offered for New Orleans alone about half the price he paid for all Louisiana.[1] Still, Bonaparte forced the west bank on Livingston. Every diplomatic object would have been gained by accepting Jefferson's *projet* of a treaty, and signing it without the change of a word. Spain would have been still in some degree protected; England would have been tempted to commit the mistake of conquering the retained territory, and thereby the United States would have been held in check; the United States would have gained all the stimulus their ambition could require for many years

[1] Madison to Livingston and Monroe, March 2, 1803; State Papers, ii. 543.

to come; and what was more important to Bonaparte,
France could not justly say that he had illegally and
ignobly sold national territory except for a sufficient
and national object.

The real reasons which induced Bonaparte to alienate the territory from France remained hidden in
the mysterious processes of his mind. Perhaps he
could not himself have given the true explanation of
his act. Anger with Spain and Godoy had a share
in it, as he avowed through Talleyrand's letter of
June 22; disgust for the sacrifices he had made, and
impatience to begin his new campaigns on the Rhine,
— possibly a wish to show Talleyrand that his policy
could never be revived, and that he had no choice
but to follow into Germany, — had still more to do
with the act. Yet it is also reasonable to believe
that the depths of his nature concealed a wish to hide
forever the monument of a defeat. As he would have
liked to blot Corsica, Egypt, and St. Domingo from
the map, and wipe from human memory the record of
his failures, he may have taken pleasure in flinging
Louisiana far off, and burying it forever from the
sight of France in the bosom of the only government
which could absorb and conceal it.

For reasons of his own, which belonged rather to
military and European than to American history,
Bonaparte preferred to deal with Germany before
crossing the Pyrenees; and he knew that meanwhile
Spain could not escape. Godoy on his side could
neither drag King Charles into a war with France,

nor could he provide the means of carrying on such
a war with success.   Where strong nations like
Austria, Russia, and Prussia were forced to crouch
before Bonaparte, and even England would have
been glad to accept tolerable terms, Spain could not
challenge attack.   The violent anger that followed
the sale of Louisiana and the rupture of the peace
of Amiens soon subsided.   Bonaparte, aware that he
had outraged the rights of Spain, became moderate.
Anxious to prevent her from committing any act of
desperation, he did not require her to take part in
the war, but even allowed her stipulated subsidies to
run in arrears; and although he might not perhaps
regret his sale of Louisiana to the United States, he
felt that he had gone too far in shaking the colonial
system.   At the moment when Cevallos made his
bitterest complaints, Bonaparte was least disposed to
resent them by war.   Both parties knew that so far
as Louisiana was concerned, the act was done and
could not be undone; that France was bound to carry
out her pledge, or the United States would take possession of Louisiana without her aid.   Bonaparte was
willing to go far in the way of conciliation, if Spain
would consent to withdraw her protest.

Of this the American negotiators knew little.
Through such complications, of which Bonaparte
alone understood the secret, the Americans moved
more or less blindly, not knowing enemies from
friends.   The only public man who seemed ever to
understand Napoleon's methods was Pozzo di Borgo,

whose ways of thought belonged to the island society in which both had grown to manhood; and Monroe was not skilled in the diplomacy of Pozzo, or even of Godoy. Throughout life, Monroe was greatly under the influence of other men. He came to Paris almost a stranger to its new society, for his only relations of friendship had been with the republicans, most of whom Bonaparte had sent to Cayenne. He found Livingston master of the situation, and wisely interfered in no way with what Livingston did. The treaty was no sooner signed than he showed his readiness to follow Livingston further, without regard to embarrassments which might result.

When Livingston set his name to the treaty of cession, May 2, 1803, he was aware of the immense importance of the act. He rose and shook hands with Monroe and Marbois. "We have lived long," said he; "but this is the noblest work of our lives." This was said by the man who in the Continental Congress had been a member of the committee appointed to draft the Declaration of Independence; and it was said to Monroe, who had been assured only three months before, by President Jefferson of the grandeur of his destinies in words he could hardly have forgotten:[1] "Some men are born for the public. Nature, by fitting them for the service of the human race on a broad scale, has stamped them with the evidences of her destination and their duty." Monroe was born for the public, and knew

[1] Jefferson to Monroe, Jan. 13, 1803; Works, iv. 455.

what destiny lay before him ; while in Livingston's
mind New York had thenceforward a candidate for
the Presidency whose claims were better than Monroe's. In the cup of triumph of which these two
men then drank deep, was yet one drop of acid.
They had been sent to buy the Floridas and New
Orleans. They had bought New Orleans ; but instead
of Florida, so much wanted by the Southern people,
they had paid ten or twelve million dollars for the
west bank of the Mississippi. The negotiators were
annoyed to think that having been sent to buy the
east bank of the Mississippi, they had bought the
west bank instead ; that the Floridas were not a part
of their purchase. Livingston especially felt the
disappointment, and looked about him for some way
to retrieve it.

Hardly was the treaty signed, when Livingston
found what he sought. He discovered that France
had actually bought West Florida without knowing
it, and had sold it to the United States without being
paid for it. This theory, which seemed at first sight
preposterous, became a fixed idea in Livingston's
mind. He knew that West Florida had not been
included by Spain in the retrocession, but that on
the contrary Charles IV. had repeatedly, obstinately,
and almost publicly rejected Bonaparte's tempting
bids for that province. Livingston's own argument
for the cession of Louisiana had chiefly rested on
this knowledge, and on the theory that without Mobile New Orleans was worthless. He recounted this

to Madison in the same letter which announced Talleyrand's offer to sell : [1] —

" I have used every exertion with the Spanish Ambassador and Lord Whitworth to prevent the transfer of the Floridas, . . . and unless they [the French] get Florida, I have convinced them that Louisiana is worth little."

In the preceding year one of the French ministers had applied to Livingston " to know what we understand in America by Louisiana ; " and Livingston's answer was on record in the State Department at Washington : [2] " Since the possession of the Floridas by Britain and the treaty of 1762, I think there can be no doubt as to the precise meaning of the terms." He had himself drafted an article which he tried to insert in Marbois's *projet*, pledging the First Consul to interpose his good offices with the King of Spain to obtain the country east of the Mississippi. As late as May 12, Livingston wrote to Madison : [3] " I am satisfied that . . . if they [the French] could have concluded with Spain, we should also have had West Florida." In his next letter, only a week afterward, he insisted that West Florida was his : [4] —

" Now, sir, the sum of this business is to recommend to you in the strongest terms, after having obtained the possession that the French commissary will give you, to

[1] Livingston to Madison, April 11, 1803; State Papers, ii. 552.

[2] Ibid., July 30, 1802; State Papers, ii. 519.

[3] Ibid., May 12, 1803; State Papers, ii. 557.

[4] Ibid., May 20, 1803; State Papers, ii. 561.

insist upon this as a part of your right, and to take possession at all events to the River Perdido.   I pledge myself that your right is good."

The reasoning on which he rested this change of
opinion was in substance the following : France had,
in early days, owned nearly all the North American
continent, and her province of Louisiana had then
included Ohio and the watercourses between the Lakes
and the Gulf, as well as West Florida, or a part of
it.   This possession lasted until the treaty of peace,
Nov. 3, 1762, when France ceded to England not
only Canada, but also Florida and all other possessions east of the Mississippi, except the Island of New
Orleans.   Then West Florida by treaty first received
its modern boundary at the Iberville.   On the same
day France further ceded to Spain the Island of New
Orleans and all Louisiana west of the Mississippi.
Not a foot of the vast French possessions on the continent of North America remained in the hands of
the King of France ; they were divided between England and Spain.

The retrocession of 1800 was made on the understanding that it referred to this cession of 1762.   The
province of Louisiana which had been ceded was
retro-ceded, with its treaty-boundary at the Iberville.
Livingston knew that the understanding between
France and Spain was complete ; yet on examination
he found that it had not been expressed in words so
clearly but that these words could be made to bear
a different meaning.   Louisiana was retroceded, he

perceived, " with the same extent that it now has in the hands of Spain, and that it had when France possessed it, and such as it should be according to the treaties subsequently entered into between Spain and other States." When France possessed Louisiana it included Ohio and West Florida : no one could deny that West Florida was in the hands of Spain ; therefore Bonaparte, in the absence of negative proof, might have claimed West Florida, if he had been acute enough to know his own rights, or willing to offend Spain, — and as all Bonaparte's rights were vested in the United States, President Jefferson was at liberty to avail himself of them.

The ingenuity of Livingston's idea was not to be disputed ; and as a ground for a war of conquest it was as good as some of the claims which Bonaparte made the world respect. As a diplomatic weapon, backed as Napoleon would have backed it by a hundred thousand soldiers, it was as effective an instrument as though it had every attribute of morality and good faith ; and all it wanted, as against Spain, was the approval of Bonaparte. Livingston hoped that after the proof of friendship which Bonaparte had already given in selling Louisiana to the United States, he might without insuperable difficulty be induced to grant this favor. Both Marbois and Talleyrand, under the First Consul's express orders, led him on. Marbois did not deny that Mobile might lie in Louisiana, and Talleyrand positively denied knowledge that Laussat's instructions contained a definition of boundaries. Bonaparte stood behind both these agents, telling them that if an obscurity did not exist about the boundary they should make one. Talleyrand went so far as to encourage the pretensions which Livingston hinted: " You have made a noble bargain for yourselves," said he, " and I suppose you will make the most of it." This was said at the time when Bonaparte was still intent on punishing Spain.

Livingston found no difficulty in convincing Monroe that they had bought Florida as well as Louisiana.[1]

" We consider ourselves so strongly founded in this conclusion, that we are of opinion the United States should act on it in all the measures relative to Louisiana in the same manner as if West Florida was comprised within the Island of New Orleans, or lay to the west of the River Iberville."

Livingston expected that " a little force,"[2] as he expressed himself, might be necessary.

" After the explanations that have been given here, you need apprehend nothing from a decisive measure; your minister here and at Madrid can support your claim, and the time is peculiarly favorable to enable you to do it without the smallest risk at home. . . . The moment is so favorable for taking possession of that country that I hope it has not been neglected, even though a little force should be necessary to effect it. Your minister must find the means to justify it."

[1] Livingston and Monroe to Madison, June 7, 1803; State Papers, ii. 563–565.

[2] Livingston to Madison, May 20, 1803; Nov. 15, 1803; State Papers, ii. 561, 573.

A little violence added to a little diplomacy would answer the purpose. To use the words which "Aristides" Van Ness was soon to utter with striking effect, the United States ministers to France " practised with unlimited success upon the Livingston maxim, —

'Rem facias, rem
Si possis recte; si non, quocunque modo, REM.'"

CHAPTER IV.

In the excitement of this rapid and half-understood foreign drama, domestic affairs seemed tame to the American people, who were busied only with the routine of daily life. They had set their democratic house in order. So short and easy was the task, that the work of a single year finished it. When the President was about to meet Congress for the second time, he had no new measures to offer.[1] " The path we have to pursue is so quiet that we have nothing scarcely to propose to our legislature." The session was too short for severe labor. A quorum was not made until the middle of December, 1802; the Seventh Congress expired March 4, 1803. Of these ten weeks, a large part was consumed in discussions of Morales's proclamation and Bonaparte's scheme of colonizing Louisiana.

On one plea the ruling party relied as an excuse for inactivity and as a defence against attack. Their enemies had said and believed that the democrats possessed neither virtue nor ability enough to carry on the government; but after eighteen months of trial, as the year 1803 began, the most severe Federalist

[1] Jefferson to Thomas Cooper, Nov. 29, 1802; Works, iv. 452.

could not with truth assert that the country had yet
suffered in material welfare from the change. Although the peace in Europe, after October, 1801,
checked the shipping interests of America, and although France and Spain, returning to the strictness
of their colonial system, drove the American flag from
their harbors in the Antilles, yet Gallatin at the close
of the first year of peace was able to tell Congress [1]
that the customs revenue, which he had estimated
twelve months before at $9,500,000, had brought into
the Treasury $12,280,000, or much more than had
ever before been realized in a single year from all
sources of revenue united. That the Secretary of the
Treasury should miscalculate by one third the product of his own taxes was strange ; but Gallatin liked
to measure the future, not by a probable mean, but
by its lowest possible extreme, and his chief aim
was to check extravagance in appropriations for objects which he thought bad. His caution increased
the popular effect of his success. Opposition became
ridiculous when it persisted in grumbling at a system
which, beginning with a hazardous reduction of taxes,
brought in a single year an immense increase in
revenue. The details of Gallatin's finance fretted the
Federalists without helping them.

The Federalists were equally unlucky in finding
other domestic grievances. The removals from office
did not shock the majority. The Judiciary was not

[1] Report of the Secretary of the Treasury, Dec. 16, 1802.
Annals of Congress, 1802–1803, 1276.

again molested. The overwhelming superiority of the democrats was increased by the admission of Ohio, Nov. 29, 1802. No man of sense could deny that the people were better satisfied with their new Administration than they ever had been with the old. Loudly as New England grumbled, the Federalists even there steadily declined in relative strength; while elsewhere an organized body of opposition to the national government hardly existed. From New York to Savannah, no one complained of being forced to work for national objects; South Carolina as well as Virginia was pleased with the power she helped to sway.

Here and there might be found districts in which Federalism tried to hold its own; but the Federalism of Delaware and Maryland was not dangerous, and even in Delaware the Federalist champion Bayard was beaten by Cæsar A. Rodney in his contest for the House, and was driven to take refuge in the Senate. Pennsylvania, New York, Virginia, and North Carolina were nearly unanimous; and beyond the mountains democracy had its own way without the trouble of a discussion. Federalism was already an old-fashioned thing; a subject of ridicule to people who had no faith in forms; a half-way house between the European past and the American future. The mass of Americans had become democratic in thought as well as act; not even another political revolution could undo what had been done. As a democrat, Jefferson's social success was sweeping and final;

but he was more than a democrat, — and in his other character, as a Virginia republican of the State-rights school, he was not equally successful.

In the short session of 1802–1803 many signs proved that the revolution of 1800 had spent its force, and that a reaction was at hand. Congress showed no eagerness to adopt the President's new economies, and dismissed, with silence almost contemptuous, his scheme for building at Washington a large dry-dock in which the navy should be stored for safety and saving. The mint was continued by law for another five years, and twenty thousand dollars were quietly appropriated for its support. Instead of reducing the navy, Congress decided to build four sixteen-gun brigs and fifteen gunboats, and appropriated ninety-six thousand dollars for the brigs alone. The appropriation of two millions as a first instalment toward paying for New Orleans and Florida was another and a longer stride in the old Federalist path of confidence in the Executive and liberality for national objects. The expenditure for 1802, excluding interest on debt, was $3,737,000. Never afterward in United States history did the annual expenditure fall below four millions. The navy, in 1802, cost $915,000; never afterward did it cost less than a million.

The reaction toward Federalist practices was more marked in the attitude of the Executive than in that of Congress. If Jefferson's favorite phrase was true, — that the Federalist differed from the Republican only in the shade more or less of power to be given the Executive,—it was hard to see how any President could be more Federalist than Jefferson himself. A resolution to commit the nation without its knowledge to an indissoluble British alliance, was more than Washington would have dared take; yet this step was taken by the President, and was sustained by Madison, Gallatin, and Robert Smith as fairly within the limits of the Constitution. In regard to another stretch of the treaty-making power, they felt with reason the gravest doubts. When the President and Cabinet decided early in January, 1803, to send Monroe with two million dollars to buy New Orleans and Florida, a question was instantly raised as to the form in which such a purchase could be constitutionally made. Attorney-General Lincoln wished to frame the treaty or convention in such language as to make France appear not as adding new territory to the United States, but as extending already existing territory by an alteration of its boundary. He urged this idea upon the President in a letter written the day of Monroe's nomination to the Senate.[1]

" If the opinion is correct," said he, " that the general government when formed was predicated on the then existing *United* States, and such as could grow out of them, and out of them only ; and that its authority is constitutionally limited to the people composing the several political State societies in that Union, and such as might be formed out of them, — would not a direct independent

[1] Lincoln to Jefferson, Jan. 10, 1803; Jefferson MSS.

purchase be extending the executive power farther, and be more alarming, and improvable by the opposition and the Eastern States, than the proposed indirect mode?"

Jefferson sent this letter to Gallatin, who treated it without favor.[1]

"If the acquisition of territory is not warranted by the Constitution," said he, "it is not more legal to acquire for one State than for the United States. . . . What could, on his construction, prevent the President and Senate, by treaty, annexing Cuba to Massachusetts, or Bengal to Rhode Island, if ever the acquirement of colo·nies should become a favorite object with governments, and colonies should be acquired? But does any constitutional objection really exist? . . . To me it would appear, (1) that the United States, as a nation, have an inherent right to acquire territory; (2) that whenever that acquisition is by treaty, the same constituted authorities in whom the treaty-making power is vested have a constitutional right to sanction the acquisition."

Gallatin not only advanced Federal doctrine, but used also what the Virginians always denounced as Federalist play on words. "The United States as a nation" had an inherent right to do whatever the States in union cared. to do; but the Republican party, with Jefferson, Madison, and Gallatin at their head, had again and again maintained that the United States *government* had the inherent right to do no act whatever, but was the creature of the States in union; and its acts, if not resulting from an expressly granted

[1] Gallatin to Jefferson, Jan. 13, 1803; Gallatin's Works, i. 112.

power, were no acts at all, but void, and not to be obeyed or regarded by the States. No foreigner, not even Gallatin, could master the theory of Virginia and New England, or distinguish between the nation of States in union which granted certain powers, and the creature at Washington to which these powers were granted, and which might be strengthened, weakened, or abolished without necessarily affecting the nation. Whether the inability to grasp this distinction was a result of clearer insight or of coarser intelligence, the fact was the same; and on this point, in spite of his speech on the Alien and Sedition Acts, Gallatin belonged to the school of Hamilton, while both were of one mind with Dallas. The chief avowed object of Jefferson's election had been to overthrow the reign of this school. No Virginian could be expected within two short years to adopt the opinions of opponents who had been so often branded as "monocrats," because of acting on these opinions. Although the Attorney-General's advice was not followed, the negotiation for New Orleans was begun on the understanding that the purchase, if made, would be an inchoate act which would need express sanction from the States in the shape of an amendment to the Constitution.

There the matter rested. At the moment of Monroe's appointment, the President, according to his letters, had little hope of quick success in the purchase of territory. His plan was to "palliate and endure," unless France should force a war upon him;

the constitutional question could wait, and it was accordingly laid aside. Yet the chief ambition of Southern statesmen in foreign affairs was to obtain the Floridas and New Orleans; and in effecting this object they could hardly escape establishing a serious precedent. Already Jefferson had ordered his ministers at Paris to buy this territory, although he thought the Constitution gave him no power to do so; he was willing to increase the national debt for this purpose, even though a national debt was a "mortal canker;" and he ordered his minister, in case Bonaparte should close the Mississippi, to make a permanent alliance with England, or in his own words to "marry ourselves to the British fleet and nation," as the price of New Orleans and Florida. Jefferson foresaw and accepted the consequences of the necessity; he repeatedly referred to them and deprecated them in his letters; but the territory was a vital object, and success there would, as he pointed out, secure forever the triumph of his party even in New England.

"I believe we may consider the mass of the States south and west of Connecticut and Massachusetts as now a consolidated body of Republicanism," — he wrote to Governor McKean in the midst of the Mississippi excitement.[1] "In Connecticut, Massachusetts, and New Hampshire there is still a Federal ascendency; but it is near its last. If we can settle happily the difficulties of the Mississippi, I think we may promise ourselves smooth seas during our time."

[1] Jefferson to Governor McKean, Feb. 19, 1803; Jefferson MSS.

What he rightly feared more than any other political
disaster was the risk of falling back to the feelings
of 1798 and 1799, "when a final dissolution of all
bonds, civil and social, appeared imminent."[1]   With
zeal which never flagged, Jefferson kept up his struggle with the New England oligarchy, whose last move
alarmed him. So sensitive was the President, that
he joined personally in the fray that distracted New
England; and while waiting for news from Monroe,
he wrote a defence of his own use of patronage, showing, under the assumed character of a Massachusetts
man, that a proportionate division of offices between
the two parties would, since the Federalists had so
much declined in numbers, leave to them even a
smaller share of Federal offices than they still possessed. This paper he sent to Attorney-General Lincoln,[2] to be published in the Boston "Chronicle;"
and there, although never recognized, it appeared.

Had the Federalists suspected the authorship, they
would have fallen without mercy upon its arguments
and its modest compliment to "the tried ability and
patriotism of the present Executive;" but the essay
was no sooner published than it was forgotten. The
"Chronicle" of June 27, 1803, contained Jefferson's
argument founded on the rapid disappearance of the
Federalist party; the next issue of the "Chronicle,"
June 30, contained a single headline, which sounded
the death-knell of Federalism altogether: "Louisiana

[1] Jefferson to Colonel Hawkins, Feb. 18, 1803; Works, iv. 565.
[2] Jefferson to Levi Lincoln, June 8, 1803; Jefferson MSS.

ceded to the United States!" The great news had arrived ; and the Federalist orators of July 4, 1803, set about their annual task of foreboding the ruin of society amid the cheers and congratulations of the happiest society the world then knew.

The President's first thought was of the Constitution. Without delay he drew up an amendment, which he sent at once to his Cabinet.[1] "The province of Louisiana is incorporated with the United States and made part thereof," began this curious paper ; "the rights of occupancy in the soil and of self-government are confirmed to the Indian inhabitants as they now exist." Then, after creating a special Constitution for the territory north of the 32d parallel, reserving it for the Indians until a new amendment to the Constitution should give authority for white ownership, the draft provided for erecting the portion south of latitude 32° into a territorial government, and vesting the inhabitants with the rights of other territorial citizens.

Gallatin took no notice of this paper, except to acknowledge receiving it.[2] Robert Smith wrote at some length, July 9, dissuading Jefferson from grafting so strange a shoot upon the Constitution.[3]

"Your great object is to prevent emigrations," said he, "excepting to a certain portion of the ceded territory. This could be effectually accomplished by a con-

[1] Amendment to the Constitution; Jefferson MSS.
[2] Gallatin to Jefferson, July 9, 1803; Works, i. 127.
[3] Robert Smith to Jefferson, July 9, 1803; Jefferson MSS.

stitutional prohibition that Congress should not erect or
establish in that portion of the ceded territory situated
north of latitude 32° any new state or territorial government, and that they should not grant to any people
excepting Indians any right or title whatever to any part
of the said portion of the said territory."

Of any jealousy between North and South which
could be sharpened by such a restriction of northern and extension of southern territory, Jefferson
was unaware. He proposed his amendment in good
faith as a means of holding the Union together by
stopping its too rapid extension into the wilderness.

Coldly as his ideas were received in the Cabinet,
Jefferson did not abandon them. Another month
passed, and a call was issued for a special meeting of
Congress October 17 to provide the necessary legislation for carrying the treaty into effect. As the
summer wore away, Jefferson imparted his opinions
to persons outside the Cabinet. He wrote, August 12,
to Breckinridge of Kentucky a long and genial letter.
Congress, he supposed,[1] after ratifying the treaty and
paying for the country, " must then appeal to *the
nation* for an additional article to the Constitution
approving and confirming an act which the nation had
not previously authorized. The Constitution has made
no provision for our holding foreign territory, still
less for incorporating foreign nations into our Union.
The Executive, in seizing the fugitive occurrence
which so much advances the good of their country,

[1] Jefferson to Breckinridge, Aug. 12, 1803; Works, iv. 498.

have done an act beyond the Constitution. The Legislature, in casting behind them metaphysical sub-tleties and risking themselves like faithful servants, must ratify and pay for it, and throw themselves on their country for doing for them unauthorized what we know they would have done for themselves had they been in a situation to do it."

Breckinridge — whose Kentucky Resolutions, hardly five years before, declared that unconstitutional as-sumptions of power were the surrender of the form of government the people had chosen, and the replacing it by a government which derived its powers from its own will — might be annoyed at finding his prin-ciples abandoned by the man who had led him to father them; and surely no leader who had sent to his follower in one year the draft of the Kentucky Resolutions could have expected to send in another the draft of the Louisiana treaty. " I suppose they must then appeal to *the nation*" were the President's words; and he underscored this ominous phrase. " We shall not be disavowed by the nation, and their act of indemnity will confirm and not weaken the Constitution by more strongly marking out its lines." The Constitution, in dealing with the matter of amend-ments, made no reference to the nation; the word itself was unknown to the Constitution, which invari-ably spoke of the *Union* wherever such an expression was needed; and on the Virginia theory Congress had no right to appeal to the nation at all, except as a nation of States, for an amendment. The language used by Jefferson was the language of centralization, and would have been rejected by him and his party in 1798 or in 1820.

On the day of writing to Breckinridge the President wrote in a like sense to Paine ; but in the course of a week despatches arrived from Paris which alarmed him.   Livingston had reason to fear a sudden change of mind in the First Consul, and was willing to hasten the movements of President and Congress. Jefferson took the alarm, and wrote instantly to warn Breckinridge and Paine that no whisper of constitutional difficulties must be heard : [1] —

" I wrote you on the 12th instant on the subject of Louisiana and the constitutional provision which might be necessary for it.   A letter received yesterday shows that nothing must be said on that subject which may give a pretext for retracting, but that we should do *sub silentio* what shall be found necessary.   Be so good, therefore, as to consider that part of my letter as confidential."

He gave the same warning to his Cabinet : [2]   " I infer that the less we say about constitutional difficulties the better ; and that what is necessary for surmounting them must be done *sub silentio.*"

He then drew up a new amendment, which he sent to the members of his Cabinet.[3]   The July draft was

[1] Jefferson to Paine, Aug. 18, 1803; Jefferson MSS.

[2] Jefferson to Madison, Aug. 18, 1803 ; to R. Smith, Aug. 23 ; Jefferson MSS.

[3] Jefferson to Madison, Aug. 25; to Lincoln, Aug. 30, 1803; Works, iv. 501–505 ; to Gallatin, Aug. 23, 1803 ; Gallatin's Works, i. 144.

long, elaborate, and almost a new Constitution in itself; the August draft was comparatively brief. " Louisiana as ceded by France to the United States is made a part of the United States. Its white inhabitants shall be citizens, and stand, as to their rights and obligations, on the same footing with other citizens of the United States in analogous situations." The whole country north of the Arkansas River was reserved for Indians until another amendment should be made; and as an afterthought Florida was to be admitted as a part of the United States " whenever it may be rightfully obtained."

These persistent attempts to preserve his own consistency and that of his party were coldly received. Jefferson found himself alone. Wilson Cary Nicholas, a prominent supporter of the Virginia Resolutions in 1798 and a senator of the United States in 1803, had a long conversation with the President, and in the early days of September wrote him a letter which might have come from Theodore Sedgwick or Roger Griswold in the days of Jay's treaty, when Federalist notions of prerogative ran highest.

" Upon an examination of the Constitution," wrote Nicholas,[1] " I find the power as broad as it could well be made (Sect. 3, Art. IV.), except that new States cannot be formed out of the old ones without the consent of the *State* to be dismembered; and the exception is a proof to my mind that it was not intended to confine the Congress in the admission of new States to what was then the ter-

[1] W. C. Nicholas to Jefferson, Sept. 3, 1803 ; Jefferson MSS.

ritory of the United States. Nor do I see anything in the Constitution that limits the treaty-making power, except the general limitations of the other powers given to the government, and the evident objects for which the government was instituted."

Had Nicholas reasoned thus in 1798 he would have been a Federalist, as he seemed conscious, for he went on to say : " I am aware that this is to us delicate ground, and perhaps my opinions may clash with the opinions given by our friends during the discussion of the British treaty." Nevertheless he argued that if this treaty was unconstitutional, all other treaties were open to the same objection, and the United States government in such a case could make no treaty at all. Finally, he begged the President to avoid giving an opinion on the subject : " I should think it very probable if the treaty should be declared by you to exceed the constitutional authority of the treaty-making power, it would be rejected by the Senate, and if that should not happen, that great use would be made with the people of a wilful breach of the Constitution."

Such reasoning in the mouths of Virginia Republicans, who had asked and gained office by pledging themselves to their people against the use of implied powers, marked a new epoch. From them the most dangerous of all arguments, the *reductio ad absurdum*, was ominous. What right had they to ask whether any constitutional grant was less complete than the people might have wished or intended ? If

the Constitution were incomplete or absurd, not the
government, but the people of the States who had
made it were the only proper authority to correct it.
Otherwise, as Nicholas had so often pointed out, their
creature would become their tyrant, as had been the
law of politics from the beginning.

Jefferson was distressed to find himself thus deserted by his closest friends on an issue which he
felt to be vital.   The principle of strict construction
was the breath of his political life.   The Pope could
as safely trifle with the doctrine of apostolic succession as Jefferson with the limits of Executive power.
If he and his friends were to interpret the treaty-
making power as they liked, the time was sure to
come when their successors would put so broad an
interpretation on other powers of the government as
to lead from step to step, until at last Virginia might
cower in blood and flames before the shadowy terror
called the war-power.   With what face could Jefferson then appear before the tribunal of history, and
what position could he expect to receive?

All this he felt in his kindly way; and with this
weight on his mind he wrote his reply to Nicholas.[1]
Beginning with the warning that Bonaparte could
not be trusted, and that Congress must act with as
little debate as possible, particularly as respected the
constitutional difficulty, he went on : —

"I am aware of the force of the observations you
make on the power given by the Constitution to Congress

[1] Jefferson to W. C. Nicholas, Sept. 7, 1803; Works, iv. 505.

to admit new States into the Union without restraining
the subject to the territory then constituting the United
States.   But when I consider that the limits of the
United States are precisely fixed by the treaty of 1783,
that the Constitution expressly declares itself to be made
for the United States, . . . I do not believe it was
meant that [Congress] might receive England, Ireland,
Holland, etc., into it, — which would be the case on your
construction. . . . I had rather ask an enlargement of
power from the nation, where it is found necessary, than
to assume it by a construction which would make our
powers boundless.   Our peculiar security is in the possession of a written Constitution.   Let us not make it a
blank paper by construction.   I say the same as to the
opinion of those who consider the grant of the treaty-
making power as boundless.   If it is, then we have no
Constitution."

From the Virginia standpoint nothing could be better said.   Jefferson in this letter made two points
clear: the first was that the admission of Louisiana
into the Union without express authority from the
States made blank paper of the Constitution; the
second was that if the treaty-making power was equal
to this act, it superseded the Constitution.   He entertained no doubts on either point, and time sustained
his view; for whether he was right or wrong in law,
the Louisiana treaty gave a fatal wound to "strict
construction," and the Jeffersonian theories never
again received general support.   In thus giving them
up, Jefferson did not lead the way, but he allowed
his friends to drag him in the path they chose.   The

leadership he sought was one of sympathy and love,
not of command ; and there was never a time·when
he thought that resistance to the will of his party
would serve the great ends he had in view. The
evils which he foresaw were remote : in the hands of
true Republicans the Constitution, even though violated, was on the whole safe ; the precedent, though
alarming, was exceptional. So it happened that after
declaring in one sentence the Constitution at an end
if Nicholas had his way, Jefferson in the next breath
offered his acquiescence in advance : —

" I confess I think it important in the present case to
set an example against broad construction by appealing
for new power to the people. If, however, our friends
shall think differently, certainly I shall acquiesce with
satisfaction, confiding that the good sense of our country
will correct the evil of construction when it shall produce
ill effects."

With these words Jefferson closed his mouth on
this subject forever. Although his future silence led
many of his friends to think that he ended by alter-
ing his opinion, and by admitting that his purchase of
Louisiana was constitutional, no evidence showed the
change ; but rather one is led to believe that when in
later life he saw what he called the evils of construction grow until he cried against them with violence
almost as shrill as in 1798, he felt most strongly
the fatal error which his friends had forced him
to commit, and which he could neither repudiate
nor defend. He had declared that he would acqui-

esce with satisfaction in making blank paper of the Constitution.

A few weeks later, Oct. 17, 1803, Congress met. The President's Message had little to say of domestic affairs. The Kaskaskia Indians had sold their territory to the United States, the revenue had again exceeded the estimate, more than three millions of debt had been paid within the year. Much was said about war in Europe and the rights and duties of neutrals, about gunboats which were no longer needed, and about the unsettled boundary in Maine and at the Lake of the Woods, but not a word about the constitutional difficulties raised by the Louisiana treaty. " With the wisdom of Congress it will rest," said Jefferson, " to take those ulterior measures which may be necessary for the immediate occupation and temporary government of the country, for its incorporation into our Union, for rendering the change of government a blessing to our newly adopted brethren, for securing to them the rights of conscience and of property, for confirming to the Indian inhabitants their occupancy and self-government." These were the points of his proposed amendment; but he gave no sign of his opinion that Congress was incompetent to deal with them, and that the Senate was equally incompetent to make the treaty valid.

There were good reasons for silence. Not only were Livingston's letters alarming, but the Marquis of Casa Yrujo, the friend and benefactor of the Administration, sent to Madison one protest after

another against the sale of Louisiana.[1] He quoted
St.-Cyr's letter of July, 1802, which bound France
not to alienate the province, and he declared that
France had never carried out the conditions of contract in regard to Tuscany, and therefore could not
rightfully treat Louisiana as her own. A probable
war with Spain stared Jefferson in the face, even if
Bonaparte should raise no new difficulties. The responsibility for a mistake was great, and no one could
blame Jefferson if he threw his burden on Congress.

[1] Yrujo to Madison, Sept. 4, Sept. 27, Oct. 12, 1803; State
Papers, ii. 569, 570.

CHAPTER V.

IF President Jefferson and Secretary Madison, who wrote the Resolutions of 1798, acquiesced, in 1803, in a course of conduct which as Jefferson believed made blank paper of the Constitution, and which, whether it did so or not, certainly made waste paper of the Virginia and Kentucky Resolutions, no one could expect that their followers would be more consistent or more rigid than themselves. Fortunately, all the more prominent Republicans of 1798 had been placed in office by the people as a result of popular approval, and were ready to explain their own views. In the Senate sat John Breckinridge of Kentucky, supposed to be the author of the Kentucky Resolutions, and known as their champion in the Kentucky legislature. From Virginia came John Taylor of Caroline, the reputed father of the Virginia Resolutions, and the soundest of strict constructionists. Twenty years later, his "Construction Construed" and "New Views of the Constitution" became the text-books of the State-rights school. His colleague was Wilson Cary Nicholas, who had also taken a prominent part in supporting the Virginia Resolutions,

and whose devotion to the principles of strict construction was beyond doubt. One of the South Carolina senators was Pierce Butler; one of those from
North Carolina was David Stone; Georgia was represented by Abraham Baldwin and James Jackson, —
stanch State-rights Republicans all. In the House a
small coterie of State-rights Republicans controlled
legislation. Speaker Macon was at their head; John
Randolph, chairman of the Ways and Means Committee, was their mouthpiece. Joseph H. Nicholson
of Maryland, and Cæsar A. Rodney of Delaware,
supported Randolph on the committee; while two
of President Jefferson's sons-in-law, Thomas Mann
Randolph and John W. Eppes, sat in the Virginia
delegation. Both in Senate and House the Southern
Republicans of the Virginia school held supremacy;
their power was so absolute as to admit no contest;
they were at the flood of that tide which had set in
three years before. In the Senate they controlled
twenty-five votes against nine; in the House, one
hundred and two against thirty-nine. Virginia ruled
the United States, and · the Republicans of 1798
ruled Virginia. The ideal moment of Republican
principles had arrived.

This moment was big with the fate of theories.
Other debates of more practical importance may
have frequently occurred, — for in truth whatever the
decision of Congress might have been, it would in
no case have affected the result that Louisiana was
to enter the Union; and this inevitable result over-

shadowed all theory, — but no debate ever took place in the Capitol which better deserved recollection.

Of extraordinary ability Congress contained but little, and owing to the meagre character of the reports, appeared to contain even less than it actually possessed ; but if no one rose to excellence either of logic or rhetoric, the speakers still dealt with the whole subject, and rounded the precedent with all the argument and illustration that a future nation could need. Both actions and words spoke with decision and distinctness till that time unknown in American politics.

The debate began first in the House, where Gaylord Griswold of New York, Oct. 24, 1803, moved for such papers as the Government might possess tending to show the value of the title to Louisiana as against Spain. Under the lead of John Randolph the House refused the call. That this decision clashed with the traditions of the Republican party was proved by the vote. With a majority of three to one, Randolph succeeded in defeating Griswold only by fifty-nine to fifty-seven ; while Nicholson, Rodney, Varnum of Massachusetts, and many other stanch Republicans voted with the Federalists.

The next day the House took up the motion for carrying the treaty into effect. Griswold began again, and without knowing it repeated Jefferson's reasoning. The framers of the Constitution, he said, " carried their ideas to the time when there might be an extended population ; but they did not carry them

forward to the time when an addition might be made
to the Union of a territory equal to the whole United
States, which additional territory might overbalance
the existing territory, and thereby the rights of the
present citizens of the United States be swallowed up
and lost." The power to admit new States referred
only to the territory existing when the Constitution
was framed ; but this right, whatever it might be,
was vested in Congress, not in the Executive. In
promising to admit Louisiana as a State into the
Union, the treaty assumed for the President power
which in any case could not have been his. Finally,
the treaty gave to French and Spanish ships special
privileges for twelve years in the port of New Orleans ;
while the Constitution forbade any preference to be
given, by any regulation of commerce or revenue, to
the ports of one State over those of another.

John Randolph next rose. Just thirty years old,
with a sarcasm of tone and manner that overbore remonstrance, and with an authority in the House that
no one contested, Randolph spoke the voice of Virginia with autocratic distinctness. His past history
was chiefly marked by the ardor with which, from
1798 to 1800, he had supported the principles of his
party and encouraged resistance to the national
government. He had gone beyond Jefferson and
Madison in willingness to back their theories by
force, and to fix by a display of Virginia power the
limit beyond which neither Executive, Congress, nor
Judiciary should pass. Even then he probably cared

little for what he called the " parchment barriers "
of the Constitution : in his mind force was the real
balance, — force of State against force of Union ; and
any measure which threatened to increase the power
of the national government beyond that of the State,
was sure of his enmity. A feather might turn the
balance, so nice was the adjustment ; and Randolph
again and again cried with violence against feathers.

In the Louisiana debate, Randolph spoke in a different tone. The Constitution, he said, could not
restrict the country to particular limits, because at
the time of its adoption the boundary was unsettled on the northeastern, northwestern, and southern
frontiers. The power to settle disputes as to limits
was indispensable ; it existed in the Constitution, had
been repeatedly exercised, and involved the power of
extending boundaries.

This argument was startling in the mouth of one
who had helped to arm the State of Virginia against
a moderate exercise of implied powers. Randolph
asserted that the right to annex Louisiana, Texas,
Mexico, South America, if need be, was involved in
the right to run a doubtful boundary line between
the Georgia territory and Florida. If this power
existed in the government, it necessarily devolved
on the Executive as the organ for dealing with foreign States. Thus Griswold's first objection was
answered.

Griswold objected in the second place that the
treaty made New Orleans a favored port. " I regard

this stipulation," replied Randolph, " as a part of the price of the territory. It was a condition which the party ceding had a right to require, and to which we had a right to assent. The right to acquire involves the right to give the equivalent demanded." Randolph did not further illustrate this sweeping principle of implied power.

After the subject had been treated by speakers of less weight, Roger Griswold of Connecticut took the floor. So long as his party had been in office, the vigor of the Constitution had found no warmer friend than he ; but believing New England to have fallen at the mercy of Virginia, he was earnest to save her from the complete extinction which he thought near at hand. Griswold could not deny that the Constitution gave the power to acquire territory : his Federalist principles were too fresh to dispute such an inherent right ; and Gouverneur Morris, as extreme a Federalist as himself, whose words had been used in the Constitution, averred that he knew in 1788 as well as he knew in 1803, that all North America must at length be annexed, and that it would have been Utopian to restrain the movement.[1] This was old Federalist doctrine, resting on " inherent rights," on nationality and broad construction, — the Federalism of President Washington, which the Republican party from the beginning denounced as monarchical. Griswold would not turn his back on it ; he still took

[1] Morris to H. W. Livingston, Nov. 25, 1803. Writings of Gouverneur Morris, iii. 185.

a liberal view of the power, and even stretched it
beyond reasonable shape to accord with Morris's idea.
" A new territory and new subjects," said he, " may
undoubtedly be obtained by conquest and by purchase ; but neither the conquest nor the purchase
can incorporate them into the Union. They must
remain in the condition of colonies, and be governed
accordingly." This claim gave the central government despotic power over its new purchase ; but it
declared that a treaty which pledged the nation to
admit the people of Louisiana into the Union must be
invalid, because it assumed that " the President and
Senate may admit at will any foreign nation into this
copartnership without the consent of the States," —
a power directly repugnant to the principles of the
compact. In substance, Griswold maintained that
either under the war power or under the treaty-
making power the government could acquire territory, and as a matter of course could hold and govern
that territory as it pleased, — despotically if necessary, or for selfish objects ; but that the President
and Senate could not admit a foreign people into
the Union, as a State. Yet to this, the treaty bound
them.

To meet this attack the Republicans put forward
their two best men, — Joseph H. Nicholson of Maryland, and Cæsar A. Rodney of Delaware. The task
was difficult, and Nicholson showed his embarrassment at the outset. " Whether the United States,"
said he, " as a sovereign and independent empire,

has a right to acquire territory is one thing; but whether they can admit that territory into the Union upon an equal footing with the other States is a question of a very different nature." He refused to discuss this latter issue; in his opinion it was not before the House.

This flinching was neither candid nor courageous; but it was within the fair limits of a lawyer's if not of a statesman's practice, and Nicholson at least saved his consistency. On the simpler question, whether " a sovereign nation," as he next said, " had a right to acquire new territory," he spoke with as much emphasis as Roger Griswold and Gouverneur Morris, and he took the same ground. The separate States had surrendered their sovereignty by adopting the Constitution; " the right to declare war was given to Congress; the right to make treaties, to the President and Senate. Conquest and purchase alone are the means by which nations acquire territory." Griswold was right, then, in the ground he had taken; but Nicholson, not satisfied with gaining his point through the treaty-making power, which was at least express, added: " The right must exist somewhere: it is essential to independent sovereignty." As it was prohibited to the States, the power was necessarily vested in the United States.

This general implication, that powers inherent in sovereignty which had not been expressly reserved to the States were vested in the national government, was not more radical centralization than

Nicholson's next point. The treaty gave to the port
of New Orleans a decided preference over all other
ports of the United States, although the Constitution
said that no preference should be given to the ports
of one State over those of another. To this objection Nicholson replied that Louisiana was not a State.
" It is a territory purchased by the United States in
their confederate capacity, and may be disposed of
by them at pleasure. It is in the nature of a colony whose commerce may be regulated without any
reference to the Constitution." The new territory,
therefore, was in the nature of a European colony ;
the United States government might regulate its
commerce without regard to the Constitution, give
its population whatever advantages Congress might
see fit, and use it to break down New England — or
slavery.

With the fecund avowal that Louisiana must be
governed by Congress at pleasure without reference
to the Constitution, Nicholson sat down ; and Cæsar
Rodney took the floor, — an able and ingenious
lawyer, who came to the House with the prestige
of defeating the Federalist champion Bayard. If
Randolph and Nicholson, like the mouse in the fable
nibbling at the cords which bound the lion of Power,
had left one strand still unsevered, the lion stood
wholly free before Rodney ended. He began by appealing to the " general welfare " clause, — a device which
the Republican party and all State-rights advocates
once regarded as little short of treason. " I cannot

perceive," said he, " why within the fair meaning
of this general provision is not included the power of
increasing our territory, if necessary for the general
welfare or common defence." This argument in such
a mouth might well have sent a chill to the marrow
of every Republican of 1798; but this was not the
whole. He next invoked the " necessary and proper "
clause, even at that early time familiar to every strict
constructionist as one of the most dangerous instruments of centralization. " Have we not also vested
in us every power necessary for carrying such a
treaty into effect, in the words of the Constitution
which give Congress the authority to ' make all laws
which shall be necessary and proper for carrying
into execution the foregoing powers, and all other
powers vested by this Constitution in the government
of the United States or in any department or officer
thereof ' ? "

One more point was affirmed by Rodney. Gaylord
Griswold had maintained that the territory mentioned
in the Constitution was the territory existing in 1789.
Rodney denied it. Congress, he said, had express
power to " make all needful rules and regulations "
respecting any and all territory ; it had no need to
infer this power from other grants. As for the
special privilege of trade accorded to New Orleans, it
violated in no way the Constitution ; it was indirectly
a benefit to all the States, and a preference to none.

The Northern democrats also supported these
views ; but the opinions of Northern democrats on

constitutional questions carried little weight. Neither among them nor among Southern Republicans did any member question what Randolph, Nicholson, and Rodney had said. Macon sat silent in his chair, while John Randolph closed the debate. As though he could not satisfy himself with leaving a doubt as to the right of Government to assume what powers it wanted, Randolph took this moment to meet Roger Griswold's assertion that the United States government could not lawfully incorporate Great Britain or France into the Union. Randolph affirmed that, so far as the Constitution was concerned, this might be done. " We cannot because we cannot."

The reply was disingenuous, but decisive. The question was not whether the States in union could lawfully admit England or France into the Union, for no one denied that the States could do what they pleased. Griswold only affirmed that the people of the States had never delegated to John Randolph or Thomas Jefferson, or to a majority of the United States Senate, the right to make a political revolution by annexing a foreign State. Jefferson agreed with Griswold that they had not; if they had, " then we have no Constitution" was his comment. Yet not a voice was raised in the Administration party against Randolph's views. After one day's debate, ninety Republicans supported Randolph with their votes, and twenty-five Federalists alone protested. Of these twenty-five, not less than seventeen were from New England.

A week afterward, Nov. 2, 1803, the Senate took up the subject. After several speeches had been made without touching deeply the constitutional difficulty, Senator Pickering of Massachusetts took the floor, and in a few words stated the extreme New England doctrine. Like Griswold and Gouverneur Morris, he affirmed the right of conquest or of purchase, and the right to govern the territory so acquired as a dependent province; but neither the President nor Congress could incorporate this territory in the Union, nor could the incorporation lawfully be effected even by an ordinary amendment to the Constitution. " I believe the assent of each individual State to be necessary for the admission of a foreign country as an associate in the Union, in like manner as in a commercial house the consent of each member would be necessary to admit a new partner into the company." With his usual skill in saying what was calculated to annoy, — a skill in which he had no superior, — he struck one truth which no other eyes would see. " I believe that this whole transaction has been purposely wrapped in obscurity by the French government. The boundary of Louisiana, for instance, on the side of Florida is in the treaty really unintelligible; and yet nothing was more easy to define."

Pickering was followed by Dayton of New Jersey, and he by the celebrated John Taylor of Caroline, the senator from Virginia, whose Resolutions of 1798, with echoes which were to ring louder and louder for

sixty years to come, had declared " deep regret that a
spirit has in sundry instances been manifested by the
federal government to enlarge its powers by forced
constructions of the constitutional charter which de-
fines them ; and that indications have appeared of
a design to expound certain general phrases . . . so
as to consolidate the States by degrees into one
sovereignty." In purchasing Louisiana, the United
States government had done an act identical with
the despotic acts of consolidated European governments, — it had bought a foreign people without their
consent and without consulting the States, and had
pledged itself to incorporate this people in the Union.
Colonel Taylor's argument, so far as it went, supported the act; and although it evaded, or tried to
evade, the most difficult points of objection, it went as
far as the farthest in the path of forced construction.
On the right to acquire territory, Taylor took the
ground taken by Joseph Nicholson in the House, —
he inferred it from the war and treaty powers: " If
the means of acquiring and the right of holding are
equivalent to the right of acquiring territory, then
this right merged from the separate States to the
United States, as indispensably annexed to the treaty-
making power and the power of making war " This
part of the Federalist scheme he adopted without
a murmur; but when he came to the next inevitable step, he showed the want of courage often felt
by honest men trying to be untrue to themselves.
This territory which the Washington government

could acquire by conquest or treaty, — what was its status ? Could the Washington government " dispose of " it, as the government was expressly permitted to dispose of the territory it already held under the Constitution ; or must Louisiana be governed extra-constitutionally by " inherent powers," as Griswold maintained ; or ought Congress to ask for new and express authority from the States ? Taylor took the first position. The treaty-making power, he said, was not defined, it was competent to acquire territory. This territory by the acquisition became a part of the Union, a portion of the territories of the United States, and might be " disposed of " by Congress without an amendment to the Constitution. Although Taylor differed with Jefferson on this point, no objection could be made to the justice of his opinion except that it left the true dispute to be settled by mere implication. The power of the government over the territory had no limits, so far as Colonel Taylor defined it ; yet it either could or could not admit the new territory as a State. If it could, the government could alter the original compact by admitting a foreign country as a State ; if it could not, either the treaty was void, or government must apply to the people of the States for new powers.

Uriah Tracy of Connecticut replied to Taylor in a speech which was probably the best on his side of the question. His opposition to the purchase was grounded on a party reason : " The relative strength which this admission gives to a Southern and Western interest is contradictory to the principles of our original Union." The President and Senate had no power to make States, and the treaty was void.

"I have no doubt but we can obtain territory either by conquest or compact, and hold it, even all Louisiana and a thousand times more if you please, without violating the Constitution. We can hold territory; but to admit the inhabitants into the Union, to make citizens of them, and States, by treaty, we cannot constitutionally do; and no subsequent act of legislation, or even ordinary amendment to our Constitution, can legalize such measures. If done at all, they must be done by universal consent of all the States or partners to our political association; and this universal consent I am positive can never be obtained to such a pernicious measure as the admission of Louisiana, — of a world, and such a world, into our Union. This would be absorbing the Northern States, and rendering them as insignificant in the Union as they ought to be, if by their own consent the measure should be adopted."

Tracy's speech was answered by Breckinridge of Kentucky, who had induced the Kentucky legislature, only five years before, to declare itself determined "tamely to submit to undelegated, and consequently unlimited, powers in no man or body of men on earth;" and to assert further that submission to the exercise of such powers "would be to surrender the form of government we have chosen, and to live under one deriving its powers from its own will, and not from our authority." When he came to deal with the same question in a new form, he glided with extreme delicacy over the thin ice of the Constitution. His answer to Tracy was an admission. He pointed out that the Federalist argument carried centralization further than it was carried by this treaty. " By his construction," said Breckinridge, " territories and citizens are considered and held as the property of the government of the United States, and may consequently be used as dangerous engines in the hands of the government against the States and people." This was true. The Federalists maintained that such territory could be held only as property, not as part of the Union; and the consequences of this doctrine, if granted, were immense. Breckinridge argued that the admission by treaty of a foreign State was less dangerous, and therefore more constitutional, than such ownership of foreign territory. The conclusion was not perfectly logical, and was the less so because he denied the power in neither case. " Could we not," he went on, quoting from Tracy's speech, " incorporate in the Union some foreign nation containing ten millions of inhabitants, — Africa, for instance, — and thereby destroy our government ? Certainly the thing would be possible if Congress would do it and the people consent to it. . . . The true construction must depend on the manifest import of the instrument and the good sense of the community." What then had become of the old Republican principle that acts of undelegated authority were no acts at all ? Or had the States really delegated to the President and two thirds of the Senate the right to "destroy our government"? If Breckinridge had expressed these ideas in his Kentucky Resolutions, American history would have contained less dispute as to the meaning of State-rights and the powers of the central government; but Breckinridge himself would have then led the Federalist, not the Republican party.

Breckinridge's speech was followed by one from Pickering's colleague, the young senator from Massachusetts, son of John Adams, the Federalist President whom Jefferson had succeeded. The Federalist majority in Massachusetts was divided; one portion followed the lead of the Essex Junto, the other and larger part yielded unwillingly to the supremacy of Alexander Hamilton and George Cabot. When in the spring of 1803 both seats of Massachusetts in the United States Senate became by chance vacant at once, the Essex Junto wished to choose Timothy Pickering for the long term. The moderate Federalists set Pickering aside, elected John Quincy Adams, then thirty-six years old, for the long term, and allowed Pickering to enter the Senate only as junior senator to a man more than twenty years younger than himself, whose father had but three years before dismissed Pickering abruptly and without explanation from his Cabinet. Neither of the senators owned a temper or character likely to allay strife. The feud between them was bitter and life-long. From the moment of their appearance in the Senate they took opposite sides.

Pickering held with Tracy, Griswold, and all the extreme Federalists that the treaty was void, and that the admission of Louisiana as a State without the separate consent of each State in the Union was a rupture of the compact, which broke the tie and left each State free to act independently of the rest. His colleague was as decided in favor of the Louisiana purchase as Pickering and Tracy were opposed to it; but he too agreed that the treaty was outside of the Constitution, and he urged the Senate to take this view. He believed that even Connecticut would approve of admitting Louisiana if the Southern majority had the courage to try the experiment. " I firmly believe, if an amendment to the Constitution, amply sufficient for the accomplishment of everything for which we have contracted, shall be proposed, as I think it ought, it will be adopted by the legislature of every State in the Union." This was in effect the view which Jefferson had pressed upon his Cabinet and friends.

Then came Wilson Cary Nicholas. Five years before, in the Virginia legislature, Nicholas had spoken and voted for the Resolutions moved by his colleague, John Taylor of Caroline. He then said that if the principle were once established that Congress had a right to use powers not expressly delegated, " the tenure by which we hold our liberty would be entirely subverted : instead of rights independent of human control, we must be content to hold by the courtesy and forbearance of those whom we have heretofore considered as the servants of the people." Instead of using the same language in 1803, he accepted his colleague's views as to the extent of the treaty-making power, and added reasoning of his own. If the spirit of New England Calvinism contained an element of self-deceit, Virginia metaphysics occasionally ran into slippery evasion, as the argument of Nicholas showed. He evaded a straightforward opinion on every point at issue. The treaty-making power was undefined, he thought, but not unlimited ; the general limitations of the Constitution applied to it, not the special limitations of power ; and of course the treaty must be judged by its conformity with the general meaning of the compact. He then explained away the apparent difficulties in the case. " If the third article of the treaty," said he, " is an engagement to incorporate the territory of Louisiana into the Union of the United States and to make it a State, it cannot be considered as an unconstitutional exercise of the treaty-making power, for it will not be asserted by any rational man that the territory is incorporated as a State by the treaty itself." This incorporation was stipulated to be done " according to the principles of the Constitution," and the States might do it or not, at their discretion : if it could not be done constitutionally, it might be done by amendment.

Nothing could be more interesting than to see the discomfort with which the champions of State-rights tossed themselves from one horn to the other of the Federalist dilemma. The Federalists cared little on which horn their opponents might choose to impale themselves, for both were equally fatal. Either Louisiana must be admitted as a State, or must be held as territory. In the first case the old Union was at an end; in the second case the national government was an empire, with "inherent sovereignty" derived from the war and treaty-making powers, — in either case the Virginia theories were exploded. The Virginians felt the embarassment, and some of them, like Nicholas, tried to hide it in a murmur of words and phrases; but the Republicans of Kentucky and Tennessee were impatient of such restraint, and slight as it was, thrust it away. The debate was closed by Senator Cocke of Tennessee, who defied opposition. "I assert," said he, "that the treaty-making powers in this country are competent to the full and free exercise of their best judgment in making treaties without limitation of power."

On this issue the vote was taken without further discussion, and by twenty-six to five the Senate passed the bill. Pickering of Massachusetts, Tracy and Hillhouse of Connecticut, and the two senators Wells and White from Delaware, were alone in opposition.

The result of these debates in the Senate and House decided only one point. Every speaker, without distinction of party, agreed that the United States government had the power to acquire new territory either by conquest or by treaty; the only difference

of opinion regarded the disposition of this territory
after it was acquired. Did Louisiana belong to the
central government at Washington, or to the States ?
The Federalists maintained that the central government, representing the States in union, might, if it
pleased, as a consequence of its inherent sovereignty,
hold the rest of America in its possession and govern
it as England governed Jamaica or as Spain was
governing Louisiana, but without the consent of the
States could not admit such new territory into the
Union. The Republicans seemed rather inclined to
think that new territory acquired by war or conquest
would become at once a part of the general territory
mentioned in the Constitution, and as such might be
admitted by Congress as a State, or otherwise disposed of as the general welfare might require, but
that in either case neither the people nor the States
had anything to do with the matter. At bottom,
both doctrines were equally fatal to the old status of
the Union. In one case the States, formed or to be
formed, east of the Mississippi had established a government which could hold the rest of the world in
despotic control, and which bought a foreign people
as it might buy cattle, to rule over them as their
owner ; in the other case, the government was equally
powerful, and might besides admit the purchased or
conquered territory into the Union as States. The
Federalist theory was one of empire, the Republican
was one of assimilation ; but both agreed that the
moment had come when the old Union must change

its character. Whether the government at Washington could possess Louisiana as a colony or admit it as a State, was a difference of no great matter if the cession were to hold good; the essential point was that for the first time in the national history all parties agreed in admitting that the government could govern.

CHAPTER VI.

HARDLY was it decided that the government had an inherent right to acquire territory and annex foreign States, when the next question forced itself on Congress for settlement, — What were the powers of Congress over the new territory?

Three paths were open. The safest was to adopt an amendment of the Constitution admitting Louisiana into the Union and extending over it the express powers of Congress as they had applied to the old territory of the United States. The second course was to assume that the new territory became, by the fact of acquisition, assimilated to the old, and might be " disposed of " in the same way. The third was to hold it apart as a peculiar estate, and govern it, subject to treaty stipulations, by an undefined power implied in the right to acquire, — on the principle that government certainly had the right to govern what it had the right to buy.

The first plan, which was in effect Jefferson's original idea, preserved the theory of the Constitution as far as was possible ; but the Republicans feared the consequences with France and Spain of throwing a doubt on the legality of the treaty. Another reason for their activity lay in the peculiarities of their character as a party. The Northern democrats, never strict constructionists, knew and cared little for the dogmas of their Southern allies. The Southern Republicans, especially those of the Virginia school, were honest in their jealousy of the central government; but as a class they were impatient of control and unused to self-restraint: they liked to do their will, and counted so surely on their own strength and honesty of purpose that they could not feel the need of a curb upon their power. None of them moved. The only man in Congress who showed a sincere wish to save what could be preserved of the old constitutional theory was Senator Adams of Massachusetts, who called upon Madison October 28, before the debate, to ask whether the Executive intended, through any member of either House, to propose an amendment of the Constitution to carry the treaty into effect.[1] Madison talked to him openly, and expressed ideas which as far as they went were the same with those of Jefferson. For his own part, said Madison, had he been on the floor of Congress he should have seen no difficulty in acknowledging that the Constitution had not provided for such a case as this; that it must be estimated by the magnitude of the object; and that those who had agreed to it must rely upon the candor of their country for justification. Probably, when the immediate pressure

[1] Documents relating to New England Federalism, pp. 156, 157; Diary of J. Q. Adams, i. 267.

of special legislation was past, the matter would be attended to; and if he should have any agency in concerting the measure, he would request its mover to consult Senator Adams. There for a month the matter rested, while Congress adopted its special legislation.

At length, November 25, Senator Adams, becoming impatient, called again on the Secretary of State, with the draft of an amendment which he meant to propose. Madison thought it too comprehensive, and suggested a simple declaration to meet the special case: " Louisiana is hereby admitted into this Union." On the same day Adams accordingly moved for a committee, but could not obtain a seconder. The Senate unanimously refused even the usual civility of a reference. No more was ever heard of amending the Constitution.

With almost unanimous consent Louisiana was taken into the Union by the treaty-making power, without an amendment. This point being fixed, Congress had also to determine whether the new territory should be governed by authority drawn from the power of acquisition, or whether it should be merged in the old territory which Congress had express right to " dispose of " and regulate at will.

By an act of sovereignty as despotic as the corresponding acts of France and Spain, Jefferson and his party had annexed to the Union a foreign people and a vast territory, which profoundly altered the relations of the States and the character of their nationality. By similar acts they governed both. Jefferson, in his special Message of October 23, requested Congress to make "such temporary provisions . . . as the case may require." A select committee, Randolph being chairman, immediately reported a Bill, emanating from the Executive.

"It was a startling Bill," was the criticism[1] of a man who shared in much legislation, "continuing the existing Spanish government; putting the President in the place of the King of Spain; putting all the territorial officers in the place of the King's officers, and placing the appointment of all these officers in the President alone without reference to the Senate. Nothing could be more incompatible with our Constitution than such a government, — a mere emanation of Spanish despotism, in which all powers, civil and military, legislative, executive, and judicial, were in the Intendant General, representing the King; and where the people, far from possessing political rights, were punishable arbitrarily for presuming to meddle with political subjects."

The Federalists immediately objected that the powers conferred on the President by this bill were unconstitutional. The Republicans replied, in effect, that the Constitution was made for States, not for territories. Rodney explained the whole intent of his party in advocating the bill: "It shows that Congress have a power in the territories which they cannot exercise in the States, and that the limitations of power found in the Constitution are applicable to

[1] Examination of the Decision of the Supreme Court in the case of Dred Scott. By Thomas H. Benton, p. 55.

States and not to territories." [1]   John Randolph defended the assumption of power on the ground of
necessity, and maintained that the government of the
United States, with respect to this territory, possessed the powers of European sovereignty: " Gentlemen will see the necessity of the United States
taking possession of this country in the capacity of
sovereigns, in the same extent as that of the existing
government of the province." The Bill passed Congress by a party vote, and was approved by Jefferson,
October 31, [2] without delay.

The Act of October 31 was a temporary measure
rather for taking possession of the territory than for
governing it. Four weeks later, Senator Breckinridge
moved for a committee to prepare a territorial form
of government for Louisiana. Two senators of the
State-rights school, — Jackson and Baldwin of Georgia, — besides Breckinridge and J. Q. Adams, were
appointed on this committee ; and they reported, December 30, a Bill that settled the principle on which
the new territory should be governed.

Breckinridge's Bill divided the purchased country
at the 33d parallel, the line which afterward divided
the State of Arkansas from the State of Louisiana.
The country north of that line was named the District
of Louisiana, and, after some dispute, was subjected
to the territorial government of the Indiana Territory,

[1] Annals of Congress, 1803–1804, p. 514.

[2] Act of October 31, 1803. Annals of Congress, 1803–1804.
App. p. 1245.

consisting of a governor, secretary, and judges without a legislature, all controlled by the Ordinance of 1787. This arrangement implied that Congress considered the new territory as assimilated to the old, and " disposed of " it by the same constitutional power.

The northern district contained few white inhabitants, and its administrative arrangements chiefly concerned Indians; but the southern district, which received the name " Territory of Orleans," included an old and established society, numbering fifty thousand persons. The territory of Ohio numbered only forty-five thousand persons by the census of 1800, while the States of Delaware and Rhode Island contained less than seventy thousand. The treaty guaranteed that " the inhabitants of the ceded territory shall be incorporated in the Union of the United States, and admitted as soon as possible, according to the principles of the Federal Constitution, to the enjoyment of all the rights, advantages, and immunities of citizens of the United States; and in the mean time they shall be maintained and protected in the free enjoyment of their liberty, property, and the religion which they profess."

Breckinridge's Bill, which was probably drawn by Madison in co-operation with the President, created a territorial government in which the people of Louisiana were to have no share. The governor and secretary were to be appointed by the President for three years ; the legislative council consisted of thirteen members to be appointed by the President without consulting the Senate, and was to be convened and prorogued by the governor as he might think proper. The judicial officers, also appointed by the President, were to hold office for four years, instead of the usual term of good behavior. The right to a jury trial was restricted to cases where the matter in controversy exceeded twenty dollars, and to capital cases in criminal prosecutions. The slave-trade was restricted by threefold prohibitions : 1. No slave could be imported from abroad ; 2. No slave could be brought into the territory from the Union who had been imported from abroad since May 1, 1798 ; 3. No slave could be introduced into the territory, " directly or indirectly," except by an American citizen " removing into said territory for actual settlement, and being, at the time of such removal, *bona fide* owner of such slave," — the penalty being three hundred dollars fine and the slave's freedom.

This Bill seemed to set the new Territory apart, as a peculiar estate, to be governed by a power implied in the right to acquire it. The debate which followed its introduction into the Senate was not reported, but the Journal mentioned that Senator Adams, Jan. 10, 1804, moved three Resolutions, to the effect that no constitutional power existed to tax the people of Louisiana without their consent, and carried but three voices with him in support of the principle.[1] Other attempts were made to arrest the exercise of

[1] Diary of J. Q. Adams (Jan. 10, 1804), i. 287.

arbitrary power without better success, and the Bill passed the Senate, Feb. 18, 1804, after six weeks consideration, by a vote of twenty to five.

Few gaps in the parliamentary history of the Union left so serious a want as was caused by the failure to report the Senate debate on this Bill; but the report of the House debate partly supplied the loss, for the Bill became there a target for attack from every quarter. Michael Leib, one of the extreme Pennsylvania democrats, began by objecting to the power given to the governor over the Louisiana legislature as "royal." His colleague, Andrew Gregg, objected altogether to the appointment of the council by the President. Varnum of Massachusetts denounced the whole system, and demanded an elective legislature. Matthew Lyon, who represented Kentucky, compared Jefferson to Bonaparte. "Do we not owe something on this score to principle?" he asked. Speaker Macon took the same ground. George W. Campbell of Tennessee was more precise. "It really establishes a complete despotism," he said; "it does not evince a single trait of liberty; it does not confer one single right to which they are entitled under the treaty; it does not extend to them the benefits of the Federal Constitution, or declare when, hereafter, they shall receive them." On the other hand Dr. Eustis, of Boston, took the ground that a despotism was necessary: "I am one of those who believe that the principles of civil liberty cannot suddenly be engrafted on a people accustomed to a

regimen of a directly opposite hue." In contradiction
to the language of the treaty and the principles of his
party, he went on to say that the people of Louisiana
had no rights: "I consider them as standing in
nearly the same relation to us as if they were a conquered country." Other speakers supported him.
The Louisianians, it was said, had shed tears when
they saw the American flag hoisted in place of the
French; they were not prepared for self-government.
When the treaty was under discussion, the speakers
assumed that the people of Louisiana were so eager
for annexation as to make an appeal to them useless;
when they were annexed, they were so degraded as
not to be worth consulting.

The House refused to tolerate such violation of
principle, and by the majority of seventy-four to
twenty-three struck out the section which vested
legislative powers in the President's nominees. John
Randolph did not vote; but his friend Nicholson and
the President's son-in-law, Thomas Mann Randolph,
were in the minority. By fifty-eight to forty-two the
House then adopted an amendment which vested
legislative powers, after the first year, in an elective
council; by forty-four to thirty-seven the restriction
on jury trials was rejected; the Act was then limited
to two years; and so altered it passed the House
March 17, 1804, several Republicans recording their
votes against it to the end.

When the Bill, thus amended, came back to the
Senate, that body, March 20, summarily disagreed

with all the changes made by the House except the limitation of time, which the Senate further reduced to one year. This change reconciled the House, not very cheerfully, to recede, and March 23 the Bill, as it passed the Senate, became law by a vote of fifty-one to forty-five. With the passage of this Act and its twin statute for collecting duties in the ceded territory, the precedent was complete. Louisiana received a government in which its people, who had been solemnly promised all the rights of American citizens, were set apart, not as citizens, but as subjects lower in the political scale than the meanest tribes of Indians, whose right to self-government was never questioned.

By these measures the Executive and the Legislature recorded their decision in regard to the powers of government over national territory. The Judiciary was not then consulted ; but twenty-five years afterward, in the year 1828, Chief-Justice Marshall was in his turn required to give an opinion, and he added the final authority of the Supreme Court to the precedent. With characteristic wisdom he claimed for the government both the constitutional and the extra-constitutional powers in question. The case concerned the rights of inhabitants of Florida, who he said —

" Do not participate in political power ; they do not share in the government till Florida shall become a State. In the mean time Florida continues to be a territory of the United States, governed by virtue of that clause in the

Constitution which empowers Congress ' to make all needful rules and regulations respecting the territory or other property belonging to the United States.' Perhaps the power of governing a territory belonging to the United States which has not, by becoming a State, acquired the means of self-government, may result necessarily from the fact that it is not within the jurisdiction of any particular State, and is within the power and jurisdiction of the United States. The right to govern may be the inevitable consequence of the right to acquire territory. Whichever may be the source whence the power is derived, the possession of it is unquestioned." [1]

The effect of such a precedent on constitutional principles was certain to be great. A government competent to interpret its own powers so liberally in one instance, could hardly resist any strong temptation to do so in others. The doctrines of " strict construction " could not be considered as the doctrines of the government after they had been abandoned in this leading case by a government controlled by strict constructionists. The time came at last when the opponents of centralization were obliged to review their acts and to discover the source of their mistakes. In 1856 the Supreme Court was again required to pronounce an opinion, and found itself confronted by the legislation of 1803–1804 and the decision of Chief-Justice Marshall in 1828. Chief-Justice Taney and his associates, in the case of Dred Scott, then reviewed the acts of Jefferson and his

[1] American Insurance Company and Others *v.* Canter (January Term, 1828), 1 Peters's Reports, 511–546.

friends in 1803–1804, and pronounced upon them the final judgment of the State-rights school.

Chief-Justice Taney affirmed the right of the government to buy Louisiana and to govern it, but not to govern it as a part of the old territory over which the Constitution gave Congress unlimited power. Louisiana was governed, according to Marshall's dictum, by a power which was " the inevitable consequence of the right to acquire territory,"— a power limited by the general purposes of the Constitution, and therefore not extending to a colonial system like that of Europe. Territory might thus be acquired ; but it was acquired in order to become a State, and not to be held as a colony and governed by Congress with absolute authority ; citizens who migrated to it " cannot be ruled as mere colonists dependent upon the will of the general government, and to be governed by any laws it may think proper to impose." The chief-justice dwelt on this point at much length ; the federal government, he said, " cannot, when it enters a territory of the United States, put off its character and assume discretionary or despotic powers which the Constitution has denied it."

Even this emphatic opinion, which implied that all the Louisiana legislation was unconstitutional, did not satisfy Justice Campbell, a Georgian, who represented the ultimate convictions of the strict constructionists. Campbell reviewed the national history in search of evidence " that a consolidated power had been inaugurated, whose subject comprehended an empire, and which had no restriction but the discretion of Congress." He held that the Constitution had been plainly and repeatedly violated; "and in reference to the precedent of 1804, the wisest statesmen protested against it, and the President more than doubted its policy and the power of the government." The Court, he said, could not undertake to conquer their scruples as the President and Congress had done. "They acknowledge that our peculiar security is in the possession of a written Constitution, and they cannot make it blank paper by construction."

This sneer at President Jefferson was almost the last official expression of strict-constructionist principles. Of its propriety the Court itself was the best judge, but its historical interest could not be denied.

If Justice Campbell and Chief-Justice Taney were right, according to the tenets of their school the legislation of 1803–1804 was plainly unconstitutional. In that case, by stronger reasoning the treaty itself was unconstitutional and void from the beginning; for not only did Jefferson's doubts to which Campbell alluded refer to the treaty and not to the legislation, but the treaty was at least equally responsible with the laws for making, in 1803, a situation which required what Campbell denounced, — "the supreme and irresistible power which is now claimed for Congress over boundless territories, the use of which cannot fail to react upon the political system of the States to its subversion."

With the law the story need not concern itself,

but the view of American history thus suggested was peculiarly interesting. If the chief-justice and his associate expressed correctly the opinions of the strict-constructionist school, the government had at some time been converted from a government of delegated powers into a sovereignty. Such was the belief of Campbell's political friends. Four years after the Dred Scott decision was declared, the State of South Carolina, in Convention, issued an "Address to the People of the Slave-holding States," justifying its act of secession from the Union.

"The one great evil," it declared, "from which all other evils have flowed, is the overthrow of the Constitution of the United States. The government of the United States is no longer the government of confederated republics, but of a consolidated democracy. It is no longer a free government, but a despotism."

If the strict constructionists held this opinion, they necessarily believed that at some moment in the past the government must have changed its character. The only event which had occurred in American history so large in its proportions, so permanent in its influence, and so cumulative in its effects as to represent such a revolution was the Louisiana purchase; and if the Louisiana purchase was to be considered as having done what the Federalists expected it to do, — if it had made a new constitution and a government of sovereign powers, — the strict constructionists were not only consenting parties to the change, they were its authors.

From every point of view, whether Justice Campbell and the secession convention of South Carolina
were right or wrong in their historical judgment, the
Louisiana purchase possessed an importance not to
be ignored. Even in 1804 the political consequences
of the act were already too striking to be overlooked.
Within three years of his inauguration Jefferson
bought a foreign colony without its consent and
against its will, annexed it to the United States by
an act which he said made blank paper of the Constitution ; and then he who had found his predecessors
too monarchical, and the Constitution too liberal in
powers, — he who had nearly dissolved the bonds of
society rather than allow his predecessor to order
a dangerous alien out of the country in a time of
threatened war, — made himself monarch of the new
territory, and wielded over it, against its protests,
the powers of its old kings. Such an experience
was final ; no century of slow and half-understood
experience could be needed to prove that the hopes
of humanity lay thenceforward, not in attempting to
restrain the government from doing whatever the
majority should think necessary, but in raising the
people themselves till they should think nothing
necessary but what was good.

Jefferson took a different view. He regarded, or
wished to regard, the Louisiana treaty and legislation
as exceptional and as forming no precedent. While
he signed the laws for governing the territory, he
warmly objected to the establishment of a branch

bank of the United States at New Orleans. "This institution is one of the most deadly hostility existing against the principles and form of our Constitution," he wrote to Gallatin;[1] "ought we to give further growth to an institution so powerful, so hostile?" Gallatin was clear that the business of the Treasury required such aid, and Jefferson again acquiesced. Gallatin was also allowed and encouraged to enforce the restrictions on the importation of slaves into Louisiana.[2] "It seems that the whole Cabinet," wrote the French *chargé* to his government, "put the utmost weight on this prohibition. Mr. Jefferson is earnestly bent on maintaining it, and his Secretary of the Treasury takes the severest measures to insure its execution."

As though the annexation of Louisiana alone made not enough change in the old established balances of the Constitution, Congress took up another matter which touched the mainspring of the compact. A new Presidential election was at hand. The narrow escape of 1800 warned the party in power not again to risk society by following the complicated arrangements of 1788. In the convention which framed the Constitution no single difficulty was more serious than that of compromising the question of power between the large and small States. Delaware, New Jersey, Rhode Island, Maryland, and Connecticut

[1] Jefferson to Gallatin, Dec. 13, 1803; Works, iv. 518.
[2] Pichon to Talleyrand, 16 Fructidor, An xii. (Sept. 3, 1804); Archives des Aff. Étr., MSS.

were well aware that the large States would take
the lion's share of power and patronage; they knew
that except by accident no citizen of theirs could
ever reach the Presidency; and as accident alone
could give the small States a chance, accident was to
them a thing of value. Whatever tended to make
their votes decisive was an additional inducement
with them to accept the Constitution. The Vice-
presidency, as originally created, more than doubled
their chance of getting the Presidency, and was invented chiefly for this purpose; but this was not all.
As the number of electoral votes alone decided between President and Vice-president, a tie-vote was
likely often to occur; and such a tie was decided by
the House of Representatives, where another bribe
was intentionally offered to the small States by giving the election to the State delegations voting as
units, so that the vote of Delaware weighed as heavily as the vote of Pennsylvania.

The alarm caused by Burr's rivalry with Jefferson
in February, 1801, satisfied the Republican party that
such a door to intrigue ought not to be left open.
Oct. 17, 1803, before the Louisiana treaty was taken
up, an amendment to the Constitution was moved by
friends of the Administration in the House. This,
which took shape at length as the Twelfth Amendment, obliged the members of the electoral college to
distinguish in their ballots the persons voted for as
President and Vice-president.

Slight as this change might appear, it tended toward centralizing powers hitherto jealously guarded. It swept away one of the checks on which the framers had counted to resist majority rule by the great States. Lessening the influence of the small States, and exaggerating the office of President by lowering the dignity of Vice-president, it made the processes of election and government smoother and more efficient, — a gain to politicians, but the result most feared by the State-rights school. The change was such as Pennsylvania or New York might naturally want; but it ran counter to the theories of Virginia Republicans, whose jealousy of Executive influence had been extreme.

Roger Griswold said with prophetic emphasis: [1] —

" The man voted for as Vice-president will be selected without any decisive view to his qualifications to administer the government. The office will generally be carried into the market to be exchanged for the votes of some large States for President; and the only criterion which will be regarded as a qualification for the office of Vice-president will be the temporary influence of the candidate over the electors of his State. . . . The momentary views of party may perhaps be promoted by such arrangements, but the permanent interests of the country are sacrificed."

Griswold held that true reform required abolition of the office; and in this opinion his old enemy John Randolph warmly agreed. In the Senate, had the question risen as a new one, perhaps a majority might

[1] Dec. 8, 1803; Annals of Congress, 1803–1804, p. 751.

have favored abolition, for the results of retaining the office were foreseen; but the discussion was hampered by the supposed popular will and by express votes of State legislatures, and Congress felt itself obliged to follow a prescribed course. The amendment was adopted by the usual party vote ; and the Federalists thenceforward were able to charge Jefferson and his party with responsibility not only for stripping the small States of an advantage which had made part of their bargain, but also for putting in the office of President, in case of vacancies, men whom no State and no elector intended for the post.

CHAPTER VII.

THE extraordinary success which marked Jefferson's foreign relations in the year 1803 was almost equally conspicuous in domestic affairs. The Treasury was as fortunate as the Department of State. Gallatin silenced opposition. Although the customs produced two millions less than in 1802, yet when the Secretary in October, 1803, announced his financial arrangements, which included the purchase-money of fifteen million dollars for Louisiana, he was able to provide for all his needs without imposing a new tax. The treaty required the issue of six-per-cent bonds for eleven million two hundred and fifty thousand dollars, redeemable after fifteen years. These were issued ; and to meet the interest and sinking fund Gallatin added from his surplus an annual appropriation of seven hundred thousand dollars to his general fund ; so that the discharge of the whole debt would take place within the year 1818, instead of eighteen months earlier, as had been intended. New Orleans was expected to provide two hundred thousand dollars a year toward the interest. Of the remaining four millions, the Treasury already held half, and Gallatin hoped

to provide the whole from future surplus, which he
actually did.

This was ideal success. On a sudden call, to pay
out four million dollars in hard money, and add seven
hundred thousand dollars to annual expenditure, without imposing a tax, and with a total revenue of eleven
millions, was a feat that warranted congratulations.
Yet Gallatin's success was not obtained without an
effort. As usual, he drew a part of his estimated
surplus from the navy. He appealed to Jefferson
to reduce the navy estimates from nine hundred thousand to six hundred thousand dollars.[1]

"I find that the establishment now consists of the
'Constitution,' the 'Philadelphia,' each 44, and five small
vessels, all of which are now out, and intended to stay
the whole year, as the crew is enlisted for two years.
In my opinion one half of the force, — namely, one
frigate and two or three small vessels, — were amply
sufficient."

Jefferson urged the reduction,[2] and Secretary Smith
consented. The navy estimates were reduced to six
hundred and fifty thousand dollars, and on the
strength of this economy Gallatin made his calculation. As he probably foresaw, the attempt failed.
Whether in any case Smith could have effected so
great a retrenchment was doubtful ; but an event
occurred which made retrenchment impossible.

[1] Remarks on the Message, Gallatin's Writings, i. 156; Gallatin
to Jefferson, Oct. 6, 1803; ibid., i. 162.

[2] Jefferson to R. Smith, Oct. 10, 1803; Jefferson MSS.

The war with Tripoli dragged tediously along, and seemed no nearer its end at the close of 1803 than eighteen months before. Commodore Morris, whom the President sent to command the Mediterranean squadron, cruised from port to port between May, 1802, and August, 1803, convoying merchant vessels from Gibraltar to Leghorn and Malta, or lay in harbor and repaired his ships, but neither blockaded nor molested Tripoli; until at length, June 21, 1803, the President called him home and dismissed him from the service. His successor was Commodore Preble, who Sept. 12, 1803, reached Gibraltar with the relief-squadron which Secretary Gallatin thought unnecessarily strong. He had the " Constitution," of 44 guns, and the " Philadelphia," of 38; the four new brigs just built, — the " Argus " and the " Syren," of 16 guns, the " Nautilus " and the " Vixen," of 14 guns ; and the " Enterprise," of 12. With this force Preble set energetically to work.

Tripoli was a feeble Power, and without much effort could be watched and blockaded; but if the other governments on the coast should make common cause against the United States, the task of dealing with them was not so easy. Morocco was especially dangerous, because its ports lay on the ocean, and could not be closed even by guarding the Straits. When Preble arrived, he found Morocco taking part with Tripoli. Captain Bainbridge, who reached Gibraltar in the " Philadelphia " August 24, some three weeks before Preble arrived, caught in the neighborhood a

Moorish cruiser of 22 guns with an American brig in its clutches. Another American brig had just been seized at Mogador. Determined to stop this peril at the outset, Preble united to his own squadron the ships which he had come to relieve, and with this combined force, — the "Constitution," 44; the "New York," 36; the "John Adams," 28; and the "Nautilus," 14, — sending the "Philadelphia" to blockade Tripoli, he crossed to Tangiers October 6, and brought the Emperor of Morocco to reason. On both sides prizes and prisoners were restored, and the old treaty was renewed. This affair consumed time; and when at length Preble got the "Constitution" under way for the Tripolitan coast, he spoke a British frigate off the Island of Sardinia, which reported that the "Philadelphia" had been captured October 21, more than three weeks before.

The loss greatly embarassed Preble. The "Philadelphia" was, next to the "Constitution," his strongest ship. Indeed he had nothing else but his own frigate and small brigs of two and three hundred tons; but the accident was such as could not fail sometimes to happen, especially to active commanders. Bainbridge, cruising off Tripoli, had chased a Tripolitan cruiser into shoal water, and was hauling off, when the frigate struck on a reef at the mouth of the harbor. Every effort was made without success to float her; but at last she was surrounded by Tripolitan gunboats, and Bainbridge struck his flag. The Tripolitans, after a few days' work, floated the frigate, and brought her under the guns of the castle. The officers became prisoners of war, and the crew, in number three hundred or more, were put to hard labor.

The affair was in no way discreditable to the squadron. Morris had been recalled in disgrace for over-caution, and Bainbridge was required to be active. The Tripolitans gained nothing except the prisoners; for at Bainbridge's suggestion Preble, some time afterward, ordered Stephen Decatur, a young lieutenant in command of the " Enterprise," to take a captured Tripolitan craft re-named the " Intrepid," and with a crew of seventy-five men to sail from Syracuse, enter the harbor of Tripoli by night, board the " Philadelphia," and burn her under the castle guns. The order was literally obeyed. Decatur ran into the harbor at ten o'clock in the night of Feb. 16, 1804, boarded the frigate within half gun-shot of the Pacha's castle, drove the Tripolitan crew overboard, set the ship on fire, remained alongside until the flames were beyond control, and then withdrew without losing a man, while the Tripolitan gunboats and batteries fired on him as rapidly as want of discipline and training would allow. Gallant and successful as the affair was, it proved only what was already well known, that the Tripolitans were no match for men like Decatur and his companions; and it left Preble, after losing in the " Philadelphia " nearly one third of his force, still strong enough to do the work that needed to be done.

The frigate had been built by the citizens of Philadelphia, and given to the government in 1799. So
far as the ship was concerned, the loss was not much
regretted, for the Republicans when in opposition had
strenuously opposed the building of frigates, and still
considered them a danger rather than a defence. Although the " Philadelphia " was the newest ship in
the service, a companion to the " Constellation," the
" Congress," and the " Chesapeake," she was never
replaced ; two 18-gun brigs, the " Hornet " and the
" Wasp," were constructed instead of one 38-gun frigate ; and these were the last sea-going vessels built
under Jefferson's administration. The true annoyance was not that a frigate had been lost, but that
the captivity and enslavement of the crew obliged
Government to rescue them and to close the war, by
a kind of expenditure which the Republican party
disliked.

Bainbridge's report of his capture, which had happened at the end of October, 1803, was sent to Congress March 20, 1804, in the last week of the session.
The President sent with it a brief Message recom-
mending Congress to increase the force and enlarge
expenses in the Mediterranean. As Gallatin never
willingly allowed his own plans for the public service to be deranged, Congress adopted a new means
for meeting the new expense. Although the Treasury
held a balance of $1,700,000, Gallatin would not
trench upon this fund, but told Randolph, who was
Chairman of the Ways and Means Committee, that

the specie in the Treasury could not be safely reduced below that amount.[1] He informed Joseph Nicholson that $150,000 was the utmost sum he could spare. The sum wanted was $750,000 per annum. A Bill was introduced which imposed an additional duty of 2½ per cent on all imports that paid duty *ad valorem.* These imports had been divided, for purposes of revenue, into three classes, taxed respectively 12½, 15, and 20 per cent; the increase raised them to 15, 17½, and 22½ per cent. The average *ad valorem* duty was before about 13½; the additional tax raised it above 16 per cent; and the Republicans preferred this method of raising money as in every way better than the system of internal taxation. After imposing the additional duty of 2½ per cent, — a duty intended to produce about $750,000, — the Bill made of it a separate Treasury account, to be called the "Mediterranean Fund," which was to last only as long as the Mediterranean war should last, when the 2½ per cent duty was to cease three months after a general peace.

The Mediterranean Fund was meant as a protest against loose expenditure, — a dike against the impending flood of extravagance. The Mediterranean war was the first failure of President Jefferson's theory of foreign relations, and the Mediterranean Fund was the measure of the error in financial form. No reproach henceforward roused more ill temper

[1] Speech of John Randolph, March 22, 1804; Annals of Congress, 1803–1804, p. 1221.

among Republicans than the common charge that
their elaborate financial precautions and formalities
were a deception, and that the Mediterranean Fund
was meant to conceal a change of principle and a
return to Federalist practices.   Even in the first
words of the debate, Roger Griswold told them that
their plausible special fund was " perfectly deceptive,"
and amounted to nothing.   John Randolph retaliated
by declaring that the Republican government consisted of men who never drew a cent from the people
except when necessity compelled it ; and Griswold
could not assert, though he might even then foresee,
that for ten years to come, Randolph would denounce
the extravagance and waste of the men whom he thus
described.

The annexation of Louisiana, the constitutional
amendment in regard to the Vice-presidency, the
change of financial practices foreshadowed by the
Mediterranean Fund, were signs of reaction toward
nationality and energy in government.   Yet the old
prejudices of the Republican party had not yet wholly
lost their force.   Especially the extreme wing, consisting of men like John Randolph and W. B. Giles,
thought that a substantial reform should be attempted.
Increase of power encouraged them to act.   The
party, stimulated by its splendid success and irresistible popularity, at length, after long hesitation,
prepared for a trial of strength with the last remnant
of Federalism, — the Supreme Court of the United
States.

A year of truce between Congress and the Supreme Court had followed the repeal of the Judiciary Act. To prevent Chief-Justice Marshall and his associates from interfering with the new arrangements, Congress in abolishing the circuit courts in 1801 took the strong measure of suspending for more than a year the sessions of the Supreme Court itself. Between December, 1801, and February, 1803, the court was not allowed to sit. Early in February, 1803, a few days before the Supreme Court was to meet, after fourteen months of separation, President Jefferson sent an ominous Message to the House of Representatives.

" The enclosed letter and affidavits," he said,[1] " exhibiting matter of complaint against John Pickering, district judge of New Hampshire, which is not within executive cognizance, I transmit them to the House of Representatives, to whom the Constitution has confided a power of instituting proceedings of redress if they shall be of opinion that the case calls for them."

The enclosed papers tended to show that Judge Pickering, owing to habits of intoxication or other causes, had become a scandal to the bench, and was unfit to perform his duties. At first sight the House of Representatives might not understand what it had to do with such a matter ; but the President's language admitted no doubt of his meaning. The Constitution said that the House of Representatives " shall

[1] Message of Feb. 3, 1803; Annals of Congress, 1802–1803, p. 460.

have the sole power of impeachment;" and " all civil
officers of the United States shall be removed from
office on impeachment for, and conviction of, treason, bribery, or other high crimes and misdemeanors." Jefferson's Message officially announced to the
House the President's opinion that Judge Pickering's
conduct was a misdemeanor within the reach of
impeachment.

The House referred the Message to a committee
of five, controlled by Joseph Nicholson and John Randolph. A fortnight later, Nicholson reported a resolution ordering the impeachment; and before the
session closed, the House, by a vote of forty-five to
eight, adopted his report, and sent Nicholson and
Randolph to the bar of the Senate to impeach Judge
Pickering of high crimes and misdemeanors. March
3, 1803, the last day of the session, the two members
delivered their message.

Precisely as the House, by the President's invitation, was about to impeach Judge Pickering, the
Supreme Court, through the Chief-Justice's mouth,
delivered an opinion which could be regarded in no
other light than as a defiance. Chief-Justice Marshall's own appointment had been one of those made
by the last President between Dec. 12, 1800, and
March 4, 1801, which Jefferson called an " outrage
on decency," [1] and which, except as concerned life
offices, he held to be " nullities." His doctrine that
all appointments made by a retiring President were

[1] Jefferson to General Knox, March 27, 1801 ; Works, iv. 386.

nullities, unless made with the consent of the President elect, rested on the argument that the retiring President was no longer selecting his own but his successor's agents. Perhaps it involved also the favorite idea that the election of 1800 was something more than a change of Presidents, — that it was a real revolution in the principle of government. Any theory was sufficient for the Executive, but executive theories did not necessarily bind the Judiciary. Among the nominations which, like the appointment of Marshall, were obnoxious to Jefferson, was that of William Marbury as justice of the peace for five years for the District of Columbia. The nomination was sent to the Senate March 2, 1801, and was approved the next day, a few hours before Jefferson took his oath of office. The commission, regularly made out, signed by the President, countersigned by John Marshall the acting Secretary of State, and duly sealed, was left with other documents on the table in the State Department, where it came into the possession of Attorney-General Lincoln, acting as President Jefferson's Secretary of State. Jefferson, having decided that late appointments were nullities, retained Marbury's commission. Marbury, at the December term of 1801, moved the Supreme Court for a Rule to Secretary Madison to show cause why a mandamus should not issue commanding him to deliver the document. The Rule was duly served, and the case argued in December, 1801; but the Judiciary Act having suspended for fourteen months the sessions of the Supreme Court, the Chief-Justice did not deliver his opinion until Feb. 24, 1803.[1]

The strongest admirers of Marshall admitted that his manner of dealing with this case was unusual. Where a judgment was to turn on a question of jurisdiction, the Court commonly considered that point as first and final. In the case of Marbury the Court had no original jurisdiction, and so decided; but instead of beginning at that point and dismissing the motion, the Court began by discussing the merits of the case, and ruled that when a commission had been duly signed and sealed the act was complete, and delivery was not necessary to its validity. Marbury's appointment was complete; and as the law gave him the right to hold for five years, independent of the Executive, his appointment was not revocable: "To withhold his commission, therefore, is an act deemed by the Court not warranted by law, but violative of a legal vested right."

This part of the decision bore the stamp of Marshall's character. The first duty of law, as he understood it, was to maintain the sanctity of pledged word. In his youth society had suffered severely from want of will to enforce a contract. The national government, and especially the judiciary, had been created to supply this want by compelling men to perform their contracts. The essence of the opinion in Marbury's case was that the Executive should be held to the performance of a contract, all the more because

[1] Cranch's Reports, i. 153.

of his personal repugnance. Marshall ruled that Marbury had to his commission a vested legal right of which the Executive could not deprive him; and although the Court could not intermeddle with the prerogatives of the Executive, it might and would command a head of department to perform a duty not depending on Executive discretion, but on particular Acts of Congress and the general principles of law. The mandamus might issue, but not from the Supreme Court, which had appellate jurisdiction only. In other words, if Marbury chose to apply for the mandamus to Judge Cranch and the District Court, he might expect the success of his application.

The decision in Marbury's case naturally exasperated Jefferson; but the chief-justice knew the point beyond which he could not go in asserting the jurisdiction of his court, and was content to leave the matter as it stood. Marbury never applied for the mandamus in the court below. The opinion in the case of Marbury and Madison was allowed to sleep, and its language was too guarded to furnish excuse for impeachment; but while the President was still sore under the discourtesy of Marshall's law, another member of the Supreme Bench attacked him in a different way. If one judge in the United States should have known the peril in which the judiciary stood, it was Justice Samuel Chase of Maryland, who had done more than all the other judges to exasperate the democratic majority. His overbearing manners had twice driven from his court the most

eminent counsel of the circuit; he had left the bench
without a quorum in order that he might make political speeches for his party; and his contempt for the
popular will was loudly expressed. In the cases of
Fries and Callender, in 1800, he had strained the law
in order to convict for the government; and inasmuch
as his energy was excess of zeal, for conviction was
certain, he had exposed himself to the charge of
over-officiousness in order to obtain the chief-justice's
chair, which was given to Marshall. That he was
not impeached after the change of administration
proved the caution of the Republican party; but by
this neglect Congress seemed to have condoned his
old offences, or at least had tacitly consented to let
their punishment depend on the judge's future good
behavior.

Unluckily Chase's temper knew no laws of caution.
He belonged to the old class of conservatives who
thought that judges, clergymen, and all others in authority should guide and warn the people. May 2,
1803, barely two months after Marshall's defiance of
the President in Marbury's case and the impeachment
of Pickering, Justice Chase addressed the grand jury
at Baltimore on the democratic tendencies of their
local and national government.[1]

" Where law is uncertain, partial, or arbitrary," he
said; " where justice is not impartially administered to
all; where property is insecure, and the person is liable
to insult and violence without redress by law, — the peo-

[1] Annals of Congress, 1804–1805, pp. 673–676.

ple are *not free*, whatever may be their form of government. To this situation I greatly fear we are fast approaching. . . . The late alteration of the Federal judiciary by the abolition of the office of the sixteen circuit judges, and the recent change in our State Constitution by the establishing of universal suffrage, and the further alteration that is contemplated in our State judiciary (if adopted) will in my judgment take away all security for property and personal liberty. The independence of the national judiciary is already shaken to its foundation, and the virtue of the people alone can restore it. . . . Our republican Constitution will sink into a mobocracy, — the worst of all possible governments. . . . The modern doctrines by our late reformers, that all men in a state of society are entitled to enjoy equal liberty and equal rights, have brought this mighty mischief upon us; and I fear that it will rapidly progress until peace and order, freedom and property, shall be destroyed."

At the moment of Justice Chase's outburst to the Baltimore grand jury, the President was at Washington deeply interested in the Louisiana business, and unaware that on the day when Chase delivered his tirade Livingston and Monroe in Paris were signing their names to a treaty which put the Administration beyond danger from such attacks. When he saw in the newspapers a report of what had been said from the bench at Baltimore, he wrote to Joseph Nicholson, in whose hands already lay the management of Pickering's impeachment: [1] —

[1] Jefferson to Nicholson, May 13, 1803; Works, iv. 486.

" You must have heard of the extraordinary charge of Chase to the grand jury at Baltimore. Ought this seditious and official attack on the principles of our Constitution and on the proceedings of a State to go unpunished ; and to whom so pointedly as yourself will the public look for the necessary measures? I ask these questions for your consideration ; for myself, it is better that I should not interfere."

" Non-intervention," according to Talleyrand, " is a word used in politics and metaphysics, which means very nearly the same thing as intervention." The event proved that non-intervention was wise policy ; but Jefferson was somewhat apt to say that it was better he should not interfere in the same breath with which he interfered. The warning that he could not officially interfere seemed to imply that the quarrel was personal ; for in the case of Pickering he had interfered with decision. If this was his view, the success of any attack upon Chase would be a gain to him, and he was so ordering as to make failure a loss only to those who undertook it. Nicholson, hot-headed though he was, did not enter readily into this hazardous venture. He reflected upon it all summer, and consulted the friends on whose support he depended. Macon wrote to him a letter of unusual length,[1] suggesting grave doubts whether a judge ought to be impeached for expressing to a grand jury political opinions which every man was at liberty to hold and express elsewhere, and closed by announc-

[1] Macon to Nicholson, Aug. 6, 1803; Nicholson MSS.

ing the conviction that if any attempt were made to impeach, Nicholson ought not to be the leader. In this opinion Macon was evidently right, for Chase's friends could not fail to suggest that Nicholson was to be rewarded by an appointment to Chase's vacant seat on the Supreme Bench ; but the House of Representatives contained no other leader whose authority, abilities, and experience warranted him in taking so prominent a part, unless it were John Randolph.

A worse champion than Randolph for a difficult cause could not be imagined. Between him and Jefferson little sympathy existed. Randolph had quarrelled with the branch of his family to which Jefferson was closely allied ; and his private feelings stood in the way of personal attachment. His intimates in Congress were not chiefly Virginians, but men like Macon of North Carolina, Joseph Bryan of Georgia, and Nicholson of Maryland, — independent followers of Virginia doctrine, who owned no personal allegiance to Jefferson. That the President should have been willing to let such a man take entire responsibility for an impeachment was natural ; but had Jefferson directed the step, he would never have selected Randolph to manage a prosecution on which the fate of his principles closely depended. Randolph was no lawyer ; but this defect was a trifling objection compared with his greater unfitness in other respects. Ill-balanced, impatient of obstacles, incapable of sustained labor or of methodical arrangement, illogical to excess, and egotistic to the verge of madness, he

was sparkling and formidable in debate or on the
hustings, where he could follow the wayward impulse
of his fancy running in the accustomed channels of
his thought; but the qualities which helped him in
debate were fatal to him at the bar.

Such was the origin of a measure which did more
to define the character of the government than any
other single event in Jefferson's first administration,
except the purchase of Louisiana. Randolph threw
himself into the new undertaking; for he sincerely
believed in the justice of his cause, and was alive to
the danger of leaving the Supreme Court in the hands
of Marshall and men of his stamp who were determined to consolidate the government. Yet the chance
of obtaining a conviction, on a charge no stronger than
that of the Baltimore address, was so slight as to
incline Randolph against risking it; and he decided
to insure success by putting the cases of Fries and
Callender in the foreground.

This was not easily done. Pickering's impeachment had been brought before the House by a Message from the President; but in Chase's case the
President preferred not to take part. Randolph was
forced to escape the difficulty by an awkward manœuvre. During the autumn and early winter of
1803 Congress was busy with Louisiana legislation,
and had no leisure for other matters; but soon after
the new year Randolph rose and said [1] that in the
course of the last session Mr. Smilie of Pennsylvania

[1] Jan. 5, 1804; Annals of Congress, 1803–1804, p. 805.

had made some statements in regard to Justice Chase's conduct which seemed to call for notice, but that want of time had precluded action. Finding his attention thus drawn to the matter, Randolph gravely continued, he had felt it his duty to investigate Smilie's charges ; and having convinced himself that ground for impeachment existed, he asked the House to appoint a committee of inquiry. Such an introduction of a great constitutional struggle was not imposing ; but party discipline was at its highest point, and after some vigorous Federalist resistance Randolph carried his motion by a vote of eighty-one to forty. Three Northern democrats voted with the Federalists ; and although the defection seemed not serious so far as concerned the scientific Dr. Samuel L. Mitchill, whose political principles were liberal enough at all times, some importance even then attached to the vote of John Smith of New York, who was about to enter the Senate and to act as one of Chase's judges.

Meanwhile Judge Pickering's trial began. The Senate, " sitting as a Court of Impeachments," listened while Nicholson, Randolph, Rodney, and six or seven other Republican members "exhibited the grand inquest of the nation." The character of a court was taken in all the forms of summons. The Secretary of the Senate signed, and the Sergeant-at-Arms served, the summons to Judge Pickering, while the witnesses were regularly subpœnaed by the Secretary, " to appear before the Senate of the United States in their capacity of a Court of Impeachments," and the subpœnas were served by the marshals of the district courts.

Judge Pickering was ordered to appear on the 2d of March, 1804 ; but when the day arrived, and the Senate was assembled, with the managers in attendance, John Pickering's name was three times called without an answer.   Vice-President Burr then submitted to the Senate a petition from Jacob Pickering, son of the impeached judge, praying the court to postpone the trial that he might have time to collect evidence with the view of showing that when the alleged crimes were committed, and two years before as well as ever since, the judge was wholly deranged, incapable of transacting any kind of business which required the exercise of reason, and therefore incapable of corruption of judgment, no subject of impeachment, and amenable to no tribunal for his actions.   With this petition a letter from Robert G. Harper was laid before the court, requesting to be allowed to appear on the part of the petitioner in support of the petition. Harper, having been invited to a seat within the bar, asked whether he might be heard, not as counsel for Judge Pickering, who being insane could give no authority for the purpose, but as agent for the petitioner, to ask a postponement.

The question threw all parties into agitation.   The managers instantly protested that Harper in such a character could not be heard.   The senators retired for consultation, and debated all day without coming to a decision. The impeaching party dreaded the alternative to which the proof of insanity must force them, — of saying either that an insane man was responsible, or that a man mentally irresponsible might still be guilty of "high crimes and misdemeanors " for purposes of impeachment. Senator Jackson of Georgia, who had always the merit of speaking with candor, avowed the fear that presently Judge Chase's friends would come and pretend that he too was mad;[1] but he could not, even with Breckinridge's help, carry his point. The Northern democrats flinched. Six of them and three Southern senators voted with the Federalists, and admitted Harper in his volunteer character.

Harper put in his testimony, which was decisive in regard to the insanity ; but when he rose to do so, the managers retired, saying that they considered themselves under no obligation to discuss a preliminary question raised by an unauthorized third party. The Senate went on with its session. The managers were obliged to maintain that insanity was no bar to impeachment, and the Northern democrats were forced to accept the doctrine.[2]

This view of impeachment, so far as concerned the judiciary, had strong arguments in its favor. Although the Constitution made judges' tenure of

[1] Diary of J. Q. Adams, i. 299.

[2] Ibid., i. 301–302. Pickering to George Cabot, Jan. 29, 1804; Pickering to Theodore Lyman, Feb. 11, 1804 ; New England Federalism, pp. 340, 344.

office dependent on their good behavior, it provided
no other means than that of impeachment for their
removal.   Even in England and in Massachusetts,
judges could be removed by the joint action of Legislature and Executive ; but this was not the case
under the Constitution of the United States.   If insanity or any other misfortune was to bar impeachment, the absurdity followed that unless a judge
committed some indictable offence the people were
powerless to protect themselves.   Even Federalists
might reasonably assume that the people had never
placed themselves in such a situation, but that in
making their judges subject to impeachment for
misdemeanors they had meant to extend the scope
of impeachment, and to include within it all cases
of misbehavior which might require a removal from
office for the good of the public service.

This ground was fairly taken by the impeachers,
though not formally expressed.   When Harper had
put in his evidence and retired, the Senate sent again
for the managers, who occupied one day in supplying
evidence, and then left their case without argument
in the hands of the court.   The Senate found itself
face to face with an issue beyond measure delicate,
which had never been discussed, but from which escape was impossible.   Acquittal of Pickering would
probably be fatal to the impeachment of Chase, and
would also proclaim that the people could not protect themselves from misbehavior in their judicial
servants.   On the other hand, conviction would vio-

late the deep principle of law and justice that an insane man was not responsible for his acts, and not amenable to any earthly tribunal. Virginians like Randolph and Wilson Cary Nicholas, or John Breckinridge, were ready to make a precedent which should fix the rule that impeachment need not imply criminality, and might be the equivalent to removal by address. The Northern democrats were not unwilling to accept this view; but their consciences revolted against saying " guilty " where no guilt was implied or proved.

To escape this objection a compromise was proposed and adopted. The Federalists would have forced senators to say in their final vote that Judge Pickering was " guilty" or "not guilty " of high crimes and misdemeanors. Senator Anderson of Tennessee eluded this challenge by moving for a yea-and-nay vote on the question whether Pickering was guilty " as charged." The nine Federalists alone opposed his motion, which was at length adopted by a majority of two to one. By a vote of nineteen to seven Judge Pickering was declared " guilty as charged " in the articles of impeachment; and by a vote of twenty to six the Senate resolved that he ought to be removed from office.

Two of the Federalist senators refused to vote, on the ground that the proceedings were irregular; Senator Bradley of Vermont, Senator Armstrong of New York, and Senator Stone of North Carolina tacitly protested by absenting themselves. In a Senate of thirty-four members only twenty-six voted, and only

nineteen voted for conviction. So confused, contradictory, and irregular were these proceedings that
Pickering's trial was never considered a sound precedent. That an insane man could be guilty of crime,
and could be punished on *ex parte* evidence, without
a hearing, with not even an attorney to act in his
behalf, seemed such a perversion of justice that the
precedent fell dead on the spot. Perhaps, from the
constitutional point of view, a more fatal objection
was that in doing what the world was sure to consider an arbitrary and illegal act, the Virginians failed
to put on record the reasons which led them to think
it sound in principle. In the Louisiana purchase they
had acted in a way equally arbitrary, but they had
given their reasons for thinking themselves in the
right. In Pickering's case not a word was publicly
spoken on either side ; a plainly extra-constitutional
act was done without recording the doctrine on which
it rested.

The Republicans showed no hesitation. John
Randolph's orders were obeyed without open protest.
Senator Bradley of Vermont talked strongly in private against them; Senator Armstrong of New York
would not support them ; barely half the Senate voted
in their favor ; but Randolph forced his party forward
without stopping to see how well his steps were
taken, or how far he was likely to go. As though
to intimidate the Senate, March 6, the day after the
managers were defeated on the vote to hear Harper,
Randolph reported to the House a resolution ordering

the impeachment of Justice Chase. March 12, the day when the Senate voted Pickering guilty, the House took up Randolph's report, and the majority, without debate, voted by seventy-three to thirty-two that Chase should be impeached. Not a Republican ventured to record a vote in the negative. The next morning Randolph again appeared at the bar of the Senate, and announced that the House of Representatives would in due time exhibit articles of impeachment against Samuel Chase.

CHAPTER VIII.

As the year 1804 began, with Louisiana annexed, the Electoral Amendment secured, and the impeachments in prospect, the Federalists in Congress wrought themselves into a dangerous state of excitement. All agreed that the crisis was at hand; democracy had nearly reached its limit; and, as Justice Chase said from the bench, peace and order, freedom and property, would soon be destroyed. They discussed in private what should be done; and among the New Englanders almost all the men of weight were found to favor the policy of at least saving New England. Of the six Federalist senators from the Eastern States, — Plumer and Olcott of New Hampshire, Pickering and Adams of Massachusetts, Tracy and Hillhouse of Connecticut, — all but Olcott and Adams thought a dissolution of the Union inevitable.[1] Among the Federalist members of the House, Roger Griswold of Connecticut was the most active; he too was convinced that New England must protect herself. Samuel Hunt of New Hampshire, and Calvin Goddard of Connecticut held the same opinion. Indeed, Pick-

[1] New England Federalism, pp. 106, 146, 342, 352; Plumer's Life of Plumer, pp. 284–311.

ering declared that he did not know "one reflecting Nov-Anglian" who held any other.

In the month of January, 1804, despair turned into conspiracy. Pickering, Tracy, Griswold, Plumer, and perhaps others of the New England delegation, agreed to organize a movement in their States for a dissolution of the Union. They wrote to their most influential constituents, and sketched a plan of action. In a letter to George Cabot, Pickering recounted the impending dangers [1] : —

"By the Philadelphia papers I see that the Supreme Court judges of Pennsylvania are to be hurled from their seats, on the pretence that in punishing one Thomas Passmore for a contempt they acted illegally and tyrannically. I presume that Shippen, Yates, and Smith are to be removed by the Governor, on the representation of the Legislature. And when such grounds are taken in the National and State legislatures to destroy the rights of the judges, whose rights can be safe? Why destroy *them*, unless as the prelude to the destruction of every influential Federalist and of every man of considerable property who is not of the reigning sect? New judges, of characters and tempers suited to the object, will be the selected ministers of vengeance."

A separation, Pickering inferred, had become necessary ; but when and how was it to be effected ?

"If Federalism is crumbling away in New England, there is no time to be lost, lest it should be overwhelmed and become unable to attempt its own relief; its last

[1] Pickering to George Cabot, Jan. 29, 1804; Lodge's Cabot, p. 337.

refuge is New England, and immediate exertion perhaps its only hope. It must begin in Massachusetts. The proposition would be welcomed in Connecticut; and could we doubt of New Hampshire? But New York must be associated; and how is her concurrence to be obtained? She must be made the centre of the confederacy. Vermont and New Jersey would follow of course, and Rhode Island of necessity. Who can be consulted, and who will take the lead? The legislatures of Massachusetts and Connecticut meet in May, and of New Hampshire in the same month, or June. The subject has engaged the contemplation of many. The Connecticut gentlemen have seriously meditated upon it. . . . Tracy has written to several of his most distinguished friends in Connecticut, and may soon receive their answers. R. Griswold, examining the finances, has found that the States above mentioned, to be embraced by the Northern confederacy, now pay as much or more of the public revenues as would discharge their share of the public debts due those States and abroad, leaving out the millions given for Louisiana."

Roger Griswold wrote a few weeks afterward to Oliver Wolcott in similar terms : [1] —

" The project which we had formed was to induce, if possible, the legislatures of the three New England States who remain Federal to commence measures which should call for a reunion of the Northern States. The extent of those measures, and the rapidity with which they shall be followed up, must be governed by circum-

[1] Roger Griswold to Oliver Wolcott, March 11, 1804; Hamilton's History of the Republic, vii. 781; New England Federalism, p. 354.

stances. The magnitude and jealousy of Massachusetts
would render it necessary that the operation should be
commenced there. If any hope can be created that New
York will ultimately support the plan, it may perhaps be
supported."

The first action, said he, must come from the Legislature of Massachusetts, which was not yet elected,
but would meet early in June. Connecticut and New
Hampshire were to follow; and to Pickering's san-
guine mind the Northern Confederacy seemed already
established. "The people of the East," he said,
"cannot reconcile their habits, views, and interests
with those of the South and West. The latter are
beginning to rule with a rod of iron."

Pickering knew that the Federalist majority in
Massachusetts was none too great. The election in
May, four months later, showed a Federalist vote of
30,000 against a Republican minority of 24,000, while
in the Legislature Harrison Gray Otis was chosen
Speaker by 129 votes to 103. Pickering knew also
that his colleague, Senator Adams, was watching his
movements with increasing ill-will, which Pickering
lost no chance to exasperate. Nothing could be more
certain than that at the first suggestion of disunion
Senator Adams and the moderate Federalists would
attack the Essex Junto with the bitterness of long-
suppressed hatred; and if they could not command
fourteen votes in the Legislature and three thousand
in the State, a great change must have occurred since
the year before, when they elected Adams to the

Senate for the long term over Pickering's head.   Pickering concealed his doings from his colleague; but Tracy was not so cautious.   Adams learned the secret from Tracy; and the two senators from Massachusetts drew farther and farther apart, in spite of the impeachments, which tended to force them together.

The Essex Junto, which sent Pickering to Washington, and to which he appealed for support, read his letter with evident astonishment.   George Cabot, Chief-Justice Parsons, Fisher Ames, and Stephen Higginson, who were the leaders consulted,[1] agreed that the scheme was impracticable; and Cabot, as gently as possible, put their common decision into words.

"All the evils you describe," he said,[2] "and many more, are to be apprehended; but I greatly fear that a separation would be no remedy, because the source of them is in the political theories of our country and in ourselves.   A separation at some period not very remote may probably take place,—— the first impression of it is even now favorably received by many; but I cannot flatter myself with the expectation of essential good to proceed from it while we retain maxims and principles which all experience, and I may add reason too, pronounce to be impracticable and absurd.   Even in New England, where there is among the body of the people more wisdom and virtue than in any other part of the United States, we are full of errors which no reasoning

[1] Cabot to Pickering, March 7, 1804; New England Federalism, p. 353.

[2] Cabot to Pickering, Feb. 14, 1804; Lodge's Cabot, p. 341.

could eradicate if there were a Lycurgus in every village. We are democratic altogether; and I hold democracy in its natural operation to be the government of the worst.

"There is no energy in the Federal party, and there could be none manifested without great hazard of losing the State government. Some of our best men in high stations are kept in office because they forbear to exert any influence, and not because they possess right principles. They are permitted to have power if they will not use it. . . . I incline to the opinion that the essential alterations which may in future be made to amend our form of government will be the consequences only of great suffering or the immediate effects of violence. If we should be made to feel a very great calamity from the abuse of power by the National Administration, we might do almost anything; but it would be idle to talk to the deaf, to warn the people of distant evils. By this time you will suppose I am willing to do nothing but submit to fate. I would not be so understood. I am convinced we cannot do what is wished; but we can do much, if we work with Nature (or the course of things), and not against her. A separation is now impracticable, because we do not feel the necessity or utility of it. The same separation then will be unavoidable when our loyalty to the Union is generally perceived to be the instrument of debasement and impoverishment. If it is prematurely attempted, those few only will promote it who discern what is hidden from the multitude."

Cabot's letter, more clearly than any writing of Alexander Hamilton himself, expressed the philosophy and marked the tactics of their school. Neither Cabot nor Hamilton was a lively writer, and the dust which has gathered deep on their doctrines dulls whatever brilliancy they once possessed; but this letter showed why Cabot was considered the wisest head in his party, to whose rebuke even Hamilton was forced to bow. For patient and willing students who have groped in search of the idea which, used by Hamilton and Jefferson, caused bitterer feeling and roused deeper terrors than civil war itself, Cabot's long and perhaps pedantic letter on the policy of disunion was full of meaning. "We shall go the way of all governments wholly popular, — from bad to worse, — until the evils, no longer tolerable, shall generate their own remedies." Democracy must end in a crisis, experience and reason pronounced it impracticable and absurd, Nature would in due time vindicate her own laws; and when the inevitable chaos should come, then conservative statesmanship could set society on a sound footing by limiting the suffrage to those citizens who might hold in their own right two thousand dollars value in land. Meanwhile disunion would be useless, and the attempt to bring it about would break up the Federalist party. "A war with Great Britain manifestly provoked by our rulers" was the only chance which Cabot foresaw of bringing the people of New England to a dissolution of the Union.

Pickering was not so intelligent as Cabot, Parsons, and Ames; his temper was harsher than theirs; he was impatient of control, and never forgot or wholly forgave those who forced him to follow another course than the one he chose. Cabot's letter showed a sense of these traits; for though it was in the nature of a command or entreaty to cease discussing disunion, if the Federalist party in Massachusetts were to be saved, it was couched in gentle language, and without affecting a tone of advice suggested ideas which ought to guide Federalists in Congress. Pickering was to wait for the crisis. Inaction was easy; and even though the crisis should be delayed five or ten years, — a case hardly to be supposed, — no step could be taken without a blunder before the public should be ready for it. With this simple and sound principle to guide them, conservatives could not go wrong. Cabot there left the matter.

Such gentleness toward a man of Pickering's temper was a mistake, which helped to cost the life of one whom conservatives regarded as their future leader in the crisis. Pickering was restive under the sense that his friends preferred other counsellors; whereas his experience and high offices, to say nothing of his ability, entitled him, as he thought, to greater weight in the party than Hamilton, Cabot, or Rufus King. Backed by Tracy, Griswold, and other men of standing, Pickering felt able to cope with opposition. His rough sense and democratic instincts warned him that the fine-drawn political theories of George Cabot and Theophilus Parsons might end in impotence. He could see no reason why Massachusetts, once corrupted, might not wallow in democratic iniquities with as much pleasure as

New York or Pennsylvania; and all that was worth saving might be lost before her democracy would consent to eat the husks of repentance and ask forgiveness from the wise and good. Cabot wanted to wait a few months or years until democracy should work out its own fate; and whenever the public should yearn for repose, America would find her Pitt and Bonaparte combined in the political grasp and military genius of Alexander Hamilton. Pickering, as a practical politician, felt that if democracy were suffered to pull down the hierarchy of New England, neither disunion nor foreign war, nor "a very great calamity" of any kind, could with certainty restore what had once been destroyed.

Cabot's argument shook none of Pickering's convictions; but the practical difficulty on which the home Junto relied was fatal unless some way of removing it could be invented. During the month of February, 1804, when the impeachment panic was at its height in Congress, Pickering, Tracy, and Plumer received letter after letter from New England, all telling the same story. The eminent Judge Tapping Reeve, of Connecticut, wrote to Tracy:[1] "I have seen many of our friends; and all that I have seen and most that I have heard from believe that we must separate, and that this is the most favorable moment." He had heard only one objection, — that the country was not prepared; but this objection,

[1] Tapping Reeve to Uriah Tracy, Feb. 7, 1804; Lodge's Cabot, p. 442.

which meant that the disunionists were a minority, was echoed from all New England. The conspirators dared not openly discuss the project. " There are few among my acquaintance," wrote Pickering's nephew, Theodore Lyman,[1] " with whom I could on that subject freely converse; there may be more ready than I am aware of." Plumer found a great majority of the New Hampshire Federalists decidedly opposed. Roger Griswold, toward the end of the session, summed up the result in his letter to Oliver Wolcott: —

" We have endeavored during this session to rouse our friends in New England to make some bold exertions in that quarter. They generally tell us that they are sensible of the danger, that the Northern States must unite; but they think the time has not yet arrived. Prudence is undoubtedly necessary; but when it degenerates into procrastination it becomes fatal. Whilst we are waiting for the time to arrive in New England, it is certain the democracy is making daily inroads upon us, and our means of resistance are lessening every day. Yet it appears impossible to induce our friends to make any decisive exertions. Under these circumstances I have been induced to look to New York."

The representatives of the wise and good looked at politics with eyes which saw no farther than those of the most profligate democrat into the morality of the game. Pickering enjoyed hearing himself called " honest Tim Pickering;" as though he were willing to imply a tinge of dishonesty in others, even in the

[1] Theodore Lyman to Pickering, Feb. 29, 1804; Lodge's Cabot, p. 446.

Puritan society of Wenham and Salem.   Griswold
was to the end of his life a highly respected citizen
of Connecticut, and died while governor of the State.
That both these worthy men should conspire to break
up the Union implied to their minds no dishonesty,
because they both held that the Republican majority
had by its illegal measures already destroyed the
Constitution which they had sworn to support; but
although such casuistry might excuse in their own
consciences the act of conspiracy, neither this reasoning nor any other consistent with self-respect warranted their next step.   Griswold's remark that the
procrastination of New England had led him to look
to New York was not quite candid; his plan had
from the first depended on New York.   Pickering
had written to Cabot at the outset, " She must be
made the centre of the confederacy."   New York
seemed, more than New England, unfit to be made
the centre of a Northern confederacy, because there
the Federalist party was a relatively small minority.
If Massachusetts and Connecticut showed fatal apa-
thy, in New York actual repulsion existed ; the extreme Federalists had no following.   To bring New
York to the Federalism of Pickering and Griswold, the Federalist party needed to recover power
under a leader willing to do its work.   The idea
implied a bargain and an intrigue on terms such as
in the Middle Ages the Devil was believed to impose
upon the ambitious and reckless.   Pickering and
Griswold could win their game only by bartering

their souls; they must invoke the Mephistopheles of politics, Aaron Burr.

To this they had made up their minds from the beginning. Burr's four years of office were drawing to a close. The Virginians had paid him the price he asked for replacing them in power; and had it been Shylock's pound of flesh, they could not have looked with greater care to see that Burr should get neither more nor less, even in the estimation of a hair, than the exact price they had covenanted to pay. In another year the debt would be discharged, and the Virginians would be free. Burr had not a chance of regaining a commanding place among Republicans, for he was bankrupt in private and public character. In New York the Clintons never ceased their attacks, with the evident wish to drive him from the party. Cheetham, after publishing in 1802 two heavy pamphlets, a "Narrative" and a "View," attempted in 1803 to crush him under the weight of a still heavier volume, containing "Nine Letters on the Subject of Aaron Burr's Political Defection." Nov. 16, 1803, the "Albany Register" at length followed Cheetham's lead; and nearly all the other democratic newspapers followed the "Register," abandoning Burr as a man who no longer deserved confidence.

Till near the close of 1803 the Vice-President held his peace. The first sign that he meant energetic retaliation was given by an anonymous pamphlet,[1]

---

[1] An Examination of the various Charges against Aaron Burr, by Aristides. December, 1803.

which won the rare double triumph of political and
literary success, in which ability and ill temper
seemed to have equal shares. The unexpected appearance of "Aristides" startled New York. This
attack recalled the scandal which Alexander Hamilton had created four years before by his pamphlet
against his own President. "Aristides" wrote with
even more bitterness than Hamilton, and the ferocity
of his assault on the personal and political characters
of the Republican leaders made the invectives of
Hamilton and Cheetham somewhat tame; but the
scandal in each case was due not so much to per-
sonalities of abuse as to breaches of confidence.
"Aristides" furnished to the enemies of the Clintons
and Livingstons an arsenal of poisoned weapons; but
what was more to the purpose, his defence of Burr
was strong. That it came directly from the Vice-
President was clear; but the pamphlet showed more
literary ability than Burr claimed, and the world
was at a loss to discover who could be held responsible for its severities. Cheetham tried in vain to
pierce the incognito. Not till long afterward was
"Aristides" acknowledged by Burr's most intimate
friend, William Peter Van Ness.

An attempt to separate what was just from what
was undeserved in Van Ness's reproaches of the
Clintons and Livingstons would be useless. The
Clintons and Livingstons, however unprincipled they
might be, could say that they were more respectable
than Burr; but though this were true so far as social

standing was concerned, they could not easily show
that as a politician the Vice-President was worse than
his neighbors. The New England Federalists knew
well that Burr was not to be trusted, but they did
not think much worse of him than they thought of
De Witt Clinton, or John Armstrong, or Edward
Livingston, at this moment removed from office by
Jefferson for failing to account for thirty thousand
dollars due to the United States Treasury. As a
politician Burr had played fast and loose with all
parties; but so had most of his enemies. Seeing
that he was about to try another cast of the dice, all
the political gamblers gathered round to help or hurt
his further fortunes; and Van Ness might fairly
have said that in the matter of principle or political
morality, none of them could show clean hands.

Although Vice-President until March, 1805, Burr
announced that he meant to offer himself as a candidate for the post of governor of New York in April,
1804. At the same time Governor Clinton privately
gave warning of his own retirement. De Witt
Clinton was annoyed at his uncle's conduct, and
tried to prevent the withdrawal by again calling
Jefferson to his aid and alarming him with fear of
Burr.

" A certain gentleman was to leave this place yesterday morning," wrote De Witt to the President.[1] " He
has been very active in procuring information as to his
probable success for governor at the next election. This,

[1] De Witt Clinton to Jefferson, Nov. 26, 1803 ; Jefferson MSS.

I believe, is his intention at present, although it is certain that if the present Governor will consent to be a candidate, he will prevail by an immense majority. . . . Perhaps a letter from you may be of singular service."

Jefferson declined to interfere, putting his refusal on the ground of Burr's candidacy.

" I should think it indeed a serious misfortune," was his reply,[1] " should a change in the administration of your government be hazarded before its present principles be well established through all its parts; yet on reflection you will be sensible that the delicacy of my situation, considering who may be competitors, forbids my intermeddling even so far as to write the letter you suggest. I can therefore only brood in silence over my secret wishes."

No real confidence ever existed between Jefferson and the Clintons. A few days after these letters were written, "Aristides" betrayed the secret that Governor Clinton, in the spring of 1800, declared Jefferson to be " an accommodating trimmer, who would change with times and bend to circumstances for the purposes of personal promotion." This revelation by " Aristides," supported by the names of persons who heard the remark, forced Governor Clinton into an awkward denial of the charge, and led to an exchange of letters [2] and to professions of confidence between him and Jefferson; but time showed that neither the Governor

[1] Jefferson to De Witt Clinton, Dec. 2, 1803; Jefferson MSS.

[2] Jefferson to Governor Clinton, Dec. 31, 1803; Works, iv. 520.

nor his nephew loved the Virginians more than they were loved by Burr.

The threads of intrigue drew together, as they were apt to do before a general election. The last week in January came. Three days before Senator Pickering wrote his conspiracy letter to George Cabot, a letter which implied co-operation with Burr in making him governor of New York, Burr asked for a private interview with Jefferson, and formally offered him the choice between friendship or enmity. The President thought the conversation so curious that he made a note of it.

" He began," said Jefferson,[1] " by recapitulating summarily that he had come to New York a stranger, some years ago; that he found the country in possession of two rich families, — the Livingstons and Clintons; . . . that since, those great families had become hostile to him and had excited the calumnies which I had seen published; that in this Hamilton had joined, and had even written some of the pieces against him. . . . He observed, he believed it would be for the interest of the Republican cause for him to retire, — that a disadvantageous schism would otherwise take place; but that were he to retire, it would be said he shrank from the public sentence, which he would never do; that his enemies were using my name to destroy him, and something was necessary from me to prevent and deprive them of that weapon, — some mark of favor from me which would declare to the world that he retired with my confidence."

[1] The Anas, Jan. 26, 1804; Works, ix. 204.

Jefferson, with many words but with his usual courtesy, intimated that he could not appoint the Vice-President to an Executive office; and Burr then united his intrigues with those of Pickering and Griswold. Thenceforth his chance of retaining power depended on the New York election; and his success in this election depended on the Federalists. Before George Cabot had yet written his answer to Pickering's questions, Pickering could no longer resist the temptation to act.

The effect of what passed at Washington was instantly felt at Albany. Toward the middle of February, about three weeks after Jefferson had civilly rejected the Vice-President's advances, Burr's friends in the New York legislature announced that they should hold a caucus February 18, and nominate him as candidate for governor. The Federalists at once called a preliminary caucus to decide whether they should support Burr. Alexander Hamilton, who happened to be engaged in law business at Albany, Feb. 16, 1804, attended the Federal caucus, and used his influence in favor of the regular Clinton candidate against Burr's pretensions. The drift of his argument was given in an abstract of reasons which he drew up for the occasion.[1] Unfortunately the strongest of these reasons was evidently personal; the leadership of Hamilton would not tolerate rivalry from Burr. Hamilton pointed out that Burr's elevation by the Federalists of New York would present him as their

[1] Hamilton's Works, vii. 851.

leader to the Federalists of New England, and would assist him to disorganize New England if so disposed; that there " the ill-opinion of Jefferson, and jealousy of the ambition of Virginia, is no inconsiderable prop of good opinions; but these causes are leading to an opinion that a dismemberment of the Union is expedient. It would probably suit Mr. Burr's views to promote this result, — to be the chief of the Northern portion; and placed at the head of the State of New York, no man would be more likely to succeed."

If the Union was to be severed, Hamilton was the intended chief of the Northern portion; but he wanted no severance that should leave the germs of the democratic disease. His philosophy was that of George Cabot, William Pitt, and Talleyrand; he waited for the whole country to come to its senses and restore sound principles, that democracy might everywhere die out or be stifled. Burr's methods were democratic, and would perpetuate in a Northern confederacy the vices of the Union; they would break up the conservative strength without weakening democracy. Within a few days the danger which Hamilton foresaw came to pass. Burr's little band of friends in the Legislature, Feb. 18, 1804, set him in nomination; and a large majority of Federalists, in defiance of Hamilton's entreaties, meant to vote for him.

As the situation became clearer, Hamilton's personal feeling became public. While at Albany, February 16, he dined with John Tayler, and at table talked of the political prospect. One of the company, Dr. Charles D. Cooper, an active partisan, wrote an account of the conversation to a certain Mr. Brown near Albany : " General Hamilton and Judge Kent have declared, in substance, that they looked upon Mr. Burr to be a dangerous man, and one who ought not to be trusted with the reins of government." The letter was printed, and went the rounds of the press.   As it roused some question and dispute, Cooper wrote again : " I could detail to you a still more despicable opinion which General Hamilton has expressed of Mr. Burr."   This letter also was printed ; the " Albany Register " of April 24 contained the correspondence.

The news of Burr's nomination reached Washington at the moment when Pickering and Tracy received answers to their disunion scheme ; and it served to keep them steady to their plan.   The Federalists, who professed to consider Hamilton their leader, seldom followed his advice ; but on this occasion they set him somewhat unkindly aside.   Too much in awe of Hamilton to say directly to his face that he must be content with the place of Burr's lieutenant, they wrote letters to that effect which were intended for his eye.

Of all Federalist leaders, moderate and extreme, Rufus King, who had recently returned from London, stood highest in the confidence of his party.   He was to be the Federalist candidate for Vice-President ; he had mixed in none of the feuds which made Hamilton obnoxious to many of his former friends ; and while

King's manners were more conciliatory, his opinions were more moderate, than those of other party leaders. To him Pickering wrote, March 4, 1804, in a tone of entreaty : —

" I am disgusted with the men who now rule, and with their measures. At some manifestations of their malignancy I am shocked. The cowardly wretch at their head, while like a Parisian revolutionary monster prating about humanity, would feel an infernal pleasure in the utter destruction of his opponents."

After avowing his hopes of disunion, Pickering next touched the New York election : [1] —

" The Federalists here in general anxiously desire the election of Mr. Burr to the chair of New York, for they despair of a present ascendency of the Federalist party. Mr. Burr alone, we think, can break your democratic phalanx, and we anticipate much good from his success. Were New York detached, as under his administration it would be, from the Virginia influence, the whole Union would be benefited. Jefferson would then be forced to observe some caution and forbearance in his measures. And if a separation should be deemed proper, the five New England States, New York, and New Jersey would naturally be united."

Rufus King was as cautious as Pickering was indiscreet. He acknowledged this letter in vague terms of compliment,[2] saying that Pickering's views " ought

[1] Pickering to Rufus King, March 4, 1804; Lodge's Cabot, p. 447.

[2] Rufus King to Pickering, March 9, 1804; Lodge's Cabot, p. 450.

to fix the attention of the real friends of liberty in this quarter of the Union, and the more so as things seem to be fast advancing to a crisis." Even King's cool head was possessed with the thought which tormented Hamilton, Cabot, Ames, Pickering, Griswold, and Tracy, — the crisis which was always coming, and which, in the midst of peace, plenty, and contentment such as a tortured world had seldom known, overhung these wise and virtuous men like the gloom of death.

A week later Roger Griswold followed Pickering's example by writing to another of Hamilton's friends, Oliver Wolcott, who apparently sent the letter to Hamilton.[1] A Congressional caucus, February 25, nominated George Clinton as the Republican candidate for Vice-President by sixty-five votes against forty-one, — Burr's friends absenting themselves. This nomination showed some division between the Northern and Southern democrats; but Griswold rightly argued that nothing could be done in Congress, — the formation of a Northern interest must begin at home, and must find its centre of union in Burr. The arguments for this course were set forth with entire candor.

"I have wished to ascertain," wrote Griswold, "the views of Colonel Burr in relation to the general government; but having had no intimacy with him myself, and finding no one on the spot calculated, or indeed author-

[1] Roger Griswold to Oliver Wolcott, March 11, 1804; Hamilton's History, vii. 781; New England Federalism, p. 354.

ized, to require an explanation, I have obtained but little information. He speaks in the most bitter terms of the Virginia faction, and of the necessity of a union at the northward to resist it; but what the ultimate objects are which he would propose, I do not know. It is apparent that his election is supported in New York on the principle of resisting Virginia and uniting the North; and it may be presumed that the support given to him by Federal men would tend to reconcile the feelings of those democrats who are becoming dissatisfied with their Southern masters. But it is worthy of great consideration whether the advantage gained in this manner will not be more than counterbalanced by fixing on the Northern States a man in whom the most eminent of our friends will not repose confidence. If Colonel Burr is elevated in New York to the office of governor by the votes of Federalism, will he not be considered, and must he not in fact become, the head of the Northern interest? His ambition will not suffer him to be second, and his office will give him a claim to the first rank."

Having proposed this question, Griswold argued it as one in which the interests of New York must yield to the larger interests behind, and decided that " unpleasant as the thing may be," Burr's election and consequent leadership of the Federalist party was " the only hope which at this time presents itself of rallying in defence of the Northern States. . . . What else can we do? If we remain inactive, our ruin is certain. Our friends will make no attempts alone. By supporting Mr. Burr we gain some support, although it is of a doubtful nature, and of which,

God knows, we have cause enough to be jealous. In short, I see nothing else left for us."

Had this been all, though it was a rude blow to Hamilton, it might have passed as a difference of opinion on a point of party policy; but Griswold's object in writing these excuses was to explain that he had already done more, and had even entered into personal relations with Colonel Burr in view of a bargain. What this bargain was to be, Griswold explained : —

" I have engaged to call on the Vice-President as I pass through New York. The manner in which he gave me the invitation appeared to indicate a wish to enter upon some explanation. He said he wished very much to see me, and to converse, but his situation in this place did not admit of it, and he begged me to call on him at New York. This took place yesterday in the library. Indeed, I do not see how he can avoid a full explanation with Federal men. His prospects must depend on the union of the Federalists with his friends, and it is certain that his views must extend much beyond the office of governor of New York. He has the spirit of ambition and revenge to gratify, and can do but little with his ' little band ' alone."

Even George Cabot deserted Hamilton, and wrote from Boston to Rufus King a long letter, in the tone of indolent speculation which irritated restless fighters like Pickering and Griswold : [1] —

" An *experiment* has been suggested by some of our friends, to which I object that it is impracticable, and

[1] George Cabot to Rufus King, March 17, 1804; Lodge's Cabot, p. 345.

if practicable would be ineffectual. The thing proposed
is obvious and natural; but it would now be thought too
bold, and would be fatal to its advocates as public men;
yet the time *may* soon come when it will be demanded
by the people of the North and East, and then it will
unavoidably take place."

He explained his favorite thesis, — the last resource
of failing protestants, — that things must be worse
before they were better; but closed by wishing success to Burr. "I should rejoice to see Burr win the
race in your State, but I cannot approve of aid being
given him by any of the *leading* Federalists."

Ten days later, March 27, Congress adjourned;
and thenceforward the intrigue centred about Burr
and Hamilton in New York. No sooner did Griswold reach that city, a week afterward, on his way
from Washington to Connecticut, than he kept his
engagement with Burr, and the conversation strengthened him in his policy.[1] Burr was cautious, but said
that in his present canvass "he must go on democrat-
ically to obtain the government; that if he succeeded,
he should administer it in a manner that would be
satisfactory to the Federalists. In respect to the
affairs of the nation, Burr said that the Northern
States must be governed by Virginia, or govern Virginia, and that there was no middle course; that
the democratic members of Congress from the East
were in this sentiment, — some of those from New
York, some of the leaders in Jersey, and likewise in

[1] Hamilton's History, vii. 787.

Pennsylvania." Further than this he would not go; and Griswold contented himself with such vague allurements.

On the other hand, Rufus King's library was the scene of grave dissensions. There Pickering went, April 8, to urge his scheme of disunion, and retired on the appearance of his colleague, Senator Adams, who for the first and last time in his life found himself fighting the battle of Alexander Hamilton, whom he disliked as decidedly as Pickering professed to love him. As the older senator left the house at his colleague's entrance, King said to Adams:[1] "Colonel Pickering has been talking to me about a project they have for a separation of the States and a Northern Confederacy; and he has also been this day talking of it with General Hamilton. Have you heard anything of it at Washington?" Adams replied that he had heard much, but not from Colonel Pickering. "I disapprove entirely of the project," said King; "and so, I am happy to tell you, does General Hamilton."

The struggle for control between Hamilton and the conspirators lasted to the eve of the election, — secret, stifled, mysterious; the intrigue of men afraid to avow their aims, and seeming rather driven by their own passions than guided by the lofty and unselfish motives which ought to inspire those whom George Cabot emphatically called the *best!* The result was a drawn battle. Hamilton prevented leading Federal-

[1] New England Federalism, p. 148.

ists from open committal of the party, but he could not prevent the party itself from voting for Burr. The election took place April 25, 1804; and although Burr succeeded in carrying to the Federalists a few hundred voters in the city of New York, where his strength lay, giving him there a majority of about one hundred in a total vote of less than three thousand, he polled but about twenty-eight thousand votes in the State against thirty-five thousand for the Clinton candidate. The Federalists gained nothing by supporting him; but only a small portion of the party refused him their aid.

The obstinacy of Pickering and Griswold in pressing Burr on the party forced Hamilton to strain his strength in order to prevent what he considered his own humiliation. That all Hamilton's doings were known to Burr could hardly be doubted. When the election closed, a new era in Burr's life began. He was not a vindictive man, but this was the second time Hamilton had stood in his way and vilified his character. Burr could have no reason to suppose that Hamilton was deeply loved; for he knew that four fifths of the Federal party had adopted his own leadership when pitted against Hamilton's in the late election, and he knew too that Pickering, Griswold, and other leading Federalists had separated from Hamilton in the hope of making Burr himself the chief of a Northern confederacy. Burr never cared for the past, — the present and future were his only thought; but his future in politics depended on his breaking

somewhere through the line of his personal enemies;
and Hamilton stood first in his path, for Hamilton
would certainly renew at every critical moment the
tactics which had twice cost Burr his prize.

Pickering and Griswold saw their hopes shattered
by the result of the New York election. They gained
at the utmost only an agreement to hold a private
meeting of leading Federalists at Boston in the following autumn;[1] and as Hamilton was to be present, he probably intended to take part only in order
to stop once for all the intrigues of these two men.
Such an assemblage, under the combined authority of
Cabot, King, and Hamilton, could not have failed to
restore discipline.

Nearly two months passed after the New York
election, when, on the morning of June 18, William
P. Van Ness, not yet known as "Aristides," appeared
in Hamilton's office. He brought a note from Vice-
President Burr, which enclosed newspaper-cuttings
containing Dr. Cooper's report of Hamilton's "despicable" opinion of Burr's character. The paragraph,
Burr said, had but very recently come to his knowledge. "You must perceive, sir, the necessity of a
prompt and unqualified acknowledgment or denial of
the use of any expression which would warrant the
assertions of Dr. Cooper." General Hamilton took
two days to consider the subject; and then replied in
what Burr thought an evasive manner, but closed
with two lines of defiance: " I trust on more reflec-

[1] Life of Plumer, p. 299.

tion you will see the matter in the same light with me; if not, I can only regret the circumstance, and must abide the consequences." [1]

These concluding words were the usual form in which men expressed themselves when they intended to accept a challenge to a duel. At first sight, no sufficient reason for accepting a challenge was shown by Hamilton's letter, which disavowed Dr. Cooper's report so far as Burr was warranted in claiming disavowal. Hamilton might without impropriety have declined to give further satisfaction. In truth, not the personal but the political quarrel drew him into the field; he knew that Burr meant to challenge, not the man, but the future political chief, and that an enemy so bent on rule must be met in the same spirit. Hamilton fought to maintain his own right to leadership, so rudely disputed by Burr, Pickering, and Griswold. He devoted some of his moments before the duel to the task of explaining, in a formal document, that he fought only to save his political influence.[2] " The ability to be in future useful, whether in resisting mischief or effecting good, in those crises of our public affairs which seem likely to happen, would probably be inseparable from a conformity with public prejudice in this particular."

Always the crisis! Yet this crisis which brought Hamilton in July to the duelling-ground at Weehawken was not the same as that which Pickering and

---

[1] Hamilton's History, vii. 806.
[2] Hamilton's History, vii. pp. 816–819.

Griswold had so lately tried to create. Pickering's disunion scheme came to a natural end on Burr's defeat in April. The legislatures of the three Federalist States had met and done nothing; all chance of immediate action was lost, and all parties, including even Pickering and Griswold, had fallen back on their faith in the " crisis " ; but the difference of opinion between Hamilton and the New Englanders was still well defined. Hamilton thought that disunion, from a conservative standpoint, was a mistake ; nearly all the New Englanders, on the contrary, looked to ultimate disunion as a conservative necessity. The last letter which Hamilton wrote, a few hours before he left his house for the duelling-ground, was a short and earnest warning against disunion, addressed to Theodore Sedgwick, one of the sternest Massachusetts Federalists of Pickering's class.[1]

" Dismemberment of our empire," said Hamilton, " will be a clear sacrifice of great positive advantages, without any counterbalancing good ; administering no relief to our real disease, which is *democracy*, — the poison of which, by a subdivision, will only be the more concentred in each part, and consequently the more virulent."

The New Englanders thought this argument unsound, as it certainly was ; for a dissolution of the American Union would have struck a blow more nearly fatal to democracy throughout the world than any other " crisis " that man could have compassed. Yet the argument showed that had Hamilton sur-

[1] Hamilton to Sedgwick, July 10, 1804; Works, vi. 567.

vived, he would probably have separated from his New England allies, and at last, like his friends Rufus King and Oliver Wolcott, would have accepted the American world as it was.

The tragedy that actually happened was a fitter ending to this dark chapter than any tamer close could have been. Early on the morning of July 11, in the brilliant sunlight of a hot summer, the two men were rowed to the duelling-ground across the river, under the rocky heights of Weehawken, and were placed by their seconds face to face. Had Hamilton acted with the energy of conviction, he would have met Burr in his own spirit; but throughout this affair Hamilton showed want of will. He allowed himself to be drawn into a duel, but instead of killing Burr he invited Burr to kill him. In the paper Hamilton left for his justification, he declared the intention to throw away his first fire. He did so. Burr's bullet passed through Hamilton's body. The next day he was dead.

As the news spread, it carried a wave of emotion over New England, and roused everywhere sensations strangely mixed. In New York the Clinton interest, guided by Cheetham, seized the moment to destroy Burr's influence forever. Cheetham affected to think the duel a murder, procured Burr's indictment, and drove him from the State. Charges were invented to support this theory, and were even accepted as history. In the South and West, on the other hand, the duel was considered as a simple "affair of honor," in which

Burr appeared to better advantage than his opponent. In New England a wail of despair arose. Even the clergy, though shocked that Hamilton should have offered the evil example of duelling, felt that they had lost their champion and sword of defence. "In those crises of our public affairs which seemed likely to happen," Hamilton's genius in council and in the field had been their main reliance ; he was to be their Washington, with more than Washington's genius, — their Bonaparte, with Washington's virtues. The whole body of Federalists, who had paid little regard to Hamilton's wishes in life, went into mourning for his death, and held funeral services such as had been granted to no man of New England birth. Orators, ministers, and newspapers exhausted themselves in execration of Burr. During the whole summer and autumn, undisturbed by a breath of discord or danger, except such as their own fears created, they bewailed their loss as the most fatal blow yet given to the hopes of society.

The death of Hamilton cleared for a time the murky atmosphere of New York and New England politics. Pickering and Griswold, Tracy and Plumer, and their associates retired into the background. Burr disappeared from New York, and left a field for De Witt Clinton to sacrifice in his turn the public good to private ambition. The bloody feuds of Burr's time never again recurred. The death of Hamilton and the Vice-President's flight, with their accessories of summer-morning sunlight on rocky and wooded heights, tranquil river, and distant city, and behind all, their dark background of moral gloom, double treason, and political despair, still stand as the most dramatic moment in the early politics of the Union.

CHAPTER IX.

PRESIDENT JEFFERSON was told from day to day of the communications that passed between Burr and the Connecticut Federalists. Of all members of the Government, the most active politician was Gideon Granger, the Postmaster-General, whose "intimacy with some of those in the secret," as Jefferson afterward testified, gave him "opportunities of searching into their proceedings."[1] Every day during this period Granger made a confidential report to the President; and at the President's request Granger warned De Witt Clinton of Burr's intrigues with the Federalists. What passed in Rufus King's library and in Burr's private room seemed known at once by Granger, and was reported within a few days to Jefferson, who received the news with his innate optimism, warranted by experience.[2]

"It will be found in this, as in all other similar cases, that crooked schemes will end by overwhelming their authors and coadjutors in disgrace, and that he alone who walks strict and upright, and who in matters of opinion

[1] Jefferson to Granger, March 9, 1814; Works, vi. 329.
[2] Jefferson to Granger, April 16, 1804; Works, iv. 542.

will be contented that others should be as free as himself, and acquiesce when his opinion is fairly overruled, will attain his object in the end."

If Jefferson and his Virginia friends in 1798, when their own opinions were overruled, had expressed the idea of acquiescence as strongly, the nation might perhaps have been saved the necessity of proving later the truth of his words ; but Jefferson could afford to treat with contempt the coalition between Burr and Pickering, because, as he wisely said, it had no cohesive force to hold it together, no common principle on which to rest. When Burr's defeat in April and Hamilton's death in July dissolved the unnatural connection, Jefferson let the secret die ; he wanted no scandal. He stood a little in awe of the extreme Federalists, whom he called incurables, and was unwilling to exasperate them without an object.

The Administration had every reason to rejoice that Burr's factious influence in the State of New York was at an end ; for other causes of anxiety gave the President more personal annoyance. The strength of the Republican party lay in the alliance between Virginia and Pennsylvania. So long as these two central States, with their forty members of Congress, remained harmonious, nothing could shake Jefferson's power; but any discord which threatened his control of Pennsylvania caused him anxiety. Hardly had Burr's schism been checked in New York by a succession of measures as energetic as De Witt Clinton could persuade Jefferson to adopt, when a

schism, that threatened greater mischief, broke out
in Pennsylvania.

In this State no social hierarchy existed such as
governed New England, nor were rich families with
political followings to be found there, as in New
York; but instead, Duane's "Aurora" shone without
break or bar over one broad democratic level. Duane
was represented in Congress by Michael Leib; while
over the State Legislature his influence was complete.
In Jefferson's Cabinet Pennsylvania was represented
by Gallatin, who had little sympathy with the "Aurora," and began his administration of the finances
by resisting Duane's demand for Federal patronage.

"The thirst for offices," to use Gallatin's own words,[1]
"too much encouraged by Governor McKean's first
measures, created a schism in Philadelphia as early as
1802. Leib, ambitious, avaricious, envious, and disappointed, blew up the flame, and watched the first opportunity to make his cause a general one. The vanity, the
nepotism, and the indiscretion of Governor McKean
afforded the opportunity. Want of mutual forbearance
among the best-intentioned and most respectable Republicans has completed the schism. Duane, intoxicated by
the persuasion that he alone had overthrown Federalism,
thought himself neither sufficiently rewarded nor respected; and possessed of an engine which gives him an
irresistible control over public opinion, he easily gained
the victory for his friends."

In the spring of 1803 the "Aurora" began to attack Gallatin and Madison, under cover of devotion to

[1] Gallatin to Badollet, Oct. 25, 1805; Adams's Gallatin, p. 331.

the President; and from this beginning Duane went on to quarrel with Governor McKean and Alexander J. Dallas, the district attorney.

The impeachment of Judge Pickering in Congress followed and in some degree imitated an impeachment by the Pennsylvania Legislature of Judge Addison, one of the five president judges of the Common Pleas. With the help of Dallas and Governor McKean, the Legislature in January, 1803, removed Judge Addison; then, inspired by Randolph's attack on Justice Chase, they turned against their Supreme Court, — at one sweep impeaching three of the judges, and addressing the Governor for the removal of H. H. Brackenridge, the fourth, because he insisted on making common cause with his associates. The alleged ground of impeachment was the arbitrary committal of a suitor for contempt of court; the real motive seemed rather to be a wish for legal reforms such as society was too unskilful to make for itself, and lawyers were slow to begin. Throughout America the bar was a sort of aristocracy, conservative to a degree that annoyed reformers of every class. Jefferson and his party raised one Republican lawyer after another to the bench, only to find that when their professions of political opinion were tested in legal form, the Republican judge rivalled Marshall in the Federalist and English tendencies of his law. The bar chose to consider the prejudice of society against their caste unreasonable; but the bar was itself somewhat unreasonable to require that an untrained and ill-led body of country farmers and local politicians should say precisely what legal reform they wanted, or know exactly what was practicable.

No sooner did the Pennsylvania Legislature begin to pull in pieces the judicial system of the State, and persecute the legal profession, than Dallas, McKean, and all the educated leaders of the Republican party broke from the mass of their followers, and attempted to check their violence. Governor McKean stopped with his veto certain measures which the Legislature had approved, and he declined to remove Judge Brackenridge when the Legislature asked him to do so. Dallas became counsel for the impeached judges. Duane and Leib raged against McKean and Dallas; a large majority of Pennsylvania Republicans followed the "Aurora;" Gallatin lost control over his State, and saw himself threatened, like his friend Dallas, with ostracism; while the outside world, roused by the noise of this faction-fight, asked what it meant, and could not understand the answer. The Federalists alone professed to explain the mystery which perplexed people less wise than themselves; they had said from the beginning that the democrats had neither virtue nor understanding to carry on the government, and must bring about a crisis at last.

After the excitement of Burr's intrigues and Hamilton's death subsided, leaving the politics of New York in comparative repose, the autumn elections in Pennsylvania began to disturb Jefferson's temper.

" Thank Heaven ! " wrote Dallas to Gallatin, in October,[1] " our election is over ! The violence of Duane has
produced a fatal division. He seems determined to destroy the Republican standing and usefulness of every
man who does not bend to his will. He has attacked me
as the author of an address which I never saw till it was
in the press. He menaces the Governor; you have
already felt his lash; and I think there is reason for
Mr. Jefferson himself to apprehend that the spirit of
Callender survives."

A struggle took place over the re-election of Leib
to Congress, which the " Aurora " carried by a few
hundred votes. Republicans of Dallas's kind, who
would not support Leib, were nicknamed " Quids "
by Duane, after the *tertium quid*, which was worth
not even a name. At least three fourths of the Republican party followed the " Aurora," and left the
" Quids " in the solitude of deserted leaders.

Jefferson's social relations were wholly with Gallatin, McKean, and Dallas, but his political strength
depended on the popular vote, which followed Duane
and Leib. At one moment he wanted to reason with
Duane, but by Gallatin's advice gave up this idea.
At length he temporized, became neutral, and left
Gallatin and Dallas to their own resources.

" I see with infinite pain," he wrote to Dr. Logan,[2]
" the bloody schism which has taken place among our
friends in Pennsylvania and New York, and will probably take place in other States. The main body of both

[1] Dallas to Gallatin, Oct. 16, 1804; Adams's Gallatin, p. 326.
[2] Jefferson to Dr. Logan, May 11, 1805 ; Works, iv. 575.

sections mean well, but their good intentions will produce great public evil.   The minority, whichever section
shall be the minority, will end in coalition with the Federalists and some compromise of principle.   Republicanism will thus lose, and royalism gain, some portion of
that ground which we thought we had rescued to good
government."

The idea that " royalism " could in any case gain support among the factions of Pennsylvania democrats
was one which could have occurred only to Jefferson,
who saw monarchy, as the New Englanders saw Anti-
christ, in every man who opposed him in politics.
Apart from this trick of words, Jefferson's theory
of his own duties failed to satisfy his followers.
Dallas was disgusted at the situation in which he
found himself left.

" It is obvious to me,"[1] he wrote to Gallatin soon
after the schism broke out, " that unless our Administration take decisive measures to discountenance the
factious spirit that has appeared ; unless some principle
of political cohesion can be introduced into our public
councils as well as at our elections ; and unless men of
character and talents can be drawn from professional
and private pursuits into the legislative bodies of our
governments, Federal and State, — the empire of Republicanism will moulder into anarchy, and the labor and
hope of our lives will terminate in disappointment and
wretchedness. . . . At present we are the slaves of men
whose passions are the object of all their actions, — I

[1] A. J. Dallas to Gallatin, Jan. 16, 1805 ; Adams's Gallatin,
p. 327.

mean your Duanes, Cheethams, Leibs, etc. They have the press in their power; and though we may have virtue to assert the liberty of the press, it is too plain that we have not spirit enough to resist the tyranny of the printers."

This last sharp sentence aimed at the President, who displeased Dallas by showing too evident a wish not to offend Duane. "The duty of an upright Administration," Jefferson told Dr. Logan,[1] " is to pursue its course steadily, to know nothing of these family dissensions, and to cherish the good principles of both parties." Had the President followed this duty in the case of Burr, the triumph of De Witt Clinton and Cheetham would have been more difficult than it was; but the President feared Burr the less because Burr's newspaper, the " Morning Chronicle," was respectable, while the "Aurora" was unscrupulous, and to cherish Duane's principles, whether good or bad, was the only way of escaping the lash of his tongue. Jefferson chose the path of caution in refusing to sustain Dallas and the " Quids " against the party and the Legislature; but during the rest of his term he was forced to endure Duane's attachment, and to feel that Madison and Gallatin were sacrificed to his own safety. Duane never hesitated to assert that he was in Jefferson's confidence and was acting in his interests,[2] and commonly he or some of his friends

[1] Jefferson to Dr. Logan, May 11, 1805 ; Works, iv. 575.

[2] Dallas to Gallatin, April 4, 1805; April 21, 1811; Adams's Gallatin, pp. 333, 439.

could show a recent letter in the President's handwriting which gave color to their assertion.

The Pennsylvania schism was not serious. Governor McKean and Dallas were alarmed when they saw the democratic system blundering in its rude way, without taking sound advice or heeding trained lawyers; but only the Federalists believed in a crisis. Society went undisturbed to its daily duties in spite of Duane's outcries and Dallas's grumbling. The only result of the Pennsylvania schism was to check the aggressive energy of the democratic movement by alarming a few of the older leaders and causing them to halt. From the day of Jefferson's inauguration this tendency toward reaction had begun, and it developed in party schisms which could not fail to hurry the process. The symptom, however unpleasant to old political leaders such as Jefferson, McKean, and Dallas, who liked the quiet enjoyment of power, was healthy for society at large; but no one could fail to be struck by the contrast which in this respect was offered by the two great sections of the country. While the mobile, many-sided, restless democracy of New England, New York, and Pennsylvania exhibited its faults, and succeeded, with much personal abuse, in thrusting out the elements foreign to its character which retarded its movement, the society of the Southern States was classically calm. Not a breath disturbed the quiet which brooded over the tobacco and cotton fields between the Potomac and Florida. A Presidential election was taking place, but the South saw only one candidate. The State legislatures quietly chose electors to vote for Jefferson and Clinton. From the St. Mary's to the Potomac and the Ohio, every electoral voice was given to Jefferson. With some surprise the public learned that Maryland gave two of eleven votes to C. C. Pinckney, who received also the three votes of Delaware. This little State even went back on its path, repudiated Cæsar A. Rodney, and returned to its favorite Bayard, who was sent by a handsome majority to his old seat in the House of Representatives. Broken for an instant only by this slight check, the tide of democratic triumph swept over the States of Pennsylvania, New Jersey, and New York, and burst upon Connecticut as though Jefferson's hope of dragging even that State from its moorings were at length to be realized. With difficulty the Connecticut hierarchy held its own; and with despair after the torrent passed by, it looked about and found itself alone. Even Massachusetts cast 29,310 votes for Jefferson, against 25,777 for Pinckney.

Rarely was a Presidential election better calculated to turn the head of a President, and never was a President elected who felt more keenly the pleasure of his personal triumph. At the close of four years of administration, all Jefferson's hopes were fulfilled. He had annihilated opposition. The slanders of the Federalist press helped to show that he was the idol of four fifths of the nation. He received one hundred and sixty-two of one hundred and seventy-six electoral votes, while in 1801 he had but seventy-three in one hundred and thirty-eight; and in the Ninth Congress, which was to meet in December, 1805, barely seven out of thirty-four senators, and twenty-five out of one hundred and forty-one representatives, would oppose his will. He described his triumph, in language studiously modest, in a letter to Volney : [1] —

" The two parties which prevailed with so much violence when you were here are almost wholly melted into one. At the late Presidential election I have received one hundred and sixty-two votes against fourteen only. Connecticut is still Federalist by a small majority, and Delaware on a poise, as she has been since 1775, and will be till Anglomany with her yields to Americanism. Connecticut will be with us in a short time. Though the people in mass have joined us, their leaders had committed themselves too far to retract. Pride keeps them hostile ; they brood over their angry passions, and give them vent in the newspapers which they maintain. They still make as much noise as if they were the whole nation."

Such success might have turned the head of any philosopher that ever sat on a throne. Easily elated, unwilling to forebode trouble, devoid of humor, and unable to see himself in any but the heroic light, President Jefferson basked in the sunshine of popularity and power as though it were no passing warmth such as had led scores of kings into disaster, but shone

[1] Jefferson to Volney, Feb. 8, 1805 ; Works, iv. 573.

by virtue of some democratic law which rested on truth that could never change. The White House was filled with an atmosphere of adulation. Flattery, gross as any that man could ask, was poured into the President's ear, but was as nothing compared with the more subtle flattery of the popular vote. No friend stopped him to ask how such a miraculous success had been brought about. Four years had not passed since Jefferson and his party had clamored against attempts to give energy to government; and no one could ever forget that they claimed and received power from the people in order to defend State-rights, restrict Executive influence, and correct strained constructions of the Constitution. Who upheld State-rights in 1804, and complained of Executive influence and strained constructions? Certainly not Jefferson or his friends, but the monarchical Federalists, who were fit inmates for an asylum. Whenever Jefferson had occasion to discuss the aims and opinions of the two parties, he did not allude to the principles set forth in 1798; not a word was said of "strict construction." The only theories opposed to his own which he could see in the political horizon were those of a few hundred conservatives of the colonial epoch.

"What, in fact," he wrote,[1] "is the difference of principle between the two parties here? The one desires to preserve an entire independence of the executive and legislative branches on each other and the dependence of both on the same source, — the free election of the

[1] Jefferson to J. F. Mercer, Oct. 9, 1804; Works, iv. 563.

people. The other party wishes to lessen the dependence of the Executive and of one branch of the Legislature on the people, some by making them hold for life, some hereditary, and some even for giving the Executive an influence by patronage or corruption over the remaining popular branch, so as to reduce the elective franchise to its minimum."

After nearly four years of Executive authority more complete than had ever before been known in American history, Jefferson could see in himself and in his principles only a negation of Executive influence. What had become of the old radical division of parties, — the line between men who wished the national government to exercise inherent powers of sovereignty and those who held to a strict observance of powers expressly delegated by the people of the States?

Jefferson said with truth that the two old parties were almost wholly melted into one; but in this fusion his own party had shown even more willingness than its opponents to mix its principles in a useful, but not noble, amalgam. His own protests in regard to the Louisiana purchase and the branch bank at New Orleans were recorded. With such evidence on their side, the moderate Federalists who in the election of 1804 gave to Jefferson the nineteen electoral votes of Massachusetts and the seven of New Hampshire, could claim that they had altered no opinion they ever held; that the government had suffered no change in principle from what it had been under President Washington; that not a Federalist measure, not even the Alien and Sedition laws, had been expressly repudiated; that the national debt was larger than it had ever been before, the navy maintained and energetically employed, the national bank preserved and its operations extended; that the powers of the national government had been increased to a point that made blank paper of the Constitution as heretofore interpreted by Jefferson, while the national territory, vastly more than doubled in extent, was despotically enlarged and still more despotically ruled by the President and Congress, in the teeth of every political profession the Republican party had ever made. Had this been the work of Federalists, it would have been claimed as a splendid triumph of Federalist principles; and the good sense of New England was never better shown than when Massachusetts and New Hampshire flung aside their prejudices and told Jefferson that they accepted his inaugural pledge to be a Federalist as they were Republicans.

Every Federalist who came over and every State that joined the majority weakened the relative influence of Virginia, and helped to dilute the principles of the pure Virginia school. The new democrats in New England, New York, and Ohio were Federalists in disguise, and cared nothing for fine-spun constitutional theories of what government might or might not do, provided government did what they wanted. They feared no corruption in which they were to have a part. They were in secret jealous of Virginia, and as devoted as George Cabot and Stephen Higginson to the interests of commerce and manufactures. A majority of the Northern democrats were men of this kind. Their dislike of Federalists was a social rather than political feeling, for Federalist manners seemed to them a wilful impertinence ; but the Varnums and Crowninshields of Massachusetts cared as little as De Witt Clinton or Aaron Burr for the notions of Speaker Macon and John Randolph. As orators and leaders the Northern democrats made a poor figure beside the Virginians ; but their votes weighed more and more heavily with every succeeding Congress, and both Randolph and Macon were becoming suspicious that these votes were too apt to be cast against the wishes of Virginia.

The second session of the Eighth Congress met on the first Monday in November, as provided by a law passed in view of Judge Chase's impeachment. The President's Message, sent to Congress Nov. 8, 1804, was as usual toned to cheerful harmony. The income had reached eleven millions and a half of dollars ; more than three million six hundred thousand dollars of the public debt had been discharged within the year, more than twelve millions since 1801 ; and the revenue was still increasing. Difficulties had risen with foreign nations, but no disturbance of the peace was to be expected. The Indians were quiet. Gunboats were in course of construction. No increase of the army was called for. Congress had only to inquire whether anything remained to be done for the public good.

The Federalists were reduced to showing that Jefferson's political success had not chastened his style; for the Message contained a number of sentences that exaggerated his peculiar faults of expression : --

" The war which was lighted up in Europe a little before our last meeting has not yet extended its flames to other nations, nor been marked by the calamities which sometimes stain the footsteps of war."

The Federalists reasonably objected to the figure of a war which not only extended flames but also made footsteps and marked them by calamities which stained. Jefferson went on to say that he had bought from the Delaware Indians the country between the Wabash and the Ohio : —

" This acquisition is important not only for its extent and fertility, but as fronting three hundred miles on the Ohio, and near half that on the Wabash. The produce of the settled country descending those rivers will no longer pass in view of the Indian frontier but in a small portion, and with the cession heretofore made by the Kaskaskias nearly consolidates our possessions north of the Ohio in a very respectable breadth from Lake Erie to the Mississippi."

Produce passing in view of a frontier in a portion and consolidating possessions in a breadth did not suit fastidious Federalists ; nor were they satisfied with the President's closing exhortation, requesting the Legislature to inquire " whether laws are provided in all cases where they are wanting." They enjoyed their jests at Jefferson's literary style ; but with the public the matter of the Message was more weighty than its manner. No kind of criticism had less political value than that wasted on the style of a public document.

Yet one thing was certainly wanting in this Message. No hint was given that Congress stood in danger of overstepping the limits of its powers, or would do well to return within them. This silence was not accidental ; it marked the moment of separation between Jefferson and the old Republicans of 1798. Speaker Macon, John Randolph, and Joseph Nicholson soon showed that they meant to take no such view of their duties.

Hardly had legislation begun, when Randolph, November 26, made a report against the remission of duties on books imported for the use of schools and colleges. The Constitution, he said, was a grant of limited powers for general objects ; its leading feature was an abhorrence of exclusive privileges ; impost must be uniform ; if Congress could exempt one class of the people from taxes, they might exempt other classes ; and although the practice had been different, and philosophical apparatus for the use of schools was actually exempt by law, he believed that law to be unconstitutional. The doctrine, which if carried to its ultimate conclusions would have left hardly a tax on the statute-book, was accepted by the same House which had supported Randolph in defending the Louisiana purchase by arguments that, in President Jefferson's opinion, left no Constitution at all. Two days afterward Randolph repeated the lesson, and his friends Macon and Nicholson came to his support. A Bill was before the House authorizing the corporation of Georgetown to construct a dam or causeway from Mason's Island to the shore of the Potomac, in order to scour the channel and improve navigation. Randolph affirmed that the Potomac was the joint property of Maryland and Virginia, over which Congress had no right to legislate; that the Bill authorized the corporation of Georgetown to lay a tax which would be unequal and oppressive, because all Georgetown property would not be equally benefited by deepening the harbor; and finally, " he hoped a prompt rejection of the Bill would serve as a general notice to the inhabitants of the District to desist from their daily and frivolous applications to Congress." Macon, Nicholson, and a number of the Virginians spoke earnestly in the same sense. " So long as I have the honor of a seat in the House," said Nicholson, " I will hold up my hands against any measure like the present, which would go to affect the rights of any of the States. If Congress have a right to interfere in the least with the free navigation of the Potomac, they have a right to stop it altogether." In reply to these exhortations the House passed the Bill by a vote of sixty-six to thirty-eight; and more than enough Republicans voted for it to have passed it without Federalist help.

The reason for this sudden decline of Randolph's influence was not far to seek. He was undertaking to act without concert with the President. While he and his friends argued on the State-rights theory at one end of Pennsylvania Avenue, Jefferson at the other end said openly, to Federalists and Republicans alike, that such arguments were mere metaphysical subtleties which ought to have no weight.[1] The next subject in debate left no longer a doubt of the cleft opening between the old Republicans of 1798 and the Republicans of the future, with Jefferson and Madison at their head. That Randolph had determined to fight for control of the party and for the principles upon which it had come into office was clear ; but the reason for the suddenness and violence of his emotion was found in the once famous story of the Yazoo Claims, which from his youth acted on his passionate temper with the force of a point of honor.

As already told, Congress seemed about to settle these claims as early as April, 1802, when the six commissioners made their Report.[2] John Randolph and his friends were then supreme. Dec. 30, 1803, a few days before the Federalists were startled by Randolph's demand for the impeachment of Judge Chase, the Northern democrats and the friends of Madison were surprised by a Resolution offered by Randolph excluding claimants under the Georgia grants of 1795 from any share in the proposed settlement. A few weeks later, Feb. 20, 1804, Randolph withdrew this Resolution, in order to introduce a series of declaratory Resolves, which, after reciting

[1] Diary of J. Q. Adams (Jan. 11, 1805), i. 331.
[2] See vol. i. p. 305.

the story of the Georgia grants, affirmed the right of
Georgia to rescind them, and forbade the appropriation
of money to the settlement of claims derived from
them. March 7, 1804, he made a long and earnest
speech on the subject; and after a sharp struggle in
a House nearly equally divided, he succeeded in
defeating action on the Bill. On the final vote of
postponement, March 12, 1804, he carried fifteen
members of the Virginia delegation with him. Of
the three Republicans from Virginia who rejected his
lead, one was John G. Jackson, brother-in-law of the
Secretary of State.

From that moment Randolph's energies quickened
in sympathy with old Republican principles; and
when he returned to Congress in November, 1804, he
and his friends began at once to take extreme ground
as champions of State-rights. He lost no chance of
enforcing his theories, whether in regard to exemp-
tions from taxes, or in denying to government power
to improve navigation within the District of Columbia,
or in reproving the people of Georgetown for pro-
posing to lay a general tax on their property for
the betterment of their river front. He found the
Administration opposed to him. " Mere metaphysical
subtleties," said Jefferson. The influence of Madison
was strong in favor of the Yazoo Compromise, and
the Northern democrats supported the Secretary. A
struggle for supremacy was imminent, and its consequences were soon felt. The impeachment of Judge
Chase was Randolph's measure, and received no sup-

port from Madison. The Yazoo Compromise was
Madison's measure, and its defeat was Randolph's
passionate wish.

The three branches of government were likely to be
at variance on a point of deep concern. No one who
knew Chief-Justice Marshall could doubt that he, and
the Supreme Bench with him, would hold that the
State of Georgia was bound by its contract with the
Land Companies. The Administration had taken
the ground that the State was not bound in law, but
that the United States should nevertheless make an
equitable compromise with the claimants. Randolph
was bent on forcing Congress to assert that a State
had the right to repudiate its own acts where it was
evident that these acts were against common morality
or public interest; and that its decision in such a case
should be final. The conflict was embittered by the
peculiarities of Randolph's character. In his eyes,
when such questions of honor were involved, every
man who opposed him seemed base. Unfortunately
the New England Mississippi Company secured the
services of Gideon Granger, the Postmaster-General,
as their agent; and Randolph's anger became intense when, at the close of the year 1804, he saw
the Postmaster-General on the floor of the House
openly lobbying for the passage of the Bill.

At length, at the end of January, 1805, the House
went into committee on the Georgia claims, and
Randolph for the first time displayed the full violence of his temper. Hitherto as a leader he had

been at times arrogant; but from this moment he began the long series of personal assaults which made him
famous, as though he were the bully of a race course,
dispensed from regarding ordinary rules of the ring,
and ready at any sudden impulse to spring at his enemies, gouging, biting, tearing, and rending his victims
with the ferocity of a rough-and-tumble fight. The
spectacle was revolting, but terrific; and until these
tactics lost their force by repetition, few men had the
nerve and quickness to resist them with success.

"Past experience has shown," he cried, "that this
is one of those subjects which pollution has sanctified."
He treated the majority of the House as corruptionists,
"As if animated by one spirit, they perform all their
evolutions with the most exact discipline, and march
in a firm phalanx directly up to their object. Is it
that men combined to effect some evil purpose, acting
on previous pledge to each other, are ever more in
unison than those who, seeking only to discover truth,
obey the impulse of that conscience which God has
placed in their bosoms?" He fell upon Granger:
"Millions of acres are easily digested by such
stomachs. Goaded by avarice, they buy only to sell,
and sell only to buy. The retail trade of fraud and
imposture yields too small and slow a profit to gratify
their cupidity. They buy and sell corruption in the
gross." He hinted that the Administration was to
blame: "Is it come to this? Are heads of executive
departments to be brought into this House, with all the
influence and patronage attached to them, to extort

from us now what was refused at the last session of
Congress ? " He closed by asserting that this was
the spirit of Federalism, and that Republicans who
yielded to it were false to their party : " Of what consequence is it that a man smiles in your face, holds
out his hand, and declares himself the advocate of
those political principles to which you are also attached, when you see him acting with your adversaries
upon other principles which the voice of the nation
has put down, and which I did hope were buried,
never to rise again in this section of the globe ? "
He maintained that the Federalist administrations had
done no act so corrupt : " If Congress shall determine to sanction this fraud upon the public, I trust in
God we shall hear no more of the crimes and follies
of the former Administration. For one, I promise
that my lips upon this subject shall be closed in
eternal silence. I should disdain to prate about the
petty larcenies of our predecessors after having given
my sanction to this atrocious public robbery."

The tirade could have no other result than a personal quarrel and a party schism. Madison and the
Administration had done nothing to deserve the attack, and of course could not trust Randolph again.
The question whether the claimants had rights which
the government would do well to compromise was
for the law to decide, and was ultimately settled by
Chief-Justice Marshall in their favor. The question
of morality, in regard to sanctioning fraud, though a
much wider issue, was not to be settled *ex parte*, but

must abide by the answer to the question of law.
Only the State-rights difficulty remained ; and even
on that delicate ground, although the right of Georgia
to repudiate her own pledges under the plea of her
own corruption were conceded, the State-rights theory
could not insist that this act must bind other States,
or affect any sovereignty except that which was directly involved. After the property in question had
been sold to the United States government,. Georgia
need not prevent the purchaser from doing what it
would with its own. Randolph could not make State-
rights serve his whole purpose in the argument, and
was obliged to rely on the charge of sanctioning corruption and fraud, — a charge irrelevant to the claim
of innocent third parties like the New Englanders,
unless he could prove their complicity, which was not
in his power.

Randolph's harangue struck at the credit of Madison ; and the conduct of the Postmaster-General in
acting as claim-agent cast a shadow of corruption
over the whole government. Madison's friends were
obliged to take up the challenge ; and his brother-
in-law, John G. Jackson of Virginia, replied to Randolph in a speech which was thought to bear evident
marks of Madison's hand. Some of Jackson's retorts
carried a sting. Randolph had dwelt much on the
silence and discipline of the majority. " When unprincipled men," said he, " acquire the ascendency,
they act in concert and are silent." " Silence and
concert, then," retorted Jackson, " are to him proofs

of corrupt motive. Is this always a correct position ?
Does the gentleman recollect that measures were
adopted a few years past without discussion, by my
political friends in conjunction with him, who were
silent and united ? " Throughout Jackson's speech
ran a tone of irritating disregard for his colleague,
" whose influence in this House is equal to the rapacity
of the speculator whose gigantic grasp has been described by him as extending from the shores of Lake
Erie to the mouth of the Mobile."   Whether Madison
meant it or not, an impression prevailed in the House
that in Jackson's speech the Secretary of State took up
Randolph's challenge with a defiance equally strong.

Randolph returned to his charges, attacking Granger
bitterly, but not yet venturing to take the single step
that remained to create a Virginia feud ; he left Jackson and Madison alone.   He bore with something like
patience the retorts which his violence drew upon him,
and his self-esteem made him proof to the insults of
democrats like Matthew Lyon, who thanked his Creator
"that he gave me the face of a man, not that of an ape
or a monkey, and that he gave me the heart of a man
also."   After a long and ill-tempered debate, Feb. 2,
1805, Randolph closed by an allusion to Madison and
Gallatin which implied hesitation.   " When I first read
their Report, I was filled with unutterable astonishment, finding men in whom I had and still have the
highest confidence recommend a measure which all the
facts and all the reasons they had collected opposed
and unequivocally condemned."   Prudence restrained

him from making a final breach with Madison ; and perhaps he was the more cautious because he felt the danger of pressing too far his influence over Virginia sentiment which to this point supported his opposition. When the House divided, a majority of sixty-three to fifty-eight sustained the compromise, and ordered the committee of claims to report a Bill ; but in the minority Randolph found by his side every Republican member of the Virginia delegation except two, one of whom was Jackson. Even the two sons-in-law of President Jefferson voted against the Yazoo claims. So strong was the current of opinion in Virginia, that Senator Giles went about Washington [1] asserting that Jefferson himself would lose an election there if he were known to favor the compromise, and that Jackson would certainly be defeated. For the moment Randolph might fairly suppose that in a contest for supremacy with the Secretary of State, his own hold on Virginia was stronger than Madison's. In spite of the majority against him, he succeeded in postponing action on the Bill.

Perhaps his temper was further restrained by another motive. The trial of Judge Chase was near at hand. Within a few days after the close of the Yazoo debate, Randolph was to open the case for the managers before the Senate ; and he had reason to fear that the Northern democrats were beginning to doubt the wisdom of this Virginia scheme.

[1] Diary of J. Q. Adams (Feb. 1, 1805), i. **343**.

CHAPTER X.

THE schisms which characterized the last year of
President Jefferson's first term increased the difficulty of convicting Justice Chase. Burr was still
Vice-President, and was sure not only to preside at
the trial, but also, unless conciliated, to encourage rebellion against the Virginians. He had warm friends
even in the Senate; and he was observed to cultivate
close social relations with John Smith, the senator
from Ohio, whose vote was likely to be necessary for
conviction. Although the two senators from New
York were no friends of Burr, one of them, Dr.
Samuel L. Mitchill, was known to oppose impeachment; and not only he, but also his colleague,
another John Smith, when members of the House,
voted against Randolph's motion for a committee
of inquiry. Senator Bradley of Vermont privately
talked with earnestness against the Pickering impeachment, and never favored that of Chase. His
colleague, Israel Smith, shared his doubts. Twenty-
three votes were required to convict, and the Republicans had but twenty-five senators against nine
Federalists. A defection of three Republican senators

would be fatal; but the votes of at least five were in doubt.

Randolph's attack on the Yazoo Republicans and on the friends of Madison took from them all desire to strengthen his influence; while, as though to complicate confusion, his assault on his own party was cheered by Duane and the " Aurora," until the Pennsylvania schism seemed about to join with a Virginia schism for the overthrow of the judiciary in the first place, and of Madison and Gallatin afterward. A collapse of the Republican party was to be feared. In the success of impeachment, the interests of Duane and Randolph were closely connected, and Duane controlled Pennsylvania as Randolph ruled Virginia. Everything tended to show that Chase's conviction would add to the power already in the hands of these two men; and hands less fitted to guide a government or less trusted by moderate Republicans could hardly be found in either party.

Duane's support of Randolph was the warmer because his own attack on the judiciary failed. The Pennsylvania judges were brought to trial in January, 1805. The managers for the Legislature, knowing no law themselves and unable to persuade any competent Pennsylvania lawyer to act as counsel, sent for Cæsar A. Rodney from Delaware to conduct the case. So important did Randolph and Nicholson at Washington think the success of the Pennsylvania impeachment, that at the end of December, 1804, they allowed Rodney to drop his work as member of Con-

gress and manager of Chase's trial, in order to hurry
to Lancaster and do battle with Dallas, Jefferson's district attorney, who was defending the judges.   After a
long struggle, Jan. 28, 1805, the Senate at Lancaster
came to a vote, and Rodney was beaten.   Thirteen
senators declared the judges guilty, — three less than
the required two thirds.

This defeat of the impeachers occurred the day
before Randolph attacked Granger and the Yazoo
claims in Congress.   During the week that preceded
Chase's trial, Randolph's bad management or ill-luck
seemed accumulating disasters on his head.   He roused
needless hatred against himself in Congress ; his alliance with Duane was unsuccessful ; he exhausted his
strength in fighting the Yazoo Bill, and was in no
condition of mind or body to meet the counsel of
Judge Chase.

Neither the Administration nor his Virginia friends
failed to support Randolph.   They made efforts to
conciliate Burr, whose opposition to the impeachment
was most feared.   Jefferson appointed J. B. Prevost
of New York, Burr's stepson, a judge of the Superior
Court at New Orleans ; James Brown, who married
Mrs. Burr's sister, was made secretary to the Louisiana Territory and sent to govern St. Louis, solely
on Burr's recommendation ; James Wilkinson, one of
Burr's most intimate friends and general-in-chief of
the army, was made governor of the Louisiana Territory, — an appointment directly opposed to Jefferson's theories about the union of civil and military

authority.[1] Besides these conciliatory compliments the President repeatedly invited Burr to dinner, and treated him with more attention than ever before;[2] both Madison and Gallatin kept up friendly relations with him; while Senator Giles of Virginia drew an Address to Governor Bloomfield of New Jersey, and caused it to be signed by all the senators who could be induced to let their names be used, requesting that a *nolle prosequi* should be entered on the indictment against Burr found by the grand jury of Bergen county.

The Virginians closed their quarrels for the moment in order to support the impeachment. William B. Giles, who came to the Senate in place of Wilson Cary Nicholas, acted as Randolph's representative in shaping the Senate's rules.[3] He canvassed its members, and dealt with those who doubted, laboring earnestly and openly to bring senators to the Virginia standpoint, as fixed by him in a speech intended to serve as guide in framing rules for the proceedings about to begin. This speech, made Dec. 20, 1804,[4] maintained that the Constitution put no limit on impeachment, but said only that the Senate should try *all* impeachments; and therefore, while any civil officer convicted of treason, bribery, or other high crimes and misdemeanors should be removed from office, in

---

[1] Jefferson to General Smith, May 4, 1806; Works, v. 13.

[2] Life of Plumer, p. 330.

[3] Diary of J. Q. Adams (Nov. 29, 30, 1804), i. 318.

[4] Boston Centinel, Jan. 9, 1805.

all other cases not enumerated the Senate might at its discretion remove, disqualify, or suspend the officer. Thus Judge Pickering had been removed, said Giles, though undoubtedly insane and incapable of committing any crime or of making his defence. " So the assumption of power on the part of the Supreme Court in issuing their process to the office of the Secretary of State, directing the Executive how a law of the United States should be executed, and the right which the courts have assumed to themselves of reviewing and passing upon the Acts of the Legislature in other cases," were matter of impeachment. In arguing this thesis Giles was obliged to take the ground that the Senate was not a court, and ought to discard all analogy with a court of justice; [1] impeachment need imply no criminality or corruption, and removal was nothing more than a notice to the impeached officer that he held opinions dangerous to the State, and that his office must be put in better hands. He induced the Senate to strike out the word "court" where it occurred in the proposed rules; [2] and at length went so far as to deny that the secretary of the Senate could administer the oath to witnesses, or that the Senate had power to authorize the secretary to administer such an oath, but must send for a magistrate competent for the purpose. Unfortunately for him, the impeachment of Judge Pickering was a precedent directly opposed to this doctrine. He was

[1] Diary of J. Q. Adams (Dec. 21, 1804), i. **322.**
[2] Ibid. (Dec. 24, 1804), i. **324, 325.**

compelled to submit while the Senate unwillingly took the forms of a court.

Giles's view of impeachment, which was the same with that of Randolph, had the advantage of being clear and consistent. The opposite extreme, afterward pressed by Luther Martin and his associate counsel for the defence, restricted impeachment to misdemeanors indictable at law, — a conclusion not to be resisted if the words of the Constitution were to be understood in a legal sense. Such a rule would have made impeachment worthless for many cases where it was likely to be most needed; for comparatively few violations of official duty, however fatal to the State, could be brought within this definition. Giles might have quoted Madison in support of the broader view; and if Madison did not understand the Constitution, any other Virginian might be excused for error. So far back as the year 1789, when Congress began to discuss the President's powers, Madison said: " I contend that the wanton removal of meritorious officers would subject him to impeachment and removal from his own high trust." Such a misdemeanor was certainly not indictable, and could not technically be brought within the words of the Constitution; it was impeachable only on Giles's theory.

The Senate became confused between these two views, and never knew on what theory it acted. Giles failed to take from its proceedings the character of a court of justice; but though calling itself a court of justice, it would not follow strict rules of law. The result was a nondescript court, neither legal nor political, making law and voting misdemeanors for itself as it went, and stumbling from one inconsistency to another.

The managers added to the confusion. They put forward no steady theory of their own as to the nature of impeachment; possibly differing in opinion, they intentionally allotted different lines of argument to each. In opening the case, Feb. 20, 1805, one of the managers, George W. Campbell of Tennessee, took the ground that "misdemeanor" in the Constitution need imply no criminality. "Impeachment," said he, "according to the meaning of the Constitution, may fairly be considered a kind of inquest into the conduct of an officer merely as it regards his office. . . . It is more in the nature of a civil investigation than of a criminal prosecution." Such seemed to be the theory of the managers and of the House; for although the articles of impeachment reported by Randolph in March, 1804, had in each case alleged acts which were inspired by an evil intent to oppress the victim or to excite odium against the Government, and were at least misdemeanors in the sense of misbehavior, Randolph at the last moment slipped into the indictment two new articles, one of which alleged no evil intent at all, while both alleged, at worst, errors in law such as every judge in the United States had committed. Article V. charged that Chase had issued a *capias* against Callender, when the law of Virginia required a summons to appear at the next court. Article VI. charged that he had, " with intent to oppress," held Callender for trial at once, contrary to the law of Virginia. Every judge on the Supreme Bench had ruled that United States courts were not bound to follow the processes of the State courts; Chief-Justice Marshall himself, as Giles threatened, must be the first victim if such an offence were a misdemeanor in constitutional law.

That a judge was impeachable for a mistake in declaring the law seemed therefore to be settled, so far as the House and its managers could decide the point. Judge Chase's counsel assumed that this principle, which had been so publicly proclaimed, was seriously meant; and one after another dwelt on the extravagance of the doctrine that a civil officer should be punished for mere error of judgment. In reply, Joseph H. Nicholson, Randolph's closest ally, repudiated the theory on which he had himself acted in Pickering's case, and which Giles, Randolph, and Campbell pressed; he even denied having heard such ground taken as that an impeachment was a mere inquest of office : —

" For myself, I am free to declare that I heard no such position taken. If declarations of this kind have been made, in the name of the managers I here disclaim them. We do contend that this is a criminal prosecution for offences committed in the discharge of high official duties, and we now support it, — not merely for the purpose of removing an individual from office, but in order that the punishment inflicted on him may deter others from pursuing the baneful example which has been set them."

The impeachment, then, was a criminal prosecution, and the Senate was a criminal court; yet no offence was charged which the law considered a misdemeanor, while error of judgment, with no imputed ill-intent, was alleged as a crime.

Staggering under this load of inconsistencies, uncertain what line of argument to pursue, and ignorant whether the Senate would be ruled by existing law or invent a system of law of its own, the managers, Feb. 9, 1805, appeared in the Senate chamber to open their case and produce their witnesses. Upon the popular imagination of the day the impeachment of Warren Hastings had taken deep hold. Barely ten years had passed since the House of Lords rendered its judgment in that famous case; and men's minds were still full of associations with Westminster Hall. The impeachment of Judge Chase was a cold and colorless performance beside the melodramatic splendor of Hastings's trial; but in the infinite possibilities of American democracy, the questions to be decided in the Senate chamber had a weight for future ages beyond any that were then settled in the House of Lords. Whether Judge Chase should be removed from the bench was a trifling matter; whether Chief-Justice Marshall and the Supreme Court should hold their power and principles against this combination of State-rights conservatives and Pennsylvania democrats was a subject for grave reflection. Men who did not see that the tide of political innovation had long since turned, and that the French revolution was no longer raging, were consumed with anxiety for the fate of Chase, and not wholly without reason ; for had Marshall been a man of less calm and certain judgment, a single mistake by him might easily have prostrated the judiciary at the feet of partisans.

By order of the Vice-President the Senate chamber was arranged in accordance with his ideas of what suited so grave an occasion. His own chair stood, like that of the chief-justice in the court-room, against the wall, and on its right and left crimson benches extended like the seats of associate judges, to accommodate the thirty-four senators, who were all present. In front of the Vice-President, on the right, a box was assigned to the managers ; on the left, a similar box was occupied by Justice Chase and his counsel. The rest of the floor was given to members of the House, foreign ministers, and other official persons. Behind these a new gallery was erected especially for ladies, and at each end of this temporary gallery boxes were reserved for the wives and families of public officers. The upper and permanent gallery was public. The arrangement was a mimic reproduction of the famous scene in Westminster Hall ; and the little society of Washington went to the spectacle with the same interest and passion which had brought the larger society of London to hear the orations of Sheridan and Burke.

Before this audience Justice Chase at last appeared with his array of counsel at his side, — Luther Martin,

Robert Goodloe Harper, Charles Lee, Philip Barton Key, and Joseph Hopkinson. In such a contest weakness of numbers was one element of strength; for the mere numbers of Congressmen served only to rouse sympathy for the accused. The contest was unequal in another sense, for the intellectual power of the House was quite unable on the field of law to cope with the half-dozen picked and trained champions who stood at the bar. Justice Chase alone was a better lawyer than any in Congress; Luther Martin could easily deal with the whole box of managers; Harper and Lee were not only lawyers, but politicians; and young Hopkinson's genius was beyond his years.

In the managers' box stood no lawyer of corresponding weight. John Randolph, who looked upon the impeachment as his personal act, was not only ignorant of law, but could not work by legal methods. Joseph H. Nicholson and Cæsar A. Rodney were more formidable; but neither of them would have outweighed any single member of Chase's counsel. The four remaining managers, all Southern men, added little to the strength of their associates. John Boyle of Kentucky lived to become chief-justice of that State, and was made district judge of the United States by a President who was one of the Federalist senators warmly opposed to the impeachment. George Washington Campbell of Tennessee lived to be a senator, Secretary of the Treasury, and minister to Russia. Peter Early of Georgia became a judge on the Supreme Bench of his own State. Christopher Clark of Virginia was

chosen only at the last moment to take the place
of Roger Nelson of Maryland, who retired. None of
them rose much above the average level of Congress;
and Chase's counsel grappled with them so closely, and
shut them within a field so narrow, that no genius
could have found room to move. From the moment
that the legal and criminal character of impeachment
was conceded, Chase's counsel dragged them hither
and thither at will.

Feb. 9, 1805, the case was opened by John Randolph.
Randolph claimed to have drawn all the articles of
impeachment with his own hand. If any one understood their character, it was he; and the respondent's
counsel naturally listened with interest for Randolph's
explanation or theory of impeachment, and for the
connection he should establish between his theory and
his charges. These charges were numerous, but fell
under few heads. Of the eight articles which Randolph presented, the first concerned the judge's conduct
at the trial of John Fries for treason in Philadelphia
in 1800; the five following articles alleged a number of offences committed during the trial of James
Thompson Callender for libel at Richmond in that
year; Article VII. charged as a misdemeanor the
judge's refusal, in the same year, to dismiss the grand
jury in Delaware before indicting a seditious printer;
finally, Article VIII. complained of the judge's harangue to the grand jury at Baltimore in May, 1803,
which it characterized as "highly indecent, extra-
judicial, and tending to prostitute the high judicial

character with which he was invested to the low purpose of an electioneering partisan."

Serious as some of these charges certainly were, — for in the case of Callender, even more than in that of Fries, Chase's temper had led him to strain, if not to violate, the law, — none of the articles alleged an offence known to the statute-books or the common law; and Randolph's first task was to show that they could be made the subject of impeachment, that they were high crimes and misdemeanors in the sense of the Constitution, or that in some sense they were impeachable. Instead of arguing this point, he contented himself by declaring the theory of the defence to be monstrous. His speech touched the articles, one by one, adding little to their force, but piling one mistake on another in its assertions of fact and assumptions of law.

Ten days passed in taking evidence before the field was cleared and the discussion began. Then, Feb. 20, 1805, Early and Campbell led for the managers in arguments which followed more or less closely in Randolph's steps, inferring criminality in the accused from the manifest tenor of his acts. Campbell ventured to add that he was not obliged to prove the accused to have committed any crime known to the law, — it was enough that he had transgressed the line of official duty with corrupt motives; but this timid incursion into the field of the Constitution was supported by no attempt at argument. "I lay it down as a settled rule of decision," said he, "that when a

man violates a law or commits a manifest breach of
his duty, an evil intent or corrupt motive must be
presumed to have actuated his conduct."

Joseph Hopkinson opened for the defence. Friends
and enemies joined in applauding the vigor of this
young man's attack. The whole effort of Chase's
counsel was to drive the impeachers within the limits
of law, and compel them to submit to the restrictions
of legal methods. Hopkinson struck into the heart
of the question. He maintained that under the Constitution no judge could be lawfully impeached or
removed from office for any act or offence for which
he could not be indicted ; " misdemeanor," he argued,
was a technical term well understood and defined,
which meant the violation of a public law, and which,
when occurring in a legal instrument like the Constitution, must be given its legal meaning. After
stating this proposition with irresistible force, he dealt
with Article I. of the impeachment, which covered
the case of Fries, and shook it to pieces with skill
very unlike the treatment of Early and Campbell.
Barton Key next rose, and dealt with Articles II., III.,
and IV., covering part of Callender's case ; he was
followed by Charles Lee, who succeeded in breaking
down Randolph's interpolated Articles V. and VI.
Then Luther Martin appeared on the scene, and the
audience felt that the managers were helpless in his
hands.

This extraordinary man — " unprincipled and impu-
dent Federalist bulldog," as Jefferson called him —

revelled in the pleasure of a fight with democrats.
The bar of Maryland felt a curious mixture of pride
and shame in owning that his genius and vices were
equally remarkable. Rough and coarse in manner
and expression, verbose, often ungrammatical, commonly more or less drunk, passionate, vituperative,
gross, he still had a mastery of legal principles and
a memory that overbalanced his faults, an audacity
and humor that conquered ill-will. In the practice
of his profession he had learned to curb his passions
until his ample knowledge had time to give the
utmost weight to his assaults. His argument at
Chase's trial was the climax of his career ; but such
an argument cannot be condensed in a paragraph.
Its length and variety defied analysis within the limits
of a page, though its force made other efforts seem
unsubstantial.

Martin covered the same ground that his associates
had taken before him, dwelling earnestly on the con-
tention that an impeachable offence must be also
indictable. Harper followed, concluding the argument for the defence, and seeming to go beyond his
associates in narrowing the field of impeachment ;
for he argued that it was a criminal prosecution,
which must be founded on some wilful violation of
a known law of the land, — a line of reasoning
which could end only in requiring the violation of
an Act of Congress. This theory did not necessarily
clash with that of Martin. No hesitation or inconsistency was shown on the side of the defence ; every

resource of the profession was used with energy and skill.

The managers then put forward their best pleaders; for they had need of all their strength. Nicholson began by disavowing the idea that impeachment was a mere inquest of office; this impeachment was, he said, a criminal prosecution intended not merely to remove, but to punish, the offender. On the other hand, he maintained that since judges held their commissions during good behavior, and could be removed only by impeachment, the Constitution must have intended that any act of misbehavior should be considered a misdemeanor. He showed the absurdities which would rise from construing the Constitution in a legal sense. His argument, though vigorous and earnest, and offering the advantages of a plausible compromise between two extreme and impracticable doctrines, yet evidently strained the language of the Constitution and disregarded law. As Nicholson himself said, he discarded legal usage: " In my judgment the Constitution of the United States ought to be expounded upon its own principles, and foreign aid ought never to be called in. Our Constitution was fashioned after none other in the known world; and if we understand the language in which it is written, we require no assistance in giving it a true exposition." He wanted a construction "purely and entirely American." In the mouth of a strict constructionist this substitution of the will of Congress for the settled rules of law had as strange a sound as Luther Martin could have wished, and offered another example of the instinct, so striking in the Louisiana debate, which not even Nicholson, Randolph, or Jefferson himself could always resist.

Rodney, the same day, followed Nicholson ; and as though not satisfied with his colleague's theory, did what Nicholson, in the name of all the managers, had a few hours before expressly disclaimed, — he adopted and pressed Giles's theory of impeachment with all the precision of language he could command.   Nicholson seemed content to assume impeachment as limited to " treason, bribery, or other high crimes and misdemeanors ; " but in his view misbehavior might be construed as a misdemeanor in a "purely and entirely American" sense.   Rodney was not satisfied with this argument, and insisted that the Constitution imposed no limit on impeachment.

" Is there a word in the whole sentence," he asked, " which expresses an idea, or from which any fair inference can be drawn, that no person shall be impeached but for ' treason, bribery, or other high crimes and misdemeanors ? ' . . . From the most cursory and transient view of this passage I submit with due deference that it must appear very manifest that there are other cases than those here specified for which an impeachment will lie and is the proper remedy."

The judges held their offices during good behavior ; the instant a judge should behave ill his office became forfeited.   To ascertain the fact " officially, or rather judicially," impeachment was provided ; the authority of the Senate was therefore coextensive with the complaint.

Rodney stated this principle broadly, but did not rest upon it; on the contrary, he accepted the respondent's challenge, and undertook to show that Chase had been guilty of crimes and misdemeanors in the technical sense of the term. Probably he was wise in choosing this alternative; for no one could doubt that his constitutional doctrine was one into which Chase's counsel were sedulously trying to drive him. If Rodney was right, the Senate was not a court of justice, and should discard judicial forms. Giles had seen this consequence of the argument, and had acted upon it, until beaten by its inevitable inconsistencies; at least sixteen senators were willing to accept the principle, and to make of impeachment an " official, or rather judicial," inquest of office. Judge Chase's counsel knew also that some half-dozen Republican senators feared to allow a partisan majority in the Senate to decide, after the fact, that such or such a judicial opinion had forfeited the judge's seat on the bench. This practice could end only in making the Senate, like the House of Lords, a court of last appeal. Giles threatened to impeach Marshall and the whole Supreme Court on Rodney's theory; and such a threat was as alarming to Dr. Mitchill of New York, or Senator Bradley of Vermont, as it was to Pickering and Tracy.

When Rodney finished, the theory of impeachment was more perplexed than ever, and but one chance remained to clear it. All the respondent's counsel had spoken in their turn; all the managers had expounded their theories : John Randolph was to close. Randolph was an invalid, overwhelmed by work and excitement, nervous, irritable, and not to be controlled. When he appeared in the box, Feb. 27, 1805, he was unprepared ; and as he spoke, he not only made his usual long pauses for recollection, but continually complained of having lost his notes, of his weakness, want of ability, and physical as well as moral incompetence. Such expressions in the mouths of other men might have passed for rhetoric; but Randolph's speech showed that he meant all he said. He too undertook to answer the argument of Luther Martin, Harper, and Hopkinson on the nature of impeachment ; but he answered without understanding it, — calling it " almost too absurd for argument," " a monstrous pretension," " a miserable quibble," but advancing no theory of his own, and supporting neither Campbell's, Nicholson's, nor Rodney's opinion. After a number of arguments which were in no sense answers, he said he would no longer worry the good sense of the Court by combating such a claim, — a claim which the best lawyers in America affirmed to be sound, and the two ablest of the managers had exhausted themselves in refuting.

Randolph's closing speech was overcharged with vituperation and with misstatements of fact and law, but was chiefly remarkable on account of the strange and almost irrational behavior of the speaker. Randolph's tall, thin figure, his penetrating eyes and shrill voice, were familiar to the society of Washington, and his violence of manner in the House only a short time before, in denouncing Granger and the Yazoo men, had prepared his audience for some eccentric outburst; but no one expected to see him, " with much distortion of face and contortion of body, tears, groans, and sobs," break down in the middle of his self-appointed task, and congratulate the Senate that this was " the last day of my sufferings and of yours." [1]

The next day the Senate debated the form of its final judgment.[2] Bayard moved that the question should be put: " Is Samuel Chase guilty or not guilty of a high crime or misdemeanor as charged in the article just read?" The point was vital; for if this form should be adopted, the Senate returned to the ground it had deserted in the case of Judge Pickering, and every senator would be obliged to assert that Chase's acts were crimes. At this crisis Giles abandoned the extreme impeachers. He made a speech repeating his old argument, and insisting that the House might impeach and the Senate convict not only for other than indictable offences, but for other than high crimes and misdemeanors; yet since in the present case the charges were avowedly for high crimes and misdemeanors, he was willing to take the question as Bayard proposed it, protesting meanwhile against its establishment as a precedent. Bayard's

[1] Diary of J. Q. Adams (Feb. 27, 1805), i. 359.
[2] Ibid., i. 361, 362.

Resolution was adopted March 1, a few moments before the hour of half-past twelve, which had been appointed for pronouncing judgment.

The Senate chamber was crowded with spectators when Vice-President Burr took the chair and directed the secretary to read the first article of impeachment. Every member of the Senate answered to his name. Tracy of Connecticut, prostrated by recent illness, was brought on a couch and supported to his seat, where his pale face added to the serious effect of the scene. The first article, which concerned the trial of Fries, was that on which Randolph had founded the impeachment, and on which the managers had thrown perhaps the greatest weight. As the roll was called, Senator Bradley of Vermont, first of the Republican members, startled the audience by saying "Not Guilty." Gaillard of South Carolina, and, to the astonishment of every one, Giles, the most ardent of impeachers, repeated the same verdict. These three defections decided the result; but they were only the beginning. Jackson of Georgia, another hot impeacher, came next; then Dr. Mitchill, Samuel Smith of Maryland, and in quick succession all the three Smiths of New York, Ohio, and Vermont. A majority of the Senate declared against the article, and the overthrow of the impeachers was beyond expectation complete.

On the second article the acquittal was still more emphatic; but on the third the impeachers rallied,— Giles, Jackson, and Samuel Smith returned to their party, and for the first time a majority appeared for conviction. Yet even with this support, the impeachers were far from obtaining the required twenty-three votes; the five recalcitrant Northern democrats stood firm; Gaillard was not to be moved, and Stone of North Carolina joined him: — the impeachers could muster but eighteen votes. They did no better on the fourth article. On the fifth, — Randolph's interpolated charge, which alleged no evil intent, — every member of the Senate voted "Not Guilty;" on the sixth, which was little more than a repetition of the fifth, only four senators could be found to condemn, and on the seventh, only ten. One chance of conviction remained, the eighth article, which covered the judge's charge to the grand jury at Baltimore in 1803. There lay the true cause of impeachment; yet this charge had been least pressed and least defended. The impeachers brought out their whole strength in its support; Giles, Jackson, Samuel Smith, and Stone united in pronouncing the judge guilty: but the five Northern democrats and Gaillard held out to the last, and the managers saw themselves deserted by nearly one fourth of the Republican senators. Nineteen voices were the utmost that could be induced to sustain impeachment.

The sensation was naturally intense; and yet the overwhelming nature of the defeat would have warranted an excitement still greater. No one understood better the meaning of Chase's acquittal than John Randolph, whose authority it overthrew. His

anger showed itself in an act which at first alarmed
and then amused his enemies.   Hurrying from the
Senate chamber to the House, he offered a Resolution
for submitting to the States an amendment to the
Constitution : " The judges of the Supreme and all
other courts of the United States shall be removed
by the President on the joint address of both Houses
of Congress."   His friend Nicholson, as though still
angrier than Randolph, moved another amendment, —
that the legislature of any State might, whenever it
thought proper, recall a senator and vacate his seat.
These resolutions were by a party vote referred to
the next Congress.

Randolph threatened in vain ; the rod was no
longer in his hands.   His overthrow before the
Senate was the smallest of his failures.   The Northern democrats talked of him with disgust ; and Senator Cocke of Tennessee, who had voted " Guilty " on
every article of impeachment except the fifth, told
his Federalist colleagues in the Senate that Randolph's vanity, ambition, insolence, and dishonesty,
not only in the impeachment but in other matters,
were such as to make the acquittal no subject for
regret.[1]   Madison did not attempt to hide his amusement at Randolph's defeat.   Jefferson held himself
studiously aloof.   To Jefferson and men of his class
Randolph seems to have alluded, in a letter written
a few weeks later, as " whimsicals," who " advocated
the leading measures of their party until they were

[1] Diary of J. Q. Adams (March 1, 1805), i. 364.

nearly ripe for execution, when they hung back, condemned the step after it was taken, and on most occasions affected a glorious neutrality."[1] Even Giles turned hostile. He not only yielded to the enemies of Randolph in regard to the form of vote to be taken on the impeachment, and fairly joined them in the vote on the first article, but he also aided in offering Randolph a rebuke on another point connected with the impeachment.

In the middle of the trial, February 15, Randolph reported to the House, and the House quickly passed, a Bill appropriating five thousand dollars for the payment of the witnesses summoned by the managers. When this Bill came before the Senate, Bayard moved to amend it by extending its provisions to the witnesses summoned by Judge Chase. The point was delicate; for if the Senate was a court, and impeachment a criminal procedure, this court should follow the rules that guided other judicial bodies; and every one knew that no court in America or in Christendom obliged the State, as a prosecutor, to pay the witnesses of the accused. After the acquittal, such a rule was either equivalent to telling the House that its charges against Chase were frivolous and should never have been presented, or it suggested that the trial had been an official inquiry into the conduct of an officer, and not a criminal procedure at law. The Republicans might properly reject the first assump-

[1] Randolph to Nicholson, April 30, 1805; Adams's Randolph, p. 157.

tion, the Federalists ought to resist the second; yet when Bayard's amendment came to a vote, it was unanimously adopted.[1] The House disagreed; the Senate insisted, and Giles led the Senate, affirming that he had drawn the form of summons, and that this form made no distinction between the witnesses for one party and the other. The argument was not decisive, for the court records showed at once by whom each witness was called; but Giles's reasoning satisfied the Senate, and led to his appointment, March 3, with Bradley, an enemy of impeachment, as conferrees to meet Randolph, Nicholson, and Early on the part of the House. They disagreed; and Randolph, with his friends, felt that Giles and the Senate had inflicted on them a grievous insult. The Report of the conference committee was received by the House at about seven o'clock on the evening of March 3, when the Eighth Congress was drawing its last breath. Randolph, who reported the disagreement, moved that the House adhere; and having thus destroyed the Bill, he next moved that the Clerk of the House should be directed to pay the witnesses, or any other expense certified by the managers, from the contingent fund. He would have carried his point, although it violated every financial profession of the Republican party, but that the House was thin, and the Federalists, by refusing to vote, prevented a quorum. At half-past nine o'clock on Sunday night, the 3d of March, 1805, the Eighth Congress

[1] Diary of J. Q. Adams (March 2, 1805), i. 367.

came to an end in a scene of total confusion and factiousness.

The failure of Chase's impeachment was a blow to the Republican party from which it never wholly recovered. Chief-Justice Marshall at length was safe; he might henceforward at his leisure fix the principles of Constitutional law. Jefferson resigned himself for the moment to Randolph's overthrow; but the momentary consolations passed away, and a life-long disappointment remained. Fifteen years later his regret was strongly expressed: —

" The Judiciary of the United States," mourned the old ex-President,[1] " is the subtle corps of sappers and miners constantly working underground to undermine the foundations of our confederated fabric. They are construing our Constitution from a co-ordination of a general and special government to a general and supreme one alone. . . . Having found from experience that impeachment is an impracticable thing, a mere scarecrow, they consider themselves secure for life; they skulk from responsibility; . . . an opinion is huddled up in conclave, perhaps by a majority of one, delivered as if unanimous, and with the silent acquiescence of lazy or timid associates, by a crafty chief-judge who sophisticates the law to his mind by the turn of his own reasoning."

The acquittal of Chase proved that impeachment was a scarecrow; but its effect on impeachment as a principle of law was less evident. No point was decided. The theory of Giles, Randolph, and Rodney

[1] Jefferson to Thomas Ritchie, Dec. 25, 1820; Works, vii. 192.

was still intact, for it was not avowedly applied to
the case. The theory of Judge Chase's counsel —
that an impeachable offence must be also indictable,
or even a violation of some known statute of the
United States — was overthrown neither by the argument nor by the judgment. So far as Constitutional
law was concerned, President Jefferson himself might
still be impeached, according to the dictum of Madison, for the arbitrary removal of a useful tide-waiter,
and Chief-Justice Marshall might be driven from the
bench, as Giles wished, for declaring the Constitution
to be above the authority of a statute; but although
the acquittal of Chase decided no point of law except
his innocence of high crimes or misdemeanors, as
charged in the indictment, it proved impeachment
to be "an impracticable thing" for partisan purposes, and it decided the permanence of those lines of
Constitutional development which were a reflection
of the common law. Henceforward the legal profession had its own way in expounding the principles
and expanding the powers of the central government
through the Judiciary.

CHAPTER XI.

THE Louisiana treaty, signed in May, 1803, was followed by two years of diplomatic activity. The necessary secrecy of diplomacy gave to every President the power to involve the country without its knowledge in dangers which could not be afterward escaped, and the Republican party neither invented nor suggested means by which this old evil of irresponsible politics could be cured; but of all Presidents, none used these arbitrary powers with more freedom and secrecy than Jefferson. His ideas of Presidential authority in foreign affairs were little short of royal. He loved the sense of power and the freedom from oversight which diplomacy gave, and thought with reason that as his knowledge of Europe was greater than that of other Americans, so he should be left to carry out his policy undisturbed.

Jefferson's overmastering passion was to obtain West Florida. To this end two paths seemed open. If he chose to conciliate, Yrujo was still ready to aid; and Spain stood in such danger between England and France that Godoy could not afford to throw the United States into the hands of either. If Jefferson

wished the friendship of Spain, he had every reason
to feel sure that the Prince of Peace would act in the
same spirit in which he had negotiated the treaty of
1795 and restored the right of deposit in 1802.   In
this case Florida must be let alone until Spain should
be willing to cede, or the United States be ready
for war.

On the other hand, the President might alienate
Spain and grasp at Florida.   Livingston and Monroe
warmly urged this policy, and were in fact its authors.
Livingston's advice would by itself have had no great
weight with Jefferson or Madison, but they believed
strongly in Monroe; and when he made Livingston's
idea his own, he gave it weight.   Monroe had been
sent abroad to buy Florida; he had bought Louisiana.   From the Potomac to the Mississippi, every
Southern man expected and required that by peace
or war Florida should be annexed to the Union;
and the annexation of Louisiana made that of Florida
seem easy.   Neither Monroe, Madison, nor Jefferson
could resist the impulse to seize it.

Livingston's plan has been described.   He did not
assert that Spain had intended to retrocede Florida to
France, or that France had claimed it as included in
the retrocession.   He knew the contrary; and tried in
vain to find some one willing to say that the country
to the Perdido ought to be included in the purchase.
He made much of Marbois's cautious encouragement
and Talleyrand's transparent manœuvres; but he was
forced at last to maintain that Spain had retroceded

West Florida to France without knowing it, that
France had sold it to the United States without
suspecting it, that the United States had bought it
without paying for it, and that neither France nor
Spain, although the original contracting parties, were
competent to decide the meaning of their own contract. Believing that Bonaparte was pledged to support the United States in their effort to obtain West
Florida, Livingston was anxious only to push Spain
to the utmost. Talleyrand allowed him to indulge in
these dreams. " I have obtained from him," wrote
Livingston to Madison,[1] " a positive promise that this
government shall aid any negotiation that shall be
set on foot" for the purchase of East Florida; while
as for Florida west of the Perdido, " the moment is so
favorable for taking possession of that country, that
I hope it has not been neglected, even though a little
force should be necessary to effect it. Your minister
must find the means to justify it."

When the letters written by Livingston and Monroe
in May, 1803, reached Washington, they were carefully studied by the President, fully understood, and
a policy quickly settled. When Jefferson wrote to
Senator Breckinridge his ideas on the unconstitution-
ality of the purchase, he spoke with equal clearness
on the course he meant to pursue toward Spain in
order to obtain Florida : [2] —

[1] Livingston to Madison, Nov. 15, 1803; State Papers, ii. 573,
574.

[2] Jefferson to Breckinridge, Aug. 12, 1803; Works, iv. 498.

" We have some claims to extend on the sea-coast westwardly to the Rio Norte or Bravo, and, better, to go eastwardly to the Rio Perdido, between Mobile and Pensacola, the ancient boundary of Louisiana.   These claims will be a subject of negotiation with Spain ; and if as soon as she is at war we push them strongly with one hand, holding out a price with the other, we shall certainly obtain the Floridas, and all in good time."

This was not Livingston's plan, but something quite distinct from it.   Livingston and Monroe wanted the President to seize West Florida, and negotiate for East Florida.   Jefferson preferred to negotiate for West Florida and to leave East Florida alone for the time.

Madison had already instructed [1] the minister at Madrid that the Floridas were not included in the treaty, " being, it appears, still held by Spain," and that the negotiation for their purchase would be conducted by Monroe at Madrid.   Instructions of the same date were instantly sent to Monroe,[2] urging him to pursue the negotiation for Florida, although owing to the large drain made on the Treasury, and to the " manifest course of events," the government was not disposed to make sacrifices for the sake of obtaining that country.   " Your inquiries may also be directed," wrote Madison, " to the question whether any, and how much, of what passes for West Florida be fairly included in the territory ceded to us by France."

[1] Madison to Pinckney, July 29, 1803; State Papers, ii. 614.
[2] Madison to Monroe, July 29, 1803; State Papers, ii. 626.

The idea that West Florida could be claimed as a part of the Louisiana purchase was a turning-point in the second Administration of Jefferson. Originating in Minister Livingston's mind, it passed from him to Monroe ; and in a few weeks the President declared the claim substantial.[1] As the summer of 1803 closed, Jefferson's plan became clear. He meant to push this claim, in connection with other claims, and to wait the moment when Spain should be dragged into the war between France and England.

These other claims were of various degrees of merit, and involved France as well as Spain. During the *quasi* war between the United States and France, before Jefferson came into power, American commerce in Spanish waters suffered severely from two causes. The first consisted in captures made by Spanish cruisers, and condemnations decided in Spanish courts ; the second was due to captures made by French cruisers, and condemned by French consuls in Spanish ports, or by courts of appeal in France, without regard to the rights or dignity of Spain. With much trouble, in August, 1802, at the time when Europe and America were waiting for the end of Leclerc's struggle with the negroes and fevers of St. Domingo, Pinckney succeeded in persuading the Prince of Peace to let the claims for Spanish depredations go before a commission for settlement ; but Godoy obstinately refused to recognize the claims for French depredations, taking the ground that Spain was in no way

[1] Jefferson to Madison, Aug. 25, 1803; Works, iv. 501.

responsible for them, had never in any way profited by them, and had no power at the time they occurred to prevent them ; that France, and France alone, had committed the offence, and should pay for it.

Pinckney resisted this reasoning as energetically as possible; but when Cevallos offered to sign a convention covering the Spanish depredations, and reserving the Franco-Spanish claims for future discussion, Pinckney properly decided to accept an offer which secured for his fellow-citizens five or ten millions of money, and which left the other claim still open.[1] The convention of Aug. 11, 1802, was sent to the Senate Jan. 11, 1803, in the excitement that followed Morales's withdrawal of the *entrepôt* at New Orleans. The Senate deferred action until the last moment of the session ; and then, March 3, 1803, after Nicholson and Randolph had appeared at the bar to impeach Judge Pickering, Pinckney's claims convention was taken up, and the nine Federalists were allowed to defeat it by the absence of Republican senators. The majority reconsidered the vote and postponed the whole subject till the next session. Thus, owing to the action of Federalist senators, when Jefferson in the following summer, after buying Louisiana, looked about for the means of buying Florida, he found these classes of claims, aggregating as he supposed between five and ten million dollars, ready to his hand. Monroe was promptly ordered to insist upon treating both classes alike, and setting both of them against the proposed

[1] Pinckney to Madison, Aug. 15, 1802; State Papers, ii. 482.

purchase of Florida. " On the subject of these claims you will hold a strong language," said Madison.[1]

A third class of claims could be made useful for the same purpose. Damages had been sustained by individuals in the violation of their right of deposit at New Orleans in the autumn of 1802.

" A distinction, however, is to be made," wrote Madison, " between the positive and specific damages sustained by individuals and the general injuries accruing from that breach of treaty. The latter could be provided for by a gross and vague estimate only, and need not be pressed as an indispensable condition. The claim however may be represented as strictly just, and a forbearance to insist on it as an item in the valuable considerations for which the cession [of Florida] is made. Greater stress may be laid on the positive and specific damages capable of being formally verified by individuals ; but there is a point beyond which it may be prudent not to insist, even here, especially as the incalculable advantage accruing from the acquisition of New Orleans will diffuse a joy throughout the western country that will drown the sense of these little sacrifices. Should no bargain be made on the subject of the Floridas, our claims of every sort are to be kept in force."

The President had not then decided to claim West Florida as included in the Louisiana purchase, and he conceived of no reason which should make Spain cling the more closely to Florida on account of the loss of New Orleans.

The news of the Louisiana purchase reached Wash-

[1] Madison to Monroe, July 29, 1803; State Papers, ii. 626.

ington early in July, 1803; Madison wrote his instructions to Monroe at the end of the same month;
Jefferson announced his policy to Breckenridge in
August. This was the harvest season of his life.
His theories were proved sound; his system of government stood in successful rivalry with that of
Bonaparte and Pitt; and he felt no doubt that his
friendship was as vital to England, France, and Spain
as all the armies and navies of the world. In the
midst of this enjoyment, September 4, he was suddenly told by the Marquis of Casa Yrujo that he had
bought stolen goods, and that Spain as the rightful
owner protested against the sale.[1]

Notwithstanding this strong measure, doubtless
taken in obedience to orders, Yrujo was still true
to his old friendship. On hearing of the cession, he
did again what he had done eight months before, in
the excitement about the *entrepôt* at New Orleans, —
he tried to smooth difficulties and quiet alarms.

"The ports of Florida," he wrote to Don Pedro Cevallos,[2] "as they would make it easy for us to annoy greatly
the American commerce in case of a war, would in like
degree furnish the Americans, if the Americans should
possess them, the same means of annoying ours, and of
carrying on an immense contraband trade from them,
especially from Pensacola and Mobile, with our provinces
in the Gulf of Mexico. This last is the chief evil which
in my opinion will result from the acquisition of Loui-

[1] Yrujo to Madison, Sept. 4 and 27, 1803 ; State Papers, ii.
569.

[2] Yrujo to Cevallos, Aug. 3, 1803 ; MSS. Spanish Archives.

siana by the Americans, and can only be diminished by numerous, watchful, and active revenue-cutters. For the rest I do not look on the alienation of Louisiana as a loss for Spain. That colony cost us much, and produced us very little."

In short, Louisiana could not be defended by Spain, while as a part of the United States it would certainly weaken, and probably dissolve, the Union. As for the protest, he told [1] his Government, even before he received Madison's reply, that nothing would come of it.

As late as Nov. 5, 1803, Yrujo continued to write in the same tone to his Government.

" The information I have received from trustworthy persons," he said,[2] " in regard to the disposition in which General Victor was coming here, and the spirit of restlessness and almost of rapine which reigned among many of the officials in his army, leave me no doubt that the military colony of the French in Louisiana would have been in reality a worse neighbor than the Americans for us. Things have now taken such a turn, that in my humble opinion if we are to lose Louisiana, the choice whether that colony shall fall into the power of one nation rather than another is not worth the expense and trouble of a war, provided we preserve the Floridas. . . . I am convinced that this Government knows perfectly the national interests, and to promote them will follow in this respect a course of conduct which in proportion as it better suits our own, should inspire us with greater confidence."

[1] Yrujo to Cevallos, Sept. 12, 1803; MSS. Spanish Archives.
[2] Yrujo to Cevallos, Nov. 5, 1803 ; MSS. Spanish Archives.

Yrujo acted the part of a true friend to both countries, in trying by such arguments to reconcile his Government to the loss of Louisiana; but there were limits to his good-will. He held that Spain could not afford to part with Florida. Yrujo went to the extreme of concession when he reconciled his Government to the loss of New Orleans, and nothing would reconcile him to the further loss of Mobile and Pensacola. Only on the theory that Spanish America was already ruined by the cession of Louisiana could Yrujo argue in favor of selling Florida.

On receiving Yrujo's protests of September 4 and 27, Jefferson's first feeling was of anger. He sent a strong body of troops to Natchez. " The Government of Spain," he wrote to Dupont de Nemours,[1] " has protested against the right of France to transfer, and it is possible she may refuse possession, and that may bring on acts of force; but against such neighbors as France there and the United States here, what she can expect from so gross a compound of folly and false faith is not to be sought in the book of wisdom." The folly of such conduct might be clear, but the charge of false faith against Spain for protesting against being deprived of her rights, seemed unjust, especially in the mouth of Jefferson, who meant to claim West Florida under a Franco-Spanish treaty which was acknowledged by all parties to have transferred Louisiana alone.

Only a week before this letter was written, the

[1] Jefferson to Dupont, Nov. 1, 1803; Works, iv. 508.

scheme of seizing West Florida had been publicly avowed by John Randolph on the floor of the House. Randolph's speech of October 24, in language as offensive to Spain as was possible in the mouth of a responsible leader, asserted, as a fact admitting no doubt, that West Florida belonged to the United States.[1] " We have not only obtained the command of the mouth of the Mississippi, but of the Mobile, with its widely extended branches ; and there is not now a single stream of note rising within the United States and falling into the Gulf of Mexico which is not entirely our own, the Appalachicola excepted." In a second speech the next day, he reiterated the statement even more explicitly and in greater detail.[2] The Republican press echoed the claim. Jefferson and Madison encouraged the manœuvre until they could no longer recede, and pushed inquiries in every direction,[3] without obtaining evidence that West Florida was, or ever had been, a part of the government of Louisiana. They even applied to Laussat,[4] the mortified and angry French commissioner whom Bonaparte had sent to receive possession of New Orleans ; and Laussat, to the annoyance of Talleyrand and Godoy, told the truth, — that the Iberville and the Rio Bravo were the boundaries fixed by his instructions, and

[1] Annals of Congress, 1803–1804, p. 415.

[2] Annals of Congress, 1803–1804, p. 440.

[3] Jefferson to William Dunbar, March 13, 1804; Works, iv. 537.

[4] Madison to Livingston, Jan. 31, 1804; State Papers, ii. 574.

therefore that West Florida was not a part of the purchase, but that Texas was.

Notwithstanding John Randolph's official declaration, when the time came for the delivery of Louisiana the Spanish governor, Dec. 20, 1803, peacefully surrendered the province to Laussat; Laussat handed it in due form to Claiborne; and Claiborne received it without asking for West Florida, or even recording a claim for it. That this silence was accidental no one pretended. The acquiescence in Spanish authority was so implicit that Madison three months afterward, at a time when both Executive and Legislature were acting on the theory that West Florida was in Louisiana, found himself obliged to explain the cause of conduct and contradictions so extraordinary. He wrote [1] to Livingston at Paris that the President had for several reasons preferred to make no demand for West Florida, —

" First, because it was foreseen that the demand would not only be rejected by the Spanish authority at New Orleans, which had in an official publication limited the cession westwardly by the Mississippi and the Island of New Orleans, but it was apprehended, as has turned out, that the French commissioner might not be ready to support the demand, and might even be disposed to second the Spanish opposition to it; secondly, because in the latter of these cases a serious check would be given to our title, and in either of them a premature dilemma would result between an overt submis-

[1] Madison to Livingston, March 31, 1804; State Papers, ii. 575.

sion to the refusal and a resort to force ; thirdly, because mere silence would be no bar to a plea at any time that a delivery of a part, particularly of the seat of the government, was a virtual delivery of the whole."

The President's silence at New Orleans was the more conspicuous because, at the moment when the province of Louisiana was thus delivered with such boundaries as Spain chose to define, Congress was legislating for Florida as an integral part of the Union.   John Randolph's official assertion that Mobile belonged to the United States under the treaty of cession, was made in the last part of October, 1803, soon after Congress met.   About a month later, November 30, he introduced a Bill nominally for giving effect to the laws of the United States within the ceded territory.   After much debate and disagreement this Bill at length passed both Houses, and Feb. 24, 1804, received the President's signature.   The fourth section directed that the territories ceded to the United States by the treaty, " and also all the navigable waters, rivers, creeks, bays, and inlets lying within the United States, which empty into the Gulf of Mexico east of the River Mississippi, shall be annexed to the Mississippi district, and shall, together with the same, constitute one district, to be called the ' District of Mississippi.' "   This provision was remarkable, because, as every one knew, no creeks, bays, or inlets lying within the United States emptied into the Gulf.   The Act by its eleventh section authorized the President, " whenever he shall deem it

expedient, to erect the shores, waters, and inlets of
the Bay and River of Mobile, and of the other rivers,
creeks, inlets, and bays emptying into the Gulf of
Mexico east of the said River Mobile, and west thereof
to the Pascagoula, inclusive, into a separate district,
and to establish such place within the same as he
shall deem expedient, to be the port of entry and
delivery for such district." This section gave the
President power of peace and war, for had he exercised it, the exercise must have been an act of war;
and John Randolph's previous declarations left no
doubt as to the meaning in which he, who reported
the Bill, meant it to be understood.

By this time Yrujo was boiling with such wrath
as a Spaniard alone could imagine or express. His
good-will vanished from the moment he saw that to
save Florida he must do battle with President, Secretary of State, Congress, and people. One insult had
followed another with startling rapidity. The President's *pêle-mêle*, of which the story will be told hereafter, wounded him personally. The cold reception
of his protest against the Louisiana cession; the cap-
tiousness of Madison's replies to his remonstrances;
the armed seizure of New Orleans with which he
was threatened; the sudden disregard of his friendship and great services; the open eagerness of the
Government to incite Bonaparte to plunder and dis-
member Spain; the rejection of the claims convention
in March, and its sudden approval by the Senate in
January, as though to obtain all the money Spain

was willing to give before taking by force territory vital to her empire ; and above all, the passage of this law annexing the Floridas without excuse or explanation, — all these causes combined to change Yrujo's ancient friendship into hatred.

In the midst of the complicated legislation about Louisiana, while the Mobile Act was under discussion, Jefferson sent to the Senate, Dec. 21, 1803, the correspondence about the Spanish claims, and among the rest an adverse opinion which Yrujo had obtained from five prominent American lawyers on an abstract case in regard to the Franco-Spanish spoliations. Madison was particularly annoyed by this legal opinion, and thought it should bring these five gentlemen within the penalties of the law passed Jan. 30, 1799, commonly known as Logan's Act. Senator Bradley of Vermont moved for a committee, which reported in favor of directing the President to institute proceedings against Jared Ingersoll, William Rawle, J. B. McKean, Peter S. Duponceau, and Edward Livingston, — five lawyers whose legal, social, and political character made a prosecution as unwise in politics as it was doubtful in law. The Senate having at the moment too many prosecutions already on its hands, let Senator Bradley's Report lie unnoticed, and soon afterward confirmed the claims convention by a vote of eighteen to eight,[1] — barely two thirds, the least factious of the Federalists joining the majority, and by this unpartisan act causing in the end more

[1] Journal of Executive Sessions, Jan. 9, 1804.

embarrassment to the party in power than the most
ingenious factiousness could have plotted. Madison,
in the midst of his measures for pressing the acquisition of Florida, sent the ratified claims convention
to Madrid. The period fixed for ratification had long
since expired, and the attitude of the United States
toward Florida had altered the feelings and interests of Spain ; but either Madison was unaware of
the change, or he wished to embarrass Godoy. He
added in his letter to Pinckney,[1] " It was judged
best, on the whole, no longer to deprive that class of
our citizens who are comprehended in the convention
of the benefit of its provisions ; " but although consenting to take what Spain was willing to give, he
spoke with contempt of the Spanish argument against
the Franco-Spanish claims, and insisted that these
should be pressed without relaxation. He even complained that Yrujo, in taking the opinion of American
lawyers, had failed in respect to the United States
government and his own.[2]

Madison seemed unconscious that Yrujo could have
any just cause of complaint, or that his Government
could resent the tone and temper of President and
Congress. The passage of the Bill which made
Mobile a collection district and a part of the Mississippi territory gave Yrujo the chance to retaliate.
About a fortnight after the President had signed this
law, Yrujo one morning entered the State Department

[1] Madison to Pinckney, Jan. 31, 1804 ; State Papers, ii. 614.
[2] Madison to Pinckney, Feb. 6, 1804; State Papers, ii. 615.

with the printed Act in his hand, and overwhelmed Madison with reproaches, which he immediately afterward supported by a note [1] so severe as to require punishment, and so able as to admit of none. He had at first, he said, regarded as " an atrocious libel " on the United States government the assertion that it had made a law which usurped the rights of Spanish sovereignty ; yet such was the case. He gave a short and clear abstract of the evidence which refuted the claim to West Florida, and closed by requesting that the law be annulled.

Madison could neither maintain the law nor annul it ; he could not even explain it away. Gallatin told the President six months afterward,[2] that " the public mind is altogether unprepared for a declaration that the terms and object of the Mobile Act had been misunderstood by Spain ; for every writer, without a single exception, who has written on the subject seems to have understood the Act as Spain did ; it has been justified by our friends on that ground." Yet Jefferson was not prepared to maintain and defend the Act in its full assertions of authority, after accepting Louisiana without asking for West Florida. Madison wrote a letter of complaint to Livingston at Paris,[3] explaining, as already quoted, the rea-

[1] Yrujo to Madison, March 7, 1804 ; MSS. State Department Archives.

[2] Gallatin to Jefferson, October, 1804 ; Gallatin's Works, i. 211.

[3] Madison to Livingston, March 31, 1804 ; State Papers, ii. 575.

sons which had induced the President to make no demand for West Florida before ascertaining the views and claiming the interposition of the French government.

" In this state of things," said he, " it was deemed proper by Congress, in making the regulations necessary for the collection of revenue in the ceded territory, and guarding against the new danger of smuggling into the United States through the channels opened by it, to include a provision for the case of West Florida by vesting in the President a power which his discretion might accommodate to events."

This interpretation of the law was not in harmony with the law itself or with Randolph's speeches ; but Madison hastened to turn from this delicate subject in order to bring another complaint against Yrujo.

" The Act had been many weeks depending in Congress with these sections, word for word, in it ; . . . it must in all probability have been known to the Marquis d'Yrujo in an early stage of its progress ; if it was not, it marks much less of that zealous vigilance over the concerns of his sovereign than he now makes the plea for his intemperate conduct. For some days, even after the Act was published in the Gazette of this city, he was silent. At length, however, he called at the office of State, with the Gazette in his hand, and entered into a very angry comment."

The Spanish minister's subsequent notes had been written with " a rudeness which no government can tolerate ; " but his conduct was chiefly of importance

" as it urges the expediency of cultivating the disposition of the French government to take our side of the question."

The President came to Madison's relief. By a proclamation issued a few weeks afterward, reciting the terms of the Act of Congress in regard to the Bay and River of Mobile, he declared all these " shores, waters, inlets, creeks, and rivers, lying *within the boundaries of the United States*," to be a collection district, with Fort Stoddert for its port of entry.[1] The italics were a part of the proclamation, and suggested that such could not have been the intent of Congress, because no part of the shores or waters of Mobile Bay, or of the other bays east of Mobile, lay within the boundaries of the United States. The evasion was a divergence from the words of the Act unwarranted by anything in the context ; and to give it authority, Jefferson, in spite of Gallatin's remonstrance, declared in his next Annual Message that the Mobile Act had been misunderstood on the part of Spain.[2]

[1] Proclamation of May 30, 1804 ; State Papers, ii. 583.
[2] Message of Nov. 8, 1804. Annals of Congress, 1804–1805, p. 11.

CHAPTER XII.

THOUGH Yrujo's language was strong, and his anonymous writings in the press were indiscreet, he had, down to the summer of 1804, laid himself open to no just official censure ; for whatever the Secretary of State might think, no one could seriously blame a foreign minister for obtaining the best legal advice in America on an abstract question of international law. The protests with which Yrujo contented himself, vigorous as they were, could neither be disavowed by his Government nor answered by Madison. Had he stopped there, his triumph would have been signal ; but fortunately for Madison, the Spaniard, with all the high qualities of his nation, had also its weaknesses, besides having the love of intrigue inherent in diplomacy. Yrujo was in his political training more American than Spanish. At home in Philadelphia, son-in-law to Governor McKean, and well acquainted with the methods of party politics, he burned to counteract the influence of the Administration press, and had no other means of doing so than by acting on Federalist editors. As no one but himself knew even a part of the truth about the Spanish imbroglio, he was obliged to be the channel for conveying his own

information to the public; and from time to time
Madison read in opposition newspapers anonymous
letters which bore plain marks of Yrujo's peculiar
style. He had already published a pamphlet on the
Louisiana cession. After his hot protest against
the Mobile Act, in March, 1804, the Spanish minister
left Washington, without taking leave of the Secretary of State. At length his indiscretions enabled
Madison to enjoy the pleasure of seeing him keenly
mortified.

Among other Federalist newspapers in Philadelphia was one called the "Political Register," edited
by a man named Jackson. In September, 1804, six
months after the passage-at-arms over the Mobile
Act, Yrujo, then in Philadelphia, asked for an interview with Jackson, and urged him to oppose the
course which the President had taken against Spain.
"If you will consent," he said, "to take elucidations
on the subject from me, I will furnish them, and I
will make you any acknowledgment." He charged
the Administration with wishing for war, and with
intriguing for a rebellion among the Spaniards of
West Florida.

That Yrujo or any other diplomatic agent was
quite ready to use money, if by doing so he could
obtain objects necessary for his purposes, need not
be doubted, — although corruption of this kind in the
affairs of the United States has left few traces even
on the most secret diplomatic records of England,
France, and Spain. In the ethical code of diplomacy

the offer of money to an editor for inserting information was no offence, but discovery was fatal ; and for
this reason perhaps Yrujo told the truth when he
afterward said that the use of money was not in his
mind. Had he meant to bribe, he would not have
exposed himself to detection, or put himself, without
need, in the hands of a person over whom he held
no power. Nevertheless, his blunder deserved the
punishment which quickly followed.

A few days after his interview with Jackson, Yrujo
left Philadelphia to visit Jefferson at Monticello.
Sept. 20, 1804, immediately after his departure, Jackson printed an affidavit narrating the attempt which
Yrujo had made upon his virtue, and detailing every
expression of the minister which could do him most
injury. As though to make Yrujo's position still more
mortifying, Jackson sent this affidavit to President
Jefferson ten days or more before publishing it : and
when Yrujo, ignorant of the betrayal, after passing
Madison's door at Montpelier without the courtesy of
stopping to inquire for the Secretary's health,[1] at last
reached Monticello, not only his host, but every one
except himself, had heard of the diplomatic scandal
to which he was a party.

Jefferson received his visitor with the usual hospitality, and said not a word on the subject. Being
obliged to return to Washington, the President left
Yrujo, two days later, under the protection of his

[1] Pichon to Talleyrand, 18 Brumaire, An xiii. (Nov. 9,
1804) ; Archives des Aff. Étr., MSS.

daughter Mrs. Randolph, and set out to meet his
Cabinet on the last day of the month at the Federal
city.   Madison was delayed at Montpelier, and could
not attend the Cabinet meeting, but wrote a few days
afterward :[1] —

"Jackson, I find, has lost no time in giving publicity
to the affair between him and Yrujo. What course the
latter will take, remains to be seen. Should circumstances of any kind be thought to urge a close of the
business with him, or any other arrangement with respect to it, why might not one of the other secretaries,
or even Mr. Wagner, be made a channel of your sentiments and determinations? . . . Should the door be
shut against further communication [through] Yrujo,
and Pinckney's situation at Madrid not be contradicted,
a direct communication with Cevallos appears to be the
next resource."

Already Madison flattered himself with the hope
that he was to be relieved from relations with the
Spaniard, whose continuance at Washington he had
asked as a favor from Don Carlos IV. only three
years before.

Jefferson's delicacy and hospitality were worthy
of a great lord of Spain, and did honor to his innate
kindliness ; but they put Yrujo in an attitude so mortifying, that when he returned to Washington and
learned what had taken place in his absence, he was
overcome with shame at finding himself charged with
calumniating his host at the moment of claiming

[1] Madison to Jefferson, Oct. 2, 1804 ; Jefferson MSS.

his hospitality. He immediately prepared a counter-statement and took it to the President, who replied that the matter was one which should properly belong to Madison. Yrujo then printed his letter in the "National Intelligencer," where Madison first saw it. For the moment the matter went no further; but Madison was fixed in his purpose of effecting Yrujo's recall, and when in the following spring he instructed his minister at Madrid to ask this favor, he alleged the affair of Jackson among the reasons which justified his request.

Pichon, who was in charge of the French legation, cordially disliked Yrujo, and did nothing to help him against Madison, although the relations between Spain and France were those of close alliance; but Madison next suffered a severe loss in the removal of Pichon, and in the arrival, Nov. 23, 1804, of the first minister sent by France to the United States since the departure of Adet in President Washington's time. The new appointment was not a happy one. Pichon had carried friendliness so far as on several serious questions to take sides with the United States government against his own, and had fallen into disfavor with Napoleon in consequence. The new minister was little likely to repeat this blunder. Napoleon liked military discipline in all things; and he sent as his minister to Washington a former general of the Republic, Louis Marie Turreau, best known for the extreme severities he was charged with having inflicted on the Vendeans in 1794. Like most of the republican generals, including even Moreau and Bernadotte, Turreau accepted the *coup d'état* of the 18th Brumaire, and was for private reasons anxious to obtain some position far removed from France. According to his own story, he had during the Vendean war been so unfortunate as to be saved from death, in a moment of extreme danger, by a woman's self-sacrifice. In token of his gratitude he married his preserver; but from that time his life became a long regret. His wife's temper was terrible; his own was querulous and morbidly depressed. Although he could speak no English, had no diplomatic experience and little taste for general society, he sought the post of minister resident at Washington in order to escape his wife. To his extreme annoyance, she followed him to America; and Washington resounded with the scandal of their quarrels, which reached the extremity of pitched battles. He wrote to his friends in the French Foreign Office that he was almost mad with mortification and despair.

Such a minister was not happily chosen for the difficult task on hand; but Bonaparte loaded him with other burdens, of a kind even more embarrassing to a diplomatist. At best, the position of a French minister in America was not agreeable. The mere difference in habits, manners, amusements, and the want of a thousand luxuries and pleasures such as made Paris dear to every Frenchman, rendered Washington a place of exile. Perhaps nothing but fear of the guillotine could have reconciled even republican Frenchmen to staying in a country where, in the words of Talleyrand, there was no Frenchman who did not feel himself a stranger ; but if this were true while France was a republic fighting the battles of American democracy, it became doubly true after Bonaparte had crushed French liberties and made himself the foremost enemy of republican ideas. Turreau arrived at Washington about six months before Bonaparte took the title of Emperor; and he found that as representative of Napoleon I. he could never hope for a friend in the United States, unless it were among a few bankrupt adventurers, who to retrieve their broken fortunes would have liked to see an 18th Brumaire at New Orleans, which should give an imperial crown and the mines of Mexico to Aaron Burr and his troop of embryo dukes and marshals.

As though to embarrass his representative to the utmost, Bonaparte deprived him of the only means by which he could win even the venal respect of a money-making people.   At one stroke the First Consul had annulled and sent to protest all the drafts drawn under Rochambeau's orders by the fiscal administrator of St. Domingo.[1]   His avowed reason was that every bill of exchange or draft on the public treasury which did not purport to rest on the authority of a letter from the minister authorizing the expenditure, should not be paid.   The true reason was that he had

[1] Note du Premier Consul, 2 Floréal, An xi. (April 22, 1803); Correspondance, viii. 288.

determined to waste no more money on St. Domingo, but to sacrifice his army there under cover of a war with England, which required all the means then at his disposal. Rochambeau's expenditures were becoming wild; but thus far his drafts on the Treasury were regularly drawn. They had been taken in good faith throughout the West Indies and in every commercial city on the American seaboard; they rested on the national credit of France, and their repudiation destroyed French credit in America, public and private. Before Turreau sailed for his post, the credit of his Government was at an end in the United States. Not only had the drafts drawn in St. Domingo been refused payment, but Pichon's had also suffered the same fate; and neither the new minister nor his consuls could find a man in Baltimore, Philadelphia, or New York to advance money on their official signatures. Turreau complained bitterly to Talleyrand of the penury and mortification to which he was condemned. In one of his despatches [1] he reported that at a tavern in Baltimore one of the French agents, not known to be such, was offered French government paper at fifty per cent discount, and at the same time five per cent premium for drafts on the British government. " In short, we are brought to such a state of affairs that private discredit follows the discredit of the nation, and I experience it for my own individual drafts."

[1] Turreau to Talleyrand, 23 Floréal, An xiii. (May 13, 1805); Archives des Aff. Étr., MSS.

Owing to these circumstances, Turreau declared
that his position was hardly tolerable; but even apart
from such matters, he found a formidable legacy of
diplomatic difficulties left by Pichon to be settled.
The question of trade with St. Domingo, of boundary
on both sides of Louisiana, the Spanish imbroglio, the
unpaid claims on France, and the repudiated drafts
negotiated by Pichon in the United States, were all
matters which Turreau was required to master and
manage; but none of them gave him more trouble
than the personal quarrel between his colleague Yrujo
and the Secretary of State.

Yrujo's affair with Major Jackson occurred in September, 1804, and Turreau, reaching Washington in
the following November, was soon obliged to take part
in Yrujo's feuds. Not only the tone of his instructions, but the increasing certainty that Spain must
side with France in the war against England, obliged
him to make common cause with the Spanish minister, who came from Philadelphia to Washington in
order to invoke his services. The result was told
in a despatch to Talleyrand: [1] —

"Following your instructions and the request of M.
d'Yrujo, I consented to an interview with him at Mr.
Madison's. . . . I had no trouble in perceiving from the
outset of the conversation that Mr. Madison and M.
d'Yrujo cordially detested each other, and in the discussion that their passions took the place of reason
and law."

[1] Turreau to Talleyrand, 6 Pluviôse, An xii. (Jan. 27, 1805);
Archives des Aff. Étr., MSS.

This discussion naturally turned on the question of West Florida; and unfortunately for Madison, Turreau's instructions on that point were emphatic in support of Spain. Turreau was obliged to enter the lists in defence of Yrujo's position.

"I mixed in the discussion only in order to represent to Mr. Madison, who is unwilling to stop at the treaty of 1762, that in general the last conventions were those which ought to guide in negotiations; otherwise, if each party invoked the antecedent ones in favor of his system, we should be forced to go back to the Deluge to find the primitive title. 'But, General!' replied Mr. Madison, 'we have a map which probably carries to the Perdido the eastern limit of Louisiana!' — 'I should be curious to see it, sir; the more, because I have one which includes Tennessee and Kentucky in Louisiana. You will agree that maps are not titles.' The Secretary of State closed this session, which lasted two long hours, by saying that if Spain had always conducted herself toward the United States as well as France had done, the difficulties would not have taken place. I did not think myself called upon to appear very grateful for this kind of cajolery."

Turreau did not want keenness of insight; and this early experience gave him no high respect either for Madison or for the American system of government. His despatch explained that the dispute was in great part due to the fact that the Louisiana purchase had been made a battle-ground in the Presidential election just ended; that the opposition, by depreciating its importance, had driven the party in power to exaggerate its value; and that, the Administration, to assure itself of victory, had committed itself to the policy of obtaining Florida by one means or another, till it could no longer recede. Yrujo's indiscretions had helped to make it impossible for Jefferson to withdraw with dignity from his position.

" For the rest," continued Turreau, " I have made every effort to reconcile M. d'Yrujo with the Secretary of State, and if I have not succeeded, it is the fault of the latter. He is dry (*sec*), spiteful (*haineux*), passionate; and his private resentments, still more than political difference, will long keep him apart from M. d'Yrujo. Nevertheless, as I am on very good terms with Mr. Madison, whom I was about to ask to dine with me, I sent my first aide-de-camp to ask him whether he would be pleased to meet the Spanish minister at dinner; and in consequence of his very civil and even obliging answer, I had them together at my table, where I again attempted a reconciliation. M. d'Yrujo would have agreed to it; but the Secretary of State cannot forgive."

Finally, Turreau called Talleyrand's attention to the question whether it was for the interest of France and Spain that Yrujo should be kept at Washington : —

" Doubtless the Government here wishes for his recall, and regards this step as the duty of the Court at Madrid, the more because Mr. Pinckney has been recalled; but ought the Spanish minister to be changed because the American government wishes it? This point deserves attention. These people here have been well spoiled; it is time to send them back to their proper place."

The quarrel with Yrujo was the more unfortunate because it happened at a moment when Charles Pinckney, the American minister at Madrid, showed extreme want of discretion. The President had not intended to leave Pinckney unassisted. After the conclusion of the Louisiana treaty, in May, 1803, Madison supposed that Monroe, in obedience to his instructions, would go at once to Madrid and take the negotiation from Pinckney's hands.[1] For reasons that will hereafter appear, Monroe decided against this step, and went to London instead. On learning the change of plan, Madison warned Pinckney [2] to make no propositions to the Spanish government, which was not yet in a humor to receive them with favor. Pinckney, restive under restraint, managed to keep up an appearance of diplomatic activity that greatly vexed the Secretary of State. Madison complained [3] to the President that his minister at Madrid teased the Spanish government on the subject of Florida, which he had been ordered not to touch without the presence or the advice of Monroe; forbidden to make but permitted to accept offers, he was continually offering to accept; while Livingston at Paris, equally restive under the imposed authority of Monroe, could not resist the temptation to stimulate Pinckney and offer advice both to France and Spain. Madison's complaints

[1] Madison to Monroe, July 29, 1803; State Papers, ii. 626. Madison to Pinckney, July 29, 1803; State Papers, ii. 614.

[2] Madison to Pinckney, Oct. 12, 1803; State Papers. ii. 570.

[3] Madison to Jefferson, April 9, 1804; Jefferson MSS.

were well founded ; but when he wrote in this sense
to Jefferson, he had not begun to appreciate the full
measure of diplomatic activity which his minister at
Madrid was capable of displaying.

Yrujo always managed to embarrass the American
government without seriously committing his own ;
but Pinckney showed no such forbearance, and by
the close of the year 1804 drew Madison into a
mortifying position. He began his activity in July,
1803, immediately after hearing that Monroe had
given up the proposed visit to Madrid, and had gone
to London. Without waiting to learn how this change
of plan and the purchase of Louisiana might affect
the President's views toward Spain, Pinckney, to use
his own words,[1] " pushed the new propositions respecting our claims in that positive and decided manner
which the circumstances of Europe and the particular
situation of Spain seemed to me to warrant." Cevallos
contented himself with parrying this attack by giving
to Pinckney the written opinion obtained by Yrujo
from the five American lawyers in support of his
argument that the United States, by their treaty with
France of Sept. 30, 1800, had renounced their right
to demand indemnity for losses sustained from French
cruisers.[2]

Both parties next appealed to the French ambassador at Madrid. The Prince of Peace, though
irritated by the sale of Louisiana, quickly saw that his

[1] Pinckney to Madison, Aug. 2, 1803 ; State Papers, ii. 597.
[2] Cevallos to Pinckney, Aug. 23, 1803; State Papers, ii. 604.

only chance of retaining Florida was to conciliate
Bonaparte; and Pinckney, who knew that the French
ambassador at Madrid had been instructed to support
Monroe in negotiating for Florida, counted on the
same aid in order to maintain a threatening attitude.
The result was soon seen. Pinckney, disturbed by the
news of Yrujo's protest against the sale of Louisiana,
turned to the French ambassador for advice.[1] Beurnonville accordingly wrote to Talleyrand for instructions; but Talleyrand had already sent to the Spanish
embassy at Paris a note of sharp remonstrance against
the protest.[2] Beurnonville, learning this, asked the
Prince of Peace for explanations; and Godoy hastened
to assure him that Bonaparte might be at ease on
this score, for orders had been sent to New Orleans to
surrender the province without opposition, and already
Yrujo had been instructed to change his tone at
Washington.[3] Soon afterward Cevallos formally notified Pinckney that the King renounced his opposition to the cession of Louisiana.[4] In due time Yrujo
sent to the State Department a formal note to the
same effect.[5]

At the cost of recognizing the Louisiana cession,

[1] Beurnonville to Talleyrand, 18 Nivôse, An xii. (Jan. 9,
1804); Archives des Aff. Étr., MSS.

[2] Talleyrand to D'Hervas, 12 Nivôse, An xii. (Jan. 3, 1804);
Archives des Aff. Étr., MSS.

[3] Beurnonville to Talleyrand, 21 Nivôse, An xii. (Jan. 12,
1804); Archives des Aff. Étr., MSS.

[4] Cevallos to Pinckney, Feb. 10, 1804; State Papers, ii. 583.

[5] Yrujo to Madison, May 15, 1804; State Papers, ii. 583.

Godoy pacified Bonaparte, who stood in need of Spanish support. From that moment Pinckney begged in vain for help from the French ambassador at Madrid, although the need of aid increased from day to day. Just as his first and least important point, the withdrawal of Yrujo's protest, was gained at Madrid, the Government at Washington created new difficulties about his path. At the moment when Beurnonville, Talleyrand, and Pinckney wrung from King Charles his adhesion to the Louisiana treaty, the Senate at Washington, Jan. 9, 1804, ratified the Spanish claims convention, which had been negotiated by Pinckney nearly eighteen months before, and had been held an entire year under consideration by the Senate. The last article of this convention provided, as usual with such instruments, that it should have no effect until ratified by both parties, and that the ratifications should be exchanged as soon as possible. So far from performing its part of the contract, the Senate had at one moment refused to ratify at all, and after reconsidering this refusal, had delayed ratification an entire year, until the relations of the two parties had been wholly changed. The idea that the King of Spain was bound to ratify in his turn, implied excessive confidence in his good-nature ; but Madison, in sending the ratified treaty to Pinckney, suggested no suspicion that Charles IV. might have changed his mind, and gave not a hint to Pinckney of the course to be followed in such a contingency. The Mobile Act had not yet become law, and Yrujo was waiting for its signature by the President before waking Madison from his dreams of doing what he pleased with Spanish property.

Early in February, 1804, Madison sent these new instructions to Pinckney, inclosing the ratified treaty, and instructing him in effect to press the reserved claims for French spoliations in Spanish ports. The despatch reached Pinckney in May, and he went at once to Cevallos for the ratification. To his great annoyance Cevallos made difficulties. During the discussion, Cevallos received from Yrujo a copy of the Mobile Act, which he sent to Pinckney May 31, with a demand for explanations. Pinckney replied in a tone little short of dictatorial.[1]

" Permit me on this subject to remind your Excellency," said he, " that on the first intelligence being received of the cession of Louisiana, I communicated verbally to your Excellency and the Prince of Peace the contents of an official letter I had received from Mr. Livingston and Mr. Monroe, informing me that they considered a great part of West Florida, as so called by the English, as included. Such letter could not have been written officially to me by them without their having been so informed by the French plenipotentiary and government."

Pinckney urged that the two subjects should be kept separate. " Do not show the United States that you have no confidence either in their honor or justice, — qualities on which they value themselves more than on power or wealth."

[1] Pinckney to Cevallos, June 1, 1804; State Papers, ii. 618.

Unfortunately Pinckney's note obliged Spain to show want of confidence in the " honor or justice " of the United States, unless indeed she meant to acquiesce in losing Florida as well as Louisiana. Pinckney next appealed to the French ambassador for help.[1] " I took the course of giving Mr. Pinckney an obliging but vague answer," said Beurnonville, writing for instructions to Talleyrand. Cevallos, on his side, wrote to Admiral Gravina, the Spanish ambassador at Paris, instructing him to remonstrate with Talleyrand against Pinckney's conduct. After a month's delay, Cevallos, in answer to Pinckney's letters, sent a sharp note,[2] offering to ratify the convention on three conditions, — one being that the reserved claim for French spoliations should be abandoned, and another that the Mobile Act should be revoked.

Without waiting for further instructions, or even consulting Monroe at London, Pinckney next wrote to Cevallos a letter which surpassed all indiscretions that Madison could have imagined. Requesting Cevallos " merely to answer this question," whether ratification was refused except on the conditions specified, he added : [3] —

" I wish to have your Excellency's answer as quickly as possible, as on Tuesday I send a courier with circular letters to all our consuls in the ports of Spain, stating to

[1] Beurnonville to Talleyrand, 18 Prairial, An xii. (June 7, 1804) ; Archives des Aff. Étr., MSS.

[2] Cevallos to Pinckney, July 2, 1804 ; State Papers, ii. 619.

[3] Pinckney to Cevallos, July 5, 1804; State Papers, ii. 620.

them the critical situation of things between Spain and the United States, the probability of a speedy and serious misunderstanding, and directing them to give notice thereof to all our citizens; advising them so to arrange and prepare their affairs as to be able to move off within the time limited by the treaty, should things end as I now expect. I am also preparing the same information for the commander of our squadron in the Mediterranean, for his own notice and government, and that of all the American merchant-vessels he may meet."

Cevallos immediately answered [1] that as he could not comprehend the motive for " breaking out in the decisions, not to say threats," of this letter, or how it was possible that Pinckney could have the authority of his government for such conduct, he should by the King's order transfer the negotiation to Washington. Pinckney rejoined by despatching his circular letter, which created a panic in the Mediterranean. He then informed Cevallos that so soon as his affairs could be arranged, he should send for his passports and quit Madrid.[2]

Although this step was in the highest degree improper, Pinckney had some excuse for his conduct. Left without instructions in the face of an emergency which might have been foreseen at Washington, he argued that his government, which had officially an-nexed West Florida, meant to support its acts with a strong hand. He thought that the issue presented

[1] Cevallos to Pinckney, July 8, 1804 ; State Papers, ii. 620.
[2] Pinckney to Cevallos, July 14, 1804 ; State Papers, ii. 621.

by Cevallos was such as the President was bound
to take up, and he knew that the only chance of carrying the points which the President had at heart
was in energetic action.   For three years he had
watched the peremptory tone of France and England
at Madrid, and had been assured by the common
voice of his diplomatic colleagues that threats alone
could extort action from the Spanish government.
He had seen the Prince of Peace, after resorting
to one subterfuge after another, repeatedly forced
to cower before the two great robbers who were
plundering Spain, and he explained to Madison the
necessity of imitating their example if the President
meant that Spain should cower before the United
States.   Perhaps he felt that Godoy looked on the
President at Washington as the jackal of Bonaparte,
and he may have wished to prove that America
could act alone.   His eager ambition to make himself
as important as the representatives of France and
England in the eyes of Europe might imply vanity,
but rested also on logic.

The first result of this energetic tone was not
what Pinckney had hoped.   Cevallos was outwardly
unmoved; Pinckney's violence only caused him to
lay aside that courtesy which was the usual mark
of Spanish manners.   His official notes were in outward form still civil enough, but in two or three
conversations Pinckney listened to a series of remarks as blunt as though Lord Harrowby were the
speaker.   Pinckney reported to Madison the tenor of

these rough rejoinders.[1] Cevallos told him that the Americans, ever since their independence, had been receiving the most pointed proofs of friendship and generosity from Spain, who, as was well known, received no benefit from them, — on the contrary, their commerce was extremely injurious to Spain; the Spanish government had ten times more trouble with them than with any other nation, and for his part, he did not wish to see the trade with the United States extended. Spain had nothing to fear from the United States, and had heard with contempt the threats of senators like Ross and Gouverneur Morris. The Americans had no right to expect much kindness from the King; in the purchase of Louisiana they had paid no attention to his repeated remonstrances against the injustice and nullity of that transaction, whereas if they had felt the least friendship they would have done so. They were well known to be a nation of calculators, bent on making money and nothing else; the French, and probably in the result all the nations having possessions in the West Indies, would be materially injured by them, for without a doubt it was entirely owing to the United States that St. Domingo was in its present situation.

Pinckney received[2] at the same time what he called secret intelligence on which he could implicitly rely,

[1] Pinckney to Madison, July 20, 1804; MSS. State Department Archives.

[2] Pinckney to Madison, July 20, 1804; MSS. State Department Archives.

that Cevallos meant to create indefinite delays to the
ratification, for Yrujo had written that neither these
nor the French spoliation claims, nor West Florida,
would induce the American government to depart from
its pacific system. France had indeed gone to the point
of advising and even commanding Spain to relinquish
her claim on Louisiana, and this was the reason why
Spain had so quietly given it up; but in regard to
the spoliations, France preferred not to see them paid,
as the more money Spain paid America the less she
could pay France, and France knew as well as Spain
how little serious was the American government in
the idea of abandoning its neutrality.

Pinckney having done his worst, found himself in
a position extremely awkward. Although he threatened to leave Spain, and proclaimed that he meant
soon to demand his passports, he did not venture to
take this last step without instructions. Cevallos,
excessively perplexed by his conduct, could not conceive that he should act thus without some definite
authority. Boldly as Cevallos talked, he was in truth
greatly alarmed by the idea of war. The French representative at Madrid wrote to Talleyrand that Pinckney had terrified the secretary beyond reason : [1] —

" The difficulty of making himself understood by M.
de Cevallos in a language with which he is not familiar,
excites Mr. Pinckney to fly out in terms beyond moderation and proper civility. He positively threatens war,

[1] Vandeul to Talleyrand, 7 Thermidor, An xii. (July 26,
1804) ; Archives des Aff. Étr., MSS.

and loudly announces his resolution shortly to demand his passports. The truth is that he is preparing to depart, and finds himself almost deprived of power to remain, not only in consequence of his personal altercation with the minister, but also of the care with which he has taken the public into his confidence. . . . M. de Cevallos seems to me to be quite seriously alarmed at the results this may have."

Ten days later the Frenchman reported that Cevallos was more uneasy than ever.[1]

" ' If the Emperor,' added M. de Cevallos, ' would but say a word, and let the United States understand that he is not pleased at seeing them abuse the advantages which they owe to their strength and to the nearness of their resources over an ally of France, this would reconcile all difficulties, and save his Majesty the necessity of exacting satisfaction for an insult which is as good as inflicted.' "

The Frenchman, having no instructions, contented himself with suggesting that the Emperor had more pressing matters on hand. " ' So,' said M. de Cevallos, 'France will have caused our actual misunderstanding with our neighbors, and we are to expect no service from her influence ! ' "

While Cevallos thus invoked the aid of France, the news of Pinckney's war slowly crossed the Atlantic. No sooner did it arrive than Yrujo in the middle of October, shortly after his attempt to seduce the patriotism of Major Jackson, wrote to the Secretary

[1] Vandeul to Talleyrand, 18 Thermidor, An xii. (Aug. 6, 1804) ; Archives des Aff. Étr., MSS.

of State a formal letter,[1] repeating what had already
been said to Pinckney at Madrid. Madison's reply
was studiously moderate and conciliatory.[2] He explained as best he could the offensive language of
the Mobile Act, and announced that a special minister would soon reach Madrid, to hasten the adjustment of all territorial disputes; he deprecated the
demand for an abandonment of the French claims,
and argued that such a condition of ratification was
not supported by international law; he urged Yrujo
to give assurances of an unqualified ratification, but
he said not a word about Pinckney's performances,
and gave it to be understood that Pinckney would be
recalled. A few days afterward he wrote to Monroe,
ordering him in haste to Spain. "The turn which
our affairs at Madrid have taken renders it expedient in the judgment of the President that you
should proceed thither without delay."[3] In another
letter, written at nearly the same time, he was more
explicit:[4] —

"Pinckney's recall has been asked by the Spanish
government, and a letter of leave goes to him. I suspect he will not return in good humor. I could not
permit myself to flatter him, and truth would not permit
me to praise him. He is well off in escaping reproof, for
his agency has been very faulty as well as feeble."

[1] Yrujo to Madison, Oct. 13, 1804; State Papers, ii. 624.
[2] Madison to Yrujo, Oct. 15, 1804; State Papers, ii. 625.
[3] Madison to Monroe, Oct. 26, 1804; State Papers, ii. 631.
[4] Madison to Monroe, Nov. 9, 1804; Works, ii. 208.

The first attempts to overawe Spain had failed. Pinckney, not disavowed but ignored, fell into the background; and once more Monroe stepped forward to rescue the Administration. When these instructions were written, he had already reached Paris on his way to Madrid; but Madison, undeterred by Pinckney's disaster, still persisted in advising him to place his main reliance " in a skilful appeal to the fears of Spain." [1]

[1] Madison to Monroe, Nov. 9, 1804; Works, ii. 208.

CHAPTER XIII.

HARDLY was the Louisiana treaty sent to America in May, 1803, when Monroe began preparations for a journey to Madrid. The outbreak of temper with which Godoy and Cevallos received the news that Spain had been secretly deprived of Louisiana, caused Bonaparte to feel that further maltreatment of his ally was for the moment unwise; and he interposed a sudden veto on Monroe's journey. "With respect to Florida, this is not the time to pursue that object," said he, when Monroe came to take leave.[1] The Consul Cambacérès echoed the warning: "You must not go to Spain at present; it is not the time; you had better defer it." The Third Consul Lebrun spoke in the same tone. Monroe took the advice, and abandoned the journey to Madrid. In July he crossed the Channel to London, and Aug. 17, 1803, was duly presented to George III. as the successor of Rufus King, who had already returned to America. Livingston remained at Paris to manage the relations with Napoleon.

[1] Monroe to Madison, July 20, 1803 ; MSS. State Department Archives.

In spite of success that should have filled his cup of ambition to overflowing, Livingston was far from satisfied. Neither the President nor the Secretary of State liked him; and to the latter he was a possible rival, who might become dangerous if the authority of President Jefferson, which was Madison's great support, should wane, and should New York claim the presidency from Virginia. Monroe distrusted Livingston, believing him to grasp at the whole credit of the Louisiana treaty, and to be intriguing to withdraw the Florida negotiation from Monroe's hands by causing its transfer from Madrid to Paris.[1] The Secretary of State was perpetually annoyed by his minister. Sometimes Livingston experimented on Spain, sometimes on England. At one moment he sent to the First Consul an indiscreet memorial that brought a remonstrance from the British government; at another he fell into a virulent quarrel with the American claims commissioners under the Louisiana treaty. His claims convention was admitted to be full of mistakes which he did not himself attempt to defend, while the American consul at Paris declared that his conduct in regard to certain claims was dictated by blind and insatiable vanity, if not by corrupt and criminal motives.[2]

Mistakes cost Livingston little serious annoyance;

[1] Monroe's Memoranda, Monroe MSS., State Department Archives.

[2] Skipwith to Madison, Feb. 21, 1804; State Department Archives.

but although he could afford to disregard British complaints or Consul Skipwith's abuse, or even the severe criticisms of the claims commissioners, he must have had more than human patience to sit quiet under the superiority of Monroe. He knew that whatever diplomatic credit was due for the Louisiana negotiation rightly belonged to him, and that Monroe had no claim to any part of it, except that of supporting and approving what was already accomplished; yet he saw the Administration and the public attribute the chief honor to his rival. He showed his wounded self-esteem in protests and statements to which the world was deaf. His old Federalist friends took malicious pleasure in telling him that his triumph had offended the vanity of Jefferson.[1]

Consoling himself with the reflection that he should insist on returning to America in the autumn of 1804, Livingston endured these annoyances as he best could, and found in the society of Robert Fulton and Joel Barlow the hope of greater fame and profit than political distinctions could possibly bring. While he watched and encouraged Fulton's experiments with the steamboat, clouds gathered more and more thickly round his diplomatic path. The First Consul had never inspired him with much confidence; but after the rupture of the Peace of Amiens, in May, 1803, Bonaparte's acts became more and more alarming to every Republican. He passed the autumn of 1803

[1] Gouverneur Morris to Livingston, Nov. 28, 1803; Sparks's Morris, iii. 188.

in preparations for a descent on England. He next effected, in February, 1804, the arrest, trial, and banishment of Moreau. The seizure and arbitrary execution of the Duc d'Enghien followed a month afterward, and finally, in May, 1804, the proclamation of the Empire.

In the midst of these events Livingston received from home the letter already quoted, in which Madison told the story of the Mobile Act, and complained of Yrujo's violent conduct. "The correspondence is chiefly of importance," said the Secretary of State, "as it urges the expediency of cultivating the disposition of the French government to take our side of the question." Livingston was personally rather inclined to the opposite course. He had little faith in obtaining favors from the Emperor, and no disposition to place the United States in the attitude of begging for them; but he had not the chief share in shaping action. A few weeks after receiving these instructions, when he heard of the *quasi* war which Pinckney in July declared at Madrid, Livingston was already expecting the arrival of his successor, General Armstrong, in the autumn.

The news from Spain reaching London, startled Monroe from his repose. As soon as he could make ready, Oct. 8, 1804, placing his legation in charge of a secretary, Monroe left London. While he waited in Paris to sound the disposition of Talleyrand, General Armstrong arrived to relieve Livingston. Thus it happened that three American ministers — Monroe,

Livingston, and Armstrong — met at Paris in November, 1804, to cope with Talleyrand, in whose hands lay the decision of Jefferson's quarrel with Spain.

The question to be decided was whether the United States government should disregard its obligations to Napoleon and act independently, or whether the President should defer to the opinion of Talleyrand and to the Emperor's will. The story of diplomatic adventure, which has so often an interest beyond what could be supposed possible from the contact of three or four quiet and elderly gentlemen meeting about a green table, or writing letters inordinately long, owes that interest in most cases to a hope or a despair, to a mystery or an elucidation; but Monroe's labors at that time offered little mystery, and less hope. Although he did not know all that was happening behind the diplomatic curtain, he knew enough to be aware that his negotiation for Florida, on the ground chosen by the President, was hopeless.

Three months had passed since Cevallos made his appeal to Talleyrand for help. " If the Emperor would but say a word," Cevallos urged;[1] "if he would make the United States understand that he will not be pleased at seeing them abuse their advantages," — this would put an end to insults like the Mobile Act and Pinckney's threats. Talleyrand's answer could not be doubtful. Angry with Jefferson, Madison, Monroe, and Livingston for their attack on

[1] Vandeul to Talleyrand, July 26 and Aug. 6, 1804; Archives des Aff. Étr., MSS.

West Florida, into which his own and his master's finessing had drawn them ; still angrier with Pinckney for the burlesque of Napoleonic manners with which he alarmed the government of Spain ; hostile at heart to Bonaparte's ultimate schemes against the Spanish empire, but determined that if Spain were to be plundered France should have the booty ; willing to repay a part of the humiliation and disappointment which the United States had twice inflicted upon him, — the instant the Spanish ambassador at Paris brought the Mobile Act to his notice, Talleyrand assured him with emphasis that the Emperor would formally oppose such pretensions on the part of the United States ;[1] and when Pinckney's conduct was reported to him, with the request that the Emperor would instruct his minister at Washington to act in concert with Yrujo in order to prevent a rupture, Talleyrand hastened to meet the wish of the Spanish government.

Cevallos made other requests. After narrating the history of Pinckney's claims convention, he touched briefly on the claim for French spoliations which the Americans so warmly urged against Spain, and he asserted that Lucien Bonaparte had given an assurance that these claims were covered by the Franco-American treaty of 1800, and therefore could not be pressed against Spain. He complained that Pinckney

[1] Gravina to Talleyrand, July 24, 1804; Archives des Aff. Étr., MSS. Cevallos to Monroe and Pinckney, 16 Feb. 1805; State Papers, ii. 643.

had used " language the most gross, the most insulting, and, so to speak, the most audacious and menacing." He called attention to the dangers which would result from allowing the boundary of Louisiana to be extended toward either Florida or Mexico ; and he begged " that orders might be sent to the French commissioner Laussat in Louisiana, enjoining him to restrain the pretensions of the Americans regarding the limits of that province, and not to show himself favorable to the wishes of the Americans, as there is reason to suspect him of doing, according to his correspondence with the Spanish commissioner."

Laussat's offence consisted in telling the American commissioners that his instructions fixed the Rio Bravo as the western boundary of Louisiana. Cevallos made no protest to Talleyrand against the truth of Laussat's statement. He tacitly admitted that Laussat was right ; but he invited Talleyrand to join in depriving the United States of Texas, which the United States had bought, and the price of which they had paid to France. That Godoy should conspire for this purpose was natural, for he had no reason to respect the Louisiana cession, and he had pledged his honor in no way to the United States ; but that he should ask Napoleon to deprive the United States of property which Napoleon himself had bought from Spain and sold to the United States, and for which he had received some millions of coin for his personal objects and ambitions, showed that the Prince of Peace understood the characters of Bonaparte and Talleyrand.

Talleyrand, who held that Bonaparte had made a mistake in selling Louisiana to the United States, and who looked upon himself as having no responsibility for the transaction, was glad to restrict what he thought the evil that had been done. Taking the complaints of Spain to the Emperor, he received permission to do what Spain requested; and during the month of August he sent from the Foreign Office a series of documents that disposed for the time of any hopes still nourished by Jefferson's diplomacy.

These three papers were too important to be forgotten. French diplomatic writings were models of concise, impassive clearness, contrasting with the diffuse and argumentative, if not disputatious, style which sometimes characterized American and Spanish official correspondence. These three short letters offered examples of French methods. The first was addressed to General Turreau at Washington, and concerned the boundaries of Louisiana toward the west: [1] —

" If the Mississippi and the Iberville trace with precision the eastern boundary of that colony, it has less precise limits to the westward. No river, no chain of mountains, separates it from the Spanish possessions; and between the last settlements of Louisiana and the first of those in the Spanish colonies are frequently to be found intervals so great as to make a line of demarcation difficult to agree upon. So Spain already appears to fear that the United States, who show an intention of

[1] Talleyrand to Turreau (No. 99), 20 Thermidor, An xii. (Aug. 8, 1804); Archives des Aff. Étr., MSS.

forcing back the western limits of Louisiana, may propose to advance in this direction to the ocean, and establish themselves on that part of the American coast which lies north of California."

Turreau was directed to divert the United States government from the idea of extension toward the west and northwest in any manner that might annoy Spain. He was to employ means of persuasion and friendly influence for this purpose, rather than to act officially ; all official action being reserved for objects directly interesting France.

The second document [1] was also addressed to Turreau, but was more decided in tone, as though the Emperor himself had dictated its language. After a brief allusion to Pinckney's claims convention and the American theory that Spain was responsible for French spoliations which she had not prevented, Talleyrand continued : —

" That convention, made under date of Aug. 11, 1802, is posterior by — months to that which France concluded with the United States, the 8th Vendemiaire, An ix. (30 Sept. 1800), and which declared that no indemnity should be given for prizes made by either of the two Powers. This Article ought to leave the Americans no hope that prizes made against them on Spanish shores would be excepted and paid for ; it would be useless for them to suppose that it is Spain from whom they seek these indemnities : Spain, who would have only the advances to

[1] Talleyrand to Turreau (No. 101), 27 Thermidor, An xii. (Aug. 15, 1804); Archives des Aff. Étr., MSS.

pay, would afterward recur to France for reimbursement.
It is, then, upon France that this charge would ultimately
fall; and as we are relieved by the convention of Sept.
30, 1800, from every kind of debt relating to prizes, we
can only with some surprise see the United States seeking
to obtain from another government a part of the indemnities which they had decidedly renounced in their convention with France. Spain had doubtless lost sight of
these considerations, and had not in view this convention
of ours, when her plenipotentiary signed that of Aug. 11,
1802, which the United States now require her to ratify.
Circumstances which have since taken place have, fortunately, furnished Spain with an occasion for retracing
the false step she took in signing this convention. The
Federal government, which by different acts relative to
the Floridas has violated the sovereign rights of Spain,
and which for more than eighteen months has refused to
ratify its convention with her, has lost the right to complain because the Court of Madrid now imitates its refusal, and insists upon making such modifications in this
treaty as the lapse of time may make it think necessary
and better suited to its rights and dignity."

After sending these instructions to Turreau, the
French Minister for Foreign Relations next turned to
Spain, and wrote a note intended to reassure Cevallos.
The peculiar interest of this document lay in the spirit
it showed toward the United States. Cevallos had
invited an understanding as to the boundaries of Louisiana to be alleged against the United States. These
boundaries, defined eighteen months before in the
secret instructions for Victor, a copy of which was

given to Laussat, declared the Rio Bravo to be the
western limit of Louisiana:[1] "Bounded on the west
by the river called Rio Bravo, from the mouth of this
stream up to the 30th parallel, beyond this point the
line of demarcation ceases to be traced, and it seems
that there has never been an agreement as to this part
of the frontier." That Laussat meant to act on these
instructions was proved by his language to Governor
Claiborne and General Wilkinson.[2] " M. Laussat con-
fidentially signified" to these two American commissioners that the territory "did not comprehend any
part of West Florida; adding at the same time that
it extended westwardly to the Rio Bravo, otherwise
called Rio del Norte." Although Cevallos had remonstrated against the indiscretion of this statement,
he had not suggested that Laussat was in error;[3] he
merely invited Talleyrand to check a subordinate
officer, in order to limit American pretensions. In
accordance with this hint, Talleyrand marked for the
Spanish government the line it was to take in resisting the American claim to territory for which France
had received the purchase money.

After defining the eastern boundary of Florida as

[1] Instructions secrètes pour le Capitaine-Général de la Louisiane, approuvées par le Premier Consul le 5 Frimaire, An xi.
(Nov. 26, 1802), Archives de la Marine, MSS.

[2] Madison to Livingston, March 31, 1804; State Papers,
ii. 575.

[3] Cf. Memoir upon the Negotiations between Spain and the
United States of America. By Don Luis de Onis, Madrid, 1820.
Washington, 1821; pp. 146, 147.

fixed by treaty at the Iberville and the Mississippi rivers, the French minister instructed the Spanish government as follows : [1] —

" The western limit of Louisiana not having been fixed in a manner equally precise by the treaties which preceded that of March 21, 1801, nor by that treaty itself, the uncertainty which prevailed in regard to the direction of its frontiers has necessarily continued since the cession made to the United States. France could not even take upon herself to indicate to the United States what ought to be that precise limit, for fear of wounding on this point the pretensions of one or the other Power directly interested in this question. It would have become the object of negotiation between his Imperial and his Catholic Majesties. To-day it can be treated only between Spain and the United States. Nevertheless, as the Americans derive their rights from France, I have been enabled to express to his Imperial Majesty's minister plenipotentiary near the United States the chief bases on which the Emperor would have planted himself in the demand for a demarcation of boundaries. Starting from the Gulf of Mexico, we should have sought to distinguish between settlements that belong to the kingdom of Mexico, and settlements that had been formed by the French or by those who succeeded them in this colony. This distinction between settlements formed by the French or by the Spaniards would have been made equally in ascending northwards. All those which are of French foundation would have belonged to Louisiana ; and since European settlements in the interior are rare and scat-

[1] Talleyrand to Gravina, 12 Fructidor, An xii. (Aug. 30, 1804); Archives des Aff. Étr., MSS.

tered, we might have imagined direct lines drawn from one to the other to connect them ; and it is to the west of this imaginary line that the boundary between Louisiana and the Spanish possessions would have been traced at such distance and in such direction as France and Spain should have agreed.   The great spaces which sometimes exist between the last French settlements and the last Spanish missions might have left still some doubts on the direction of the boundary to be traced between them, but with the views of friendship and conciliation which animate their Majesties, these difficulties would have been soon smoothed away."

Such were, according to Talleyrand, the conciliatory intentions which should have animated his Imperial Majesty.   They were widely different from the positive instructions formally approved by the First Consul Nov. 26, 1802, which ordered Victor and Laussat to consider the Rio Bravo as the boundary of their command.   The difference was the whole province of Texas.

On another point Talleyrand reassured the Spanish government.

" In any case," said he, " the Court of Madrid would appear to have no ground for the fear it shows that the United States may make use of their possession of Louisiana in order to form settlements on the northwest coast of America.   Whatever boundary may be agreed upon between Spain and the United States, the line will necessarily be so far removed from the western coast of America as to relieve the Court of Madrid from any anxiety on that score."

Yet no one knew better than Talleyrand the instincts of the American people, and their ambition to use the entire continent for their experiments! He knew that the First Consul, by his instructions to Laussat, had given, so far as he could, the authority of both French and Spanish governments to the claim of the United States that Louisiana stretched westwardly to the Rio Bravo, and on the northwest indefinitely to a line yet to be fixed. He knew that Laussat, who hated the Spaniards more than he did the Americans, had betrayed the secret. If Talleyrand hoped to repress American ambition, he must have calculated on the effects of force or fear, or he must have been overwhelmed by the immensity of the scale on which the Americans were acting. The doctrine of contiguity, on which the United States could rest their most plausible claim to Oregon, was as valid then as it ever afterward became; and if Talleyrand did not appreciate it, Godoy proved himself the more sagacious statesman.

By Sept. 1, 1804, these precautionary measures were completed, and Talleyrand could wait for the coming of Monroe and Armstrong. About the middle of October Monroe appeared in Paris. His instructions, sent from Washington before the news of Pinckney's extravagances had reached America, obliged him to insist upon the right to West Florida as "a *sine quâ non*, and no price to be given for it;" [1] to insist, also, upon the right to Texas, but with a

---

[1] Jefferson to Madison, July 5, 1804; Works, iv. 550.

border-land to be kept unsettled for thirty years ; and
to offer two million dollars for East Florida beyond
the Perdido.   The Cabinet then for the first time
decided to commit itself to the doctrine that West
Florida was a part of the Louisiana purchase,[1] alleging as its ostensible reason, not so much the abstract
justice of the title, as the wish to avoid acknowledging Spanish land-grants made in Florida since the
Louisiana cession.

" It is indispensable," wrote Madison, April 15, 1804,
"that the United States be not precluded from such a
construction [of the treaty]. — first, because they consider the right as well founded ; secondly and principally,
because it is known that a great proportion of the most
valuable lands between the Mississippi and the Perdido
have been granted by Spanish officers since the cession
was made by Spain.   These illicit speculations cannot
otherwise be frustrated than by considering the territory
as included in the cession made by Spain."

The hope that Spain might submit to these concessions rested on the belief that she could not afford
to quarrel with the United States.   Foreseeing that
she must soon be drawn into the war with England,
the President from the first looked forward to that
event, believing that the same reasons which as he
supposed had forced Bonaparte to cede Louisiana,
must reconcile Spain to the cession of Florida.

[1] Madison to Monroe, April 15, 1804 ; State Papers, ii. 627.
Madison to Monroe and Pinckney, July 8, 1804 ; State Papers, ii.
630.

" Should she be engaged in the war," wrote Madison to Monroe, " or manifestly threatened with that situation, she cannot fail to be the more anxious for a solid accommodation on all points with the United States, and the more willing to yield, for that purpose, to terms which, however proper in themselves, might otherwise be rejected by her pride and misapplied jealousy."

The first part of this calculation was realized even before Monroe quitted London. Oct. 1, 1804, a British squadron seized the Spanish treasure-ships on their voyage from America; and no one doubted that Spain must declare war. She did so a few weeks later, December 12, before Monroe reached Madrid. The effect of this new disaster on what Madison called her " misapplied jealousy " remained to be seen.

The only published record of Monroe's stay in Paris is contained in a note dated Nov. 8, 1804, which he persuaded Livingston to convey to Talleyrand. Although Livingston's temper was peculiar, and his diplomacy under ordinary circumstances restless, he was well acquainted with the men who governed France; and he had little faith in another man's ability to do what he had himself attempted in vain. That Livingston should be jealous of Monroe's presence in Paris was natural; for the American minister at London was not accredited to the Emperor, and his interference could do nothing but harm to the actual minister at Paris. When asked to act as medium for Monroe's proposed communications with

Talleyrand, Livingston made objections. Not until Armstrong arrived, about November 1, did the ministers agree upon the terms of the note, and send it to its address. Monroe had then been one month absent from London.

Nothing could be more courteous than the tone of Monroe's letter, which ignored Pinckney's conduct, and breathed a spirit of benevolence.[1] The object of writing was to ask the Emperor's good offices in support of the negotiation to be opened at Madrid ; and in order to reach this end, Monroe touched on the story of his present mission, recounting the causes of the previous quarrel with Spain, and alluding to West Florida, the spoliation claims, the claims for damages rising from Morales's occlusion of the Mississippi, and to the Mobile Act, which, as Monroe admitted, was intended to authorize the taking immediate possession of Florida. The only offensive idea suggested in the note was that the Spanish occupation of Florida implied an aggression against the United States, "which tends to provoke hostility and lead to war."

The note combining the diplomacy of three ministers was sent; and the three diplomatists waited in fear of what would follow, dreading nothing so much as Talleyrand's answer. They had reason to know that it would be unfavorable, and that at least on the question of West Florida Talleyrand had already committed himself against the United States. They

[1] Monroe to Talleyrand, Nov. 8, 1804 ; State Papers, ii. 634.

were told, too, that on reading their note Napoleon showed great irritation. Besides this, they had other causes of alarm. Within three days after Monroe's arrival at Paris, Marbois, his best friend among Napoleon's ministers, told him that the question was one of money : [1] " Such was the situation of Spain at this time, that he was persuaded if we would make her suitable pecuniary accommodations we might succeed." M. Hauterive, another gentleman within the circle of government, soon afterward repeated the remark : " Spain must cede territory ; the United States must pay money." Care was taken to let Monroe understand that once this principle should be agreed upon, France would cause the negotiation to be transferred to Paris. Armstrong soon afterward wrote to Madison, alluding to the story in regard to the Emperor : [2] —

" This country has determined to convert the negotiation into a job, and to draw from it advantages merely pecuniary to herself, or, in other language, to her agents. It is this venality that explains her present reserve, the degree of excitement displayed by the Emperor on reading the note, and the marked incivility with which Mr. Monroe was treated by Talleyrand. Since his departure, repeated intimations have been given to me that if certain persons could be sufficiently gratified, the negotiation should be transferred hither, and brought to a close with which we should have no reason to find fault."

[1] Monroe to Madison, Dec. 16, 1804; MSS. State Department Archives.

[2] Armstrong to Madison, Dec. 24, 1804 ; MSS. State Department Archives.

Monroe, though honest as any man in public life, and more courageous in great emergencies than some of his friends or rivals, was commonly not quick at catching an idea, nor did he see it at last from a great elevation ; but in this instance the idea was thrust so persistently into his face, that had he been blind he could not have missed it. Nothing could more clearly explain his situation than the language of the diary in which he recorded, for the President's benefit, the daily course of his conduct.

" No other alternative," he explained,[1] " presented itself to me than to abandon the object and return to London, or to submit to the terms which it was sufficiently well understood France was willing to accept, and seemed in some measure to dictate, which amounted to this : that we should create a new loan of about seventy millions of livres, and transfer the same to Spain, who would immediately pass them over to France, in consideration of which we should be put in possession of the disputed territory, under stipulations which should provide for the adjustment of the ultimate right there, and reimbursement of the money by instalment in seven years."

" To submit to the terms proposed was altogether out of the question," continued Monroe. Having led his Government to take the ground that West Florida had already been bought, he could not enter into a negotiation to buy it a second time. His instructions

[1] Diary at Aranjuez, April 22, 1805 ; MSS. State Department Archives.

made this point a *sine quâ non* of negotiation. Recognizing that under these circumstances further
effort was useless, or in his own words that no other
alternative presented itself but to abandon the object
and return to London, Monroe intimated to Talleyrand that he meant not only to pay no money, but
also to negotiate in spite of Napoleon; and started
for Madrid.

"I did not hesitate," he wrote home,[1] "in many informal communications, the substance of which I was
persuaded were made known to those in power, to declare
most solemnly that I would sanction no measure which
contemplated a payment of money to Spain in any transaction we might have with her in the affair, — by which
was meant, by creation of stock or otherwise which took
the money from our people; that neither the state of
things between the parties, the example of France in
a similar case, or my instructions, permitted it. These
conversations were with a person who possessed the
confidence of certain persons in power, as well as my
own, though they were not of a nature to compromit
either party. That circumstance enabled me to speak
with the utmost freedom, and perhaps to say things
which it might have been difficult to press directly in the
same manner to the parties themselves."

In thus defying France, Monroe, if he resembled
European diplomatists, must have aimed at giving
his Government an opportunity to break with the
Emperor and to proceed against Florida by means

[1] Monroe to Madison, Dec. 16, 1804; MSS. State Department
Archives.

of force. That he should have still hoped for success in negotiating at Madrid was hardly possible.
Armstrong thought his chance desperate.[1]

" Mr. Monroe has no doubt communicated to you,"
he wrote to the Secretary of State, " the motives which
induced him to leave England in prosecution of his
mission to Spain, and while here to attempt to draw
from this Government some new declaration in support
of our construction of the late treaty. With this view a
note was prepared and transmitted through Livingston,
the receipt of which was acknowledged by Mr. Talleyrand
with a promise that ' an answer should be given to it as
soon as the Emperor should have signified his will on the
subject.' Having waited nearly a month, and no answer
being given, having some reason to believe that any declaration from this Court now would be less favorable
than those already made, and fearful lest something
might be lost at Madrid, while nothing could be gained
here, he set out on the 8th instant for Spain. I have
but little hope, however, that he will be able to do more
than fulfil the forms of his mission."

Armstrong preferred, as he expressed it, " an effort
(which cannot fail) to do the business at home."
He had already discovered that the Emperor was
personally irritated with the Americans, that he took
no pains to conceal it, and that this irritation was a
cause of his reserve.

" I have employed every means in my power to ascertain the cause of this cause, and have learned from a

[1] Armstrong to Madison, Dec. 24, 1804 ; MSS. State Department Archives.

person sufficiently near him to know the fact, that this temper originated in representations made by Leclerc and others from St. Domingo; that it has since been kept alive by the incident of the war in that country, the trade carried on between it and the United States, the freedom with which he is treated in our press, the matrimonial connection of Jerome, and, above all, the support which principles he wishes to extinguish in France receive from the progressing prosperity of the United States."

With Napoleon in this frame of mind; with Godoy and Cevallos in a humor far worse; and with Talleyrand in such a temper as not to allow of his treating Monroe with civility, — the American plenipotentiary departed to Madrid, hoping that something might occur to overcome his difficulties. During his journey, Charles IV. declared war against England. This long-foreseen event, which should have brought Spain to terms with the United States, in fact threw her only at the feet of Napoleon. Henceforward every offence to Spain was an offence to France, which the Emperor was the more bound to resent because by treaty he must regard a war upon Charles IV. as a war upon himself.

Talleyrand was not vindictive, but he had been twice mortified by the failure of his policy toward America. If his callous cheek could burn, it was still red with the blow which the last President of the United States had struck it; and no waters of oblivion could drown in his memory the cry of distress with which he had then begged for mercy. He had been again overthrown by the present President, and obliged to sell Louisiana, turn his back on the traditions of France, and shut up his far-reaching mind within the limit of his master's artillery politics. Day by day he saw more clearly that soldiership, and not statecraft, was to guide the destinies of France, and that the new *régime* was but revolution without ideas. He had probably begun already to feel that the presence of his coldly silent face was becoming irksome to a will which revolted at the memory of a remonstrance. Talleyrand was corrupt, — perhaps he thought himself more corrupt than he was; but his political instincts were sounder than his private morality. He was incarnate conservatism; but he was wider-minded and more elevated in purpose than Napoleon. He had no faith in Napoleon's methods, and was particularly hostile to his projects against Spain; but in respect to Monroe and his mission, Talleyrand's ideas coincided with those of the Emperor; and when two such men marked out a victim, his chance of escape was small.

Talleyrand was not to blame that Monroe's note remained unanswered before Monroe left Paris. About ten days after receiving it Talleyrand made to the Emperor a report on the subject, so cool and clear as to read like a mathematical demonstration.[1]

" The United States," he began, " who wish to negotiate at Madrid under the auspices of France for the ac-

[1] Rapport à l'Empereur, 28 Brumaire, An xii. (Nov. 19, 1804); Archives des Aff. Étr., MSS.

quisition of Florida, have acquired little title to the good offices of the Emperor by the sharpness of tone and the want of civility (*égards*) with which they have conducted themselves toward Spain."

After enumerating the threats and aggressions of the United States government against Spain during the last three years, the report disposed of the American claims, one by one, in few words. First, the spoliations, which had been formally abandoned by treaty; second, the claim for losses rising from the interruption of *entrepôt* at New Orleans, which "should be terminated by the treaty of cession, — the acquisition of an immense country might throw out of view some anterior losses;" finally, the claim to West Florida, — a species of attack on the Emperor's dignity and good faith which merited some expression of his displeasure. To support this view, Talleyrand related the history of the French negotiation for West Florida and its failure, commenting on the manner in which the Americans had fabricated their claim, and coming at last to a conclusion studiously moderate, and evidently in harmony with the views of Hauterive as expressed to Monroe. Talleyrand rarely wrote such papers with his own hand; probably they were drawn up under his directions by Hauterive, or some other subordinate of the Office, in the form of suggestions rather than advice.

"According to such evidence, no one can suppose the United States to be convinced of the justice of their rights; and we are warranted in thinking that the Federal government, as a result of confidence in its own strength, of its ambition, and its ascendency in America, raises pretensions to a part of Florida in order to show itself afterward more exacting toward Spain. The Emperor will feel that justice requires him not to recognize such pretensions. If he should assist by his good offices an ar-rangement between the United States and Spain, he would wish good faith and impartiality for its base.

Only. in case the United States should desist from their unjust pretensions to West Florida, and return to the forms of civility and decorum, — from which in their relations with each other governments should never depart, — could the Emperor allow himself to second at the Court of Madrid the project of acquisition of the two Floridas. Then perhaps the Emperor might think that this country is less suited to Spain now that it is separated from her other colonies, and that it is better suited to the United States because a part of their Western rivers cross the Floridas before flowing into the Gulf of Mexico; and finally, that Spain may see in her actual situation, and in the expenses entailed on her by the war, some motives for listening to the offers of the Federal government."

Talleyrand had great need to insist on "the forms of civility and decorum from which governments should never depart"! Perhaps Talleyrand already foresaw the scene, said to have occurred some two years later, when Napoleon violently denounced him to his face as "a silk stocking stuffed with filth," and the minister coldly retaliated by the famous phrase, "Pity that so great a man should be so ill brought up!" The task of teaching manners to

Jefferson was not Napoleon's view of his own func-
tions in the world. He probably gave more attention
to the concluding lines of the report, which suggested
that he should decide whether a Spanish colony, made
worthless by an arbitrary act of his own, could be
usefully employed in sustaining his wars.

This report, dated Nov. 19, 1804, lay some weeks in
the Emperor's hands. Monroe left Paris for Madrid
December 8, and still no answer had been sent to his
note. He wrote from Bordeaux, December 16, a long
and interesting letter to Madison, and resumed his
journey. He could hardly have crossed the Bidassoa
when Armstrong received from Talleyrand, December 21, the long-expected answer,[1] which by declaring
the claim to West Florida emphatically unfounded
struck the ground from under Monroe's feet, and left
him to repent at leisure his defiance of Talleyrand's
advice. Under the forms of perfect courtesy, this letter contained both sarcasm and menace. Talleyrand
expressed curiosity to learn the result of Monroe's
negotiation : —

" This result his Imperial Majesty will learn with real
interest. He saw with pain the United States commence
their difficulties with Spain in an unusual manner, and
conduct themselves toward the Floridas by acts of violence which, not being founded in right, could have no
other effect but to injure the lawful owner. Such an aggression gave the more surprise to his Majesty because

[1] Talleyrand to Armstrong, Dec. 21, 1804 ; State Papers,
ii. 635.

the United States seemed in this measure to avail themselves of their treaty with France as an authority for
their proceedings, and because he could scarcely reconcile with the just opinion which he entertains of the
wisdom and fidelity of the Federal government a course
of proceedings which nothing can authorize toward a
Power which has long occupied, and still occupies, one
of the first ranks in Europe."

Madison and Monroe, as well as Jefferson, in the
course of their diplomacy had many mortifications to
suffer ; but they rarely received a reprimand more
keen than this. Yet its sharpness was so delicately
covered by the habitual forms of Talleyrand's diplomacy that Americans, who were accustomed to hear
and to use strong language, hardly felt the wound
it was intended to inflict. After hearing Yrujo denounce an act of their government as an " atrocious
libel," they were not shocked to hear Talleyrand
denounce the same act as one of violence which
nothing could authorize. The force of Talleyrand's
language was more apparent to Godoy than to Madison, for it bore out every expression of Yrujo and
Cevallos. The Prince of Peace received a copy of
Talleyrand's note at the moment when Monroe, after almost a month of weary winter travel, joined
Pinckney, who had for six months been employed
only in writing letter after letter begging for succor
and support. Don Pedro Cevallos, with this public
pledge in his hand, and with secret French pledges
covering every point of the negotiation in his desk,

could afford to meet with good humor the first visit of the new American plenipotentiary.

Pinckney's humiliation was extreme. After breaking off relations with Cevallos and pledging himself to demand his passports and to leave Spain, he had been reduced to admit that his Government disavowed him ; and not only was he obliged to remain at Madrid, but also to sue for permission to resume relations with Cevallos. The Spanish government good-naturedly and somewhat contemptuously permitted him to do so ; and he was only distressed by the fear that Monroe might refuse to let him take part in the new negotiation, for he was with reason confident that Monroe would be obliged to follow in his own footsteps, — that the' United States could save its dignity and influence only by war.

At the beginning of the new year, Jan. 2, 1805, Monroe entered Madrid to snatch Florida from the grasp of Spain and France. The negotiation fell chiefly within Jefferson's second term, upon which it had serious results. But while Monroe, busy at Madrid with a quarrel which could lead only to disappointment or war, thus left the legation at London for eight months to take care of itself, events were occurring which warned President Jefferson that the supreme test of his principles was near at hand, and that a storm was threatening from the shores of Great Britain compared with which all other dangers were trivial.

CHAPTER XIV.

FOR eighteen years after 1783 William Pitt guided England through peace and war with authority almost as absolute as that of Don Carlos IV. or Napoleon himself. From him and from his country President Jefferson had much to fear and nothing to gain beyond a continuance of the good relations which President Washington, with extreme difficulty, had succeeded in establishing between the two peoples. So far as England was concerned, this understanding had been the work of Pitt and Lord Grenville, who rather imposed it on their party than accepted it as the result of any public will. The extreme perils in which England then stood inspired caution ; and of this caution the treaty of 1794 was one happy result. So long as the British government remained in a cautious spirit, America was safe ; but should Pitt or his successors throw off the self-imposed restraints on England's power, America could at the utmost, even by a successful war, gain nothing materially better than a return to the arrangements of 1794.

The War of Independence, which ended in the definitive treaty of 1783, naturally left the English people in a state of irritation and disgust toward

America; and the long interregnum of the Confedera-
tion, from 1783 to 1789, allowed this disgust to ripen
into contempt. When at length the Constitution of
1789 restored order in the American chaos, England
felt little faith in the success of the experiment. She
waited for time to throw light on her interests.

This delay was natural; for American independence
had shattered into fragments the commercial system
of Great Britain, and powerful interests were combined
to resist further concession. Before 1776 the colonies
of England stretched from the St. Lawrence to the
Mississippi, and across the Gulf of Mexico to the coast
of South America, mutually supporting and strength-
ening each other. Jamaica and the other British
islands of the West Indies drew their most necessary
supplies from the Delaware and the Hudson. Boston
and New York were in some respects more important
to them than London itself. The timber, live-stock,
and provisions which came from the neighboring continent were essential to the existence of the West Indian planters and negroes. When war cut off these
supplies, famine and pestilence followed. After the
peace of 1783 even the most conservative English
statesmen were obliged to admit that the strictness of
their old colonial system could not be maintained, and
that the United States, though independent, must be
admitted to some of the privileges of a British colony.
The government unwillingly conceded what could not
be refused, and the West Indian colonists compelled
Parliament to relax the colonial system so far as to

allow a restricted intercourse between their islands and the ports of the United States. The relaxation was not a favor to the United States, — it was a condition of existence to the West Indies; not a boon, but a right which the colonists claimed and an Act of Parliament defined.[1]

The right was dearly paid for. The islands might buy American timber and grain, but they were allowed to make return only in molasses and rum. Payment in sugar would have been cheaper for the colonists, and the planters wished for nothing more earnestly than to be allowed this privilege; but as often as they raised the prayer, English shipowners cried that the navigation laws were in peril, and a chorus of familiar phrases filled the air, all carrying a deep meaning to the English people. " Nursery of seamen " was one favorite expression; " Neutral frauds " another; and all agreed in assuming that at whatever cost, and by means however extravagant, the navy must be fed and strengthened. Under the cover of supporting the navy any absurdity could be defended; and in the case of the West Indian trade, the British shipowner enjoyed the right to absurdities sanctioned by a century and a half of law and custom. The freight on British sugars belonged of right to British shippers, who could not be expected to surrender of their own accord, in obedience to any laws of political economy, a property which was the source of their incomes. The colonists asked permission to refine their own

[1] 28 George III. c. 6.

sugar; but their request not only roused strong opposition from the shipowners who wanted the bulkier freight, but started the home sugar-refiners to their feet, who proved by Acts of Parliament that sugar-refining was a British and not a colonial right. The colonist then begged a reduction of the heavy duty on sugar; but English country gentlemen cried against a measure which might lead to an increase of the income-tax or the imposition of some new burden on agriculture. In this dilemma the colonists frankly said that only their weakness, not their will, prevented them from declaring themselves independent, like their neighbors at Charleston and Philadelphia.

Even when the qualified right of trade was conceded, the colonists were not satisfied; and the concession itself laid the foundation of more serious changes. From the moment that American produce was admitted to be a necessity for the colonists, it was clear that the Americans must be allowed a voice in the British system. Discussion whether the Americans had or had not a right to the colonial trade was already a long step toward revolution. One British minister after another resented the idea that the Americans had any rights in the matter; yet when they came to practical arrangements the British statesmen were obliged to concede that they were mistaken. From the necessity of the case, the Americans had rights which never could be successfully denied. Parliament struggled to prevent the rebel Americans from sharing in the advantages of the colonial system from which they had rebelled; but unreasonable as it was that the United States should be rewarded for rebellion by retaining the privileges of subjects, this was the inevitable result. Geography and Nature were stronger than Parliament and the British navy.

At first Pitt hoped that the concession to the colonists might entail no concession to the United States; while admitting a certain hiatus in the colonial system, he tried to maintain the navigation laws in their integrity. The admission of American produce into the West Indies was no doubt an infraction of the protectionist principle on which all the civilized world, except America, founded its economical ideas; but in itself it was not serious. To allow the flour, potatoes, tobacco, timber, and horses of the American continent to enter the harbors of Barbadoes and Jamaica; to allow in turn the molasses and rum of the islands to be sent directly to New York and Boston, — harmed no one, and was advantageous to all parties, so long as British ships were employed to carry on the trade. At first this was the case. The Act of Parliament allowed only British subjects, in British-built ships, to enter colonial ports with American produce. Whether the United States government would long tolerate such legislation without countervailing measures was a question which remained open for a time, while the system itself had a chance to prove its own weakness. The British shipping did not answer colonial objects. Again and again the colonists found themselves on the verge of starvation; and always in this emergency the colonial governors threw open their ports by proclamation to American shipping, while with equal regularity Parliament protected the governors by Acts of Indemnity. To this extent the navigation system suffered together with the colonial system, but in theory it was intact. Ministry, Parliament, and people clung to the navigation laws as their ark of safety; and even the colonists conceded that although they had a right to eat American wheat and potatoes, they had no right to eat those which came to them in the hold of a Marblehead schooner.

Such a principle, however convenient to Great Britain, was not suited to the interests of New England shippers. In peace their chances were comparatively few, and the chief diplomatic difficulties between European governments and the United States had their source in the American attempt to obtain legal recognition of trade which America wished to maintain with the colonies; but in war the situation changed, and more serious disputes occurred. Then the French and Spanish West Indian ports were necessarily thrown open to neutral commerce, because their own ships were driven from the ocean by the superiority of the British navy. Besides the standing controversy about the admission of American produce to British islands, the British government found itself harassed by doubts to what extent it might safely admit the Americans into the French or Spanish West Indies, and allow them to carry French property, as though their flag were competent to protect whatever was under it.

Granting that an article like French sugar might be carried in a neutral vessel, there were still other articles, called contraband, which ought not to be made objects of neutral commerce; and England was obliged to define the nature of contraband. She was also forced to make free use of the right of blockade. These delicate questions were embittered by another and more serious quarrel. The European belligerents claimed the right to the military service of their subjects, and there was no doubt that their right was perfect. In pursuance of the claim they insisted upon taking their seamen from American merchant-vessels wherever met on the high seas. So far as France was concerned, the annoyance was slight; but the identity of race made the practice extremely troublesome as concerned England.

At the outbreak of the French wars, Nov. 6, 1793, the British government issued instructions directing all British armed vessels to seize every neutral ship they should meet, loaded with the produce of a French colony or carrying supplies for its use.[1] These orders were kept secret for several weeks, until the whole American commerce with the Antilles, and all American ships found on the ocean, laden in whole or in part with articles of French colonial produce or for French colonial use, were surprised and swept into British harbors, where they were condemned by British admiralty courts, on the ground known as the " Rule of the War of 1756," — that because trade between

[1] Additional Instructions of Nov. 6, 1793; State Papers, i. 430.

the French colonies and the United States was illegal
in peace, it was illegal in war. From the point of
view in which European Powers regarded their colonies, much could be said in support of this rule.
A colony was almost as much the property of its
home government as a dockyard or a military station.
France and Spain could hardly complain if England
chose to treat the commerce of such government-
stations as contraband ; but a rule which might perhaps be applied by European governments to each
other worked with great injustice when applied to
the United States, who had no colonies, and made no
attempt to build up a navy or support an army by
such means. Taken in its broadest sense, the European colonial system might be defined by the descrip-
tion which the best of British commentators gave to
that of England,[1] — a " policy pursued for rendering
the foreign trade of the whole world subservient to the
increase of her shipping and navigation."   American
Independence was a protest against this practice ; and
the first great task of the United States was to overthrow and destroy the principle, in order to substitute freedom of trade.   America naturally objected to
becoming a martyr to the rules of a system which she
was trying to revolutionize.

When these British instructions of Nov. 26, 1793,
became known in the United States, the Government
of President Washington imposed an embargo, threatened retaliation, and sent Chief-Justice Jay to London

[1] Reeves's Law of Shipping and Navigation, part ii. chap. iii.

as a last chance of maintaining peace. On arriving there, Jay found that Pitt had already voluntarily retreated from his ground, and that new Orders, dated Jan. 8, 1794, had been issued, exempting from seizure American vessels engaged in the direct trade from the United States to the French West Indies. In the end, the British government paid the value of the confiscated vessels. The trade from the United States to Europe was not interfered with; and thus American ships were allowed to carry French colonial produce through an American port to France, while Russian or Danish ships were forbidden by England to carry such produce to Europe at all, although their flags and harbors were as neutral as those of the United States. America became suddenly a much favored nation, and the enemies of England attributed this unexpected kindness to fear. In truth it was due to a natural mistake. The British Treasury calculated that the expense and trouble of carrying sugar and coffee from Martinique or St. Domingo to Boston, of landing it, paying duties, re-embarking it, receiving the drawback, and then carrying it to Bordeaux or Brest, would be such as to give ample advantages to English vessels which could transship more conveniently at London. The mistake soon became apparent. The Americans quickly proved that they could under these restrictions carry West Indian produce to Europe not only more cheaply than British ships could do it, but almost as quickly; while it was a positive advantage on the return voyage to make double freight by stopping at an American port.   The consequence of this discovery was seen in the sudden increase of American shipping, and was largely due to the aid of British seamen, who found in the new service better pay, food, and treatment than in their own, and comparative safety from the press-gang and the lash.   At the close of the century the British flag seemed in danger of complete exclusion from the harbors of the United States.   In 1790 more than 550 British ships, with a capacity of more than 115,000 tons, had entered inward and outward, representing about half that number of actual vessels; in 1799 the custom-house returns showed not 100 entries, and in 1800 about 140, representing a capacity of 40,000 tons.   In the three years 1790–1792, the returns showed an average of some 280 outward and inward entries of American ships with a capacity of 54,000 tons; in 1800 the entries were 1,057, with a capacity of 236,000 tons.   The Americans were not only beginning to engross the direct trade between their own ports and Europe, but were also rapidly obtaining the indirect carrying-trade between the West Indies and the European continent, and even between one European country and another.   The British government began to feel seriously uneasy.   At a frightful cost the people of England were striving to crush the navies and commerce of France and Spain, only to build up the power of a dangerous rival beyond the ocean.

Doubtless the British government would have taken measures to correct its mistake, if the political situ-

ation had not hampered its energies. Chief-Justice
Jay, in 1794, negotiated a treaty with Lord Grenville
which was in some respects very hard upon the United
States, but was inestimably valuable to them, because
it tied Pitt's hands and gave time for the new American Constitution to acquire strength. Ten years of
steady progress were well worth any temporary concessions, even though these concessions exasperated
France, and roused irritation between her and the
United States which in 1798 became actual hostility.
The prospect that the United States would become the
ally of England was so fair that Pitt dared not disturb it. His government was in a manner forced to
give American interests free play, and to let American
shipping gain a sudden and unnatural enlargement.
His liberality was well paid. For a moment France
drove the United States to reprisals; and as the
immediate consequence, St. Domingo became practically independent, owing to the support given by the
United States to Toussaint. Even the reconciliation
of France with America effected by Bonaparte and
Talleyrand in 1800 did not at first redress the balance. Not till the Peace of Amiens, in 1802, did
France recover her colonies; and not till a year later
did Bonaparte succeed, by the sacrifice of Louisiana, in
bringing the United States back to their old attitude
of jealousy toward England.

Nevertheless, indications had not been wanting that
England was aware of the advantage she had given to
American commerce, and still better of the advantages

which had been given it by Nature.   All the Acts of
Parliament on the statute-book could not prevent the
West Indies from being largely dependent on the
United States ; yet the United States need not be
allowed the right to carry West Indian produce to
France, — a right which depended only on so-called
international law, and was worthless unless supported
by the stronger force.   A new Order was issued,
Jan. 25, 1798, which admitted European neutrals to
enemies' colonies, and allowed them to bring French
colonial produce to England or to their own ports.
This Order was looked upon as a side-blow at American shipping, which was not allowed the same privilege
of sailing direct from the Antilles to Europe.   The
new Order was justified on the ground that the old
rule discriminated in favor of American merchants,
whose competition might be injurious to the commercial interests of England.[1]

Further than this the British government did not
then go; on the contrary, it officially confirmed the existing arrangement.   The British courts of admiralty
conformed closely to the rules of their political chiefs.
Sir William Scott, better known as Lord Stowell, whose
great reputation as a judge was due to the remarkable
series of judgments in which he created a new system
of admiralty law, announced with his usual clearness
the rules by which he meant to be guided.   In the
case of the " Emmanuel," in November, 1799, he explained the principle on which the law permitted

[1] Appendix to 4 Robinson, 6.

neutrals to carry French produce from their own
country to France. " By importation," he said, " the
produce became part of the national stock of the neutral country; the inconveniences of aggravated delay
and expense were a safeguard against this right becoming a special convenience to France or a serious
abridgement of belligerent rights." Soon afterward,
in the case of the " Polly," April 29, 1800, he took
occasion to define what he meant by importation into
a neutral country. He said it was not his business to
decide what was universally the test of a *bona fide*
importation; but he was strongly disposed to hold
that it would be sufficient if the goods were proved
to have been landed and the duties paid; and he
did accordingly rule that such proof was sufficient
to answer the fair demands of his court.

Rufus King, then American minister in London,
succeeded in obtaining from Pitt an express acceptance of this rule as binding on the government. On
the strength of a report [1] from the King's Advocate,
dated March 16, 1801, the British Secretary of State
notified the American minister that what Great Britain
considered as the general principle of colonial trade
had been relaxed in a certain degree in consideration
of the present state of commerce. Neutrals might
import French colonial produce, and convey it by re-
exportation to France. Landing the goods and paying
the duties in America legalized the trade, even though

[1] Advocate-General's Report, March 16, 1801; State Papers,
ii. 491.

these goods were at once re-shipped and forwarded to France on account of the same owners.

With this double guaranty Jefferson began his administration, and the American merchants continued their profitable business. Not only did they build and buy large numbers of vessels, and borrow all the capital they could obtain, but doubtless some French and Spanish merchants, besides a much greater number of English, made use of the convenient American flag. The Yankees exulted loudly over the decline of British shipping in their harbors; the British masters groaned to see themselves sacrificed by their own government; and the British admirals complained bitterly that their prize-money was cut off, and that they were wearing out their lives in the hardest service, in order to foster a commerce of smugglers and perjurers, whose only protection was the flag of a country that had not a single line-of-battle ship to fly it.

Yet President Jefferson had reason to weigh long and soberly the pointed remark with which the King's Advocate began his report, — that the general principle with respect to the colonial trade had been to a certain extent relaxed in consideration of the present state of commerce. No doubt the British pretension, as a matter of international law, was outrageous. The so-called rule of 1756 was neither more nor less than a rule of force; but when was international law itself anything more than a law of force? The moment a nation found itself unable to show some kind of physical defence for its protection, the wisdom of Grotius and Bynkershoek could not prevent it from being plundered; and how could President Jefferson complain merely because American ships were forbidden by England to carry French sugars to France, when he looked on without a protest while England and France committed much greater outrages on every other country within their reach?

President Jefferson believed that the United States had ample means to resist any British pretension. As his letters to Paine and Logan showed, he felt that European Powers could be controlled through the interests of commerce.[1]   He was the more firmly convinced by the extraordinary concessions which Pitt had made, and by the steady encouragement he gave to the American merchant.   Jefferson felt sure that England could not afford to sacrifice a trade of some forty million dollars, and that her colonies could not exist without access to the American market.   What need to spend millions on a navy, when Congress, as Jefferson believed, already grasped England by the throat, and could suffocate her by a mere turn of the wrist!

This reasoning had much in its favor.   To Pitt the value of the American trade at a time of war with France and Spain was immense; and when taken in connection with the dependence of the West Indian colonies on America, it made a combination of British interests centring in the United States which

[1] See vol. i. p. 214.

much exceeded the entire value of all England's other branches of foreign commerce. Its prospective value was still greater if things should remain as they were, and if England should continue to undersell all rivals in articles of general manufacture. England could well afford to lose great sums of money in the form of neutral freights rather than drive Congress to a protective system which should create manufactures of cotton, woollen, and iron. These were motives which had their share in the civility with which England treated America; and year by year their influence should naturally have increased.

Of all British markets the American was the most valuable; but next to the American market was that of the West Indies. In some respects the West Indian was of the two the better worth preserving. From head to foot the planters and their half-million negroes were always clad in cottons or linens made by the clothiers of Yorkshire, Wiltshire, or Belfast. Every cask and hoop, every implement and utensil, was supplied from the British Islands. The sailing of a West Indian convoy was " an epoch in the diary of every shop and warehouse throughout the Kingdom."[1] The West Indian colonies employed, including the fisheries, above a thousand sail of shipping and twenty-five thousand seamen. While America might, and one day certainly would, manufacture for herself, the West Indies could not even dream of it; there the only profitable or practicable industry was cultivation of

[1] Thoughts on Commerce and Colonies, by Charles Bosanquet.

the soil, and the chief article of cultivation was the sugar-cane. Rival industries to those of Great Britain were impossible; the only danger that threatened British control was the loss of naval supremacy or the revolt of the negroes.

A great majority of British electors would certainly have felt no hesitation in deciding, as between the markets of the United States and of the West Indies, that if a choice must be made, good policy required the government to save at all hazards the West Indies. Both as a permanent market for manufactures and as a steady support for shipping, the West Indian commerce held the first place in British interests. This fact needed to be taken into account by the United States government before relying with certainty on the extent to which Great Britain could be controlled by the interests involved in the American trade. At the most critical moment all Jefferson's calculations might be upset by the growth of a conviction in England that the colonial system was in serious danger; and to make this chance stronger, another anxiety was so closely connected with it as to cause incessant alarm in the British mind.

The carrying-trade between the French West Indies and Europe which had thus fallen into American hands, added to the natural increase of national exports and imports, required a large amount of additional shipping; and what was more directly hostile to English interests, it drew great numbers of British sailors into the American merchant-service. The desertion of British seamen and the systematic encouragement offered to deserters in every seaport of the Union were serious annoyances, which the American government was unable to excuse or correct. Between 1793 and 1801 they reached the proportions of a grave danger to the British service. Every British government packet which entered the port of New York during the winter before Jefferson's accession to power lost almost every seaman in its crew; and neither people nor magistrates often lent help to recover them. At Norfolk the crew of a British ship deserted to an American sloop-of-war, whose commander, while admitting the fact, refused to restore the men, alleging his construction of official orders in his excuse.[1] In most American harbors such protection as the British shipmaster obtained sprang from the personal good-will of magistrates, who without strict legal authority consented to apply, for the benefit of the foreign master, the merchant-shipping law of the United States; but in one serious case even this voluntary assistance was stopped by the authority of a State government.

This interference was due to the once famous dispute over Jonathan Robbins, which convulsed party politics in America during the heated election of 1800. Thomas Nash, a boatswain on the British frigate "Hermione," having been ringleader in conspiracy and murder on the high seas, was afterward identified in the United States under the name and with the papers

[1] Thornton to Grenville, March 7, 1801; MSS. British Archives.

of Jonathan Robbins of Danbury, in Connecticut. On
a requisition from the British minister, dated June 3,
1799, he was delivered under the extradition clause
of Jay's treaty, and was hung. The Republican party,
then in opposition, declared that Robbins, or Nash, was
in their belief an American citizen whose surrender
was an act of base subservience to Great Britain.
An effigy of Robbins hanging to a gibbet was a favorite electioneering device at public meetings. The
State of Virginia, having a similar grievance of its
own, went so far as to enact a law[1] which forbade,
under the severest penalties, any magistrate who
acted under authority of the State to be instrumental
in transporting any person out of its jurisdiction.
As citizens of the Union, sworn to support the Constitution, such magistrates were equally bound with
the Federal judges to grant warrants of commit-
ment, under the Twenty-seventh Article of Jay's
treaty, against persons accused of specified crimes.
The Virginia Act directly contravened the treaty ;
while indirectly it prevented magistrates from granting warrants against deserters and holding them in
custody, so that every English vessel which entered a
Virginia port was at once abandoned by her crew,
who hastened to enter the public or private ships of
the United States.[2]

The captain of any British frigate which might

[1] Act of Jan. 21, 1801, Statutes at Large of Virginia, New
Series, ii. 302.
[2] Thornton to Grenville, June 1, 1802; MSS. British Archives.

happen to run into the harbor of New York, if he
went ashore, was likely to meet on his return to the
wharf some of his boat's crew strolling about the
town, every man supplied with papers of American
citizenship. This was the more annoying, because
American agents in British ports habitually claimed
and received the benefit of the British law; while so
far as American papers were concerned, no pretence
was made of concealing the fraud, but they were
issued in any required quantity, and were transferred
for a few dollars from hand to hand.

Not only had the encouragement to desertion a
share in the decline of British shipping in American
harbors, but it also warranted, and seemed almost
to render necessary, the only countervailing measure
the British government could employ. Whatever happened to the merchant-service, the British navy could
not be allowed to suffer. England knew no conscription for her armies, because for centuries she
had felt no need of general military service; but at
any moment she might compel her subjects to bear
arms, if circumstances required it. Her necessities
were greater on the ocean. There, from time imme-
morial, a barbarous sort of conscription, known as
impressment, had been the ordinary means of supplying the royal navy in emergencies; and every
seafaring man was liable to be dragged at any moment
from his beer-cellar or coasting-vessel to man the guns
of a frigate on its way to a three-years' cruise in the
West Indies or the Mediterranean. Mere engage-

ment in a foreign merchant-service did not release
the British sailor from his duty.   When the captain
of a British frigate overhauled an American merchant-
vessel for enemy's property or contraband of war, he
sent an officer on board who mustered the crew, and
took out any seamen whom he believed to be British.
The measure, as the British navy regarded it, was
one of self-protection.   If the American government
could not or would not discourage desertion, the naval
commander would recover his men in the only way
he could.   Thus a circle of grievances was established
on each side.   Pitt's concessions to the United States
irritated the British navy and merchant-marine, while
they gave great profits to American shipping; the
growth of American shipping stimulated desertions
from the British service to the extent of injuring its
efficiency; and these desertions in their turn led to
a rigorous exercise of the right of impressment.   To
find some point at which this vicious circle could be
broken was a matter of serious consequence to both
countries, but most so to the one which avowed that
it did not mean to protect its interests by force.

Great Britain could have broken the circle by increasing the pay and improving the condition of her
seamen; but she was excessively conservative, and the
burdens already imposed on her commerce were so
great that she could afford to risk nothing.   In the
face of a combined navy like that of Spain and France,
her control of the seas at any given point, such as
the West Indies, was still doubtful; and in the face

of American competition, her huge convoys suffered under great disadvantage. Conscious of her own power, she thought that the United States should be first to give way. Had the American government been willing to perform its neutral obligations strictly, the circle might have been broken without much trouble; but the United States wished to retain their advantage, and preferred to risk whatever England might do rather than discourage desertion, or enact and enforce a strict naturalization law, or punish fraud. The national government was too weak to compel the States to respect neutral obligations, even if it had been disposed to make the attempt.

The practice of impressment brought the two governments to a deadlock on an issue of law. No one denied that every government had the right to command the services of its native subjects, and as yet no one ventured to maintain that a merchant-ship on the high seas could lawfully resist the exercise of this right; but the law had done nothing to define the rights of naturalized subjects or citizens. The British government might, no doubt, impress its own subjects; but almost every British sailor in the American service carried papers of American citizenship, and although some of these were fraudulent, many were genuine. The law of England, as declared from time out of mind by every generation of her judges, held that the allegiance of a subject was indefeasible, and therefore that naturalization was worthless. The law of the United States, as declared by Chief-Justice

Ellsworth in 1799, was in effect the same;[1] he held
that no citizen could dissolve the compact of protection and defence between himself and society without
the consent or default of the community.   On both
sides the law was emphatic to the point that naturalization could not bind the government which did
not consent to it ; and the United States could hardly
require England to respect naturalization papers which
the Supreme Court of the United States declared itself
unable to respect in a similar case.   Nevertheless,
while courts and judges declare what the law is or
ought to be, they bind only themselves, and their
decisions have no necessary effect on the co-ordinate
branches of government.   While the judges laid down
one doctrine in Westminster Hall, Parliament laid
down another in St. Stephen's chapel ; and no one
could say whether the law or the statute was final.
The British statute-book contained Acts of Parliament as old as the reign of Queen Anne[2] to encourage the admission of foreign seamen into the British
navy, offering them naturalization as an inducement.
American legislation went not quite so far, but by
making naturalization easy it produced worse results.
A little perjury, in no wise unsafe, was alone required
in order to transform British seamen into American
citizens ; and perjury was the commonest commodity
in a seaport.   The British government was forced to

[1] Trial of Isaac Williams, Hartford, 1799; Wharton's State
Trials, 653.   Shanks *v.* Dupont, 3 Peters, 242.

[2] 6 Anne, c. 20.

decide whether papers so easily obtained and transferred should be allowed to bar its claims on the services of its subjects, and whether it could afford to become a party to the destruction of its own marine, even though the United States should join with France and carry on endless war.

That there were some points which not even the loss of American trade would bring England to concede was well known to Jefferson; and on these points he did not mean to insist. Setting the matter of impressment aside, the relations between England and America had never been better than when the new President took office March 4, 1801. The British government seemed earnest in conciliation, and lost no opportunity of showing its good-will. Under the Sixth Article of Jay's treaty, a commission had been appointed to settle long-standing debts due to British subjects, but held in abeyance by State legislation in contravention of the treaty of 1783. After long delays the commission met at Philadelphia and set to work, but had made little progress when the two American commissioners, with the President's approval, in the teeth of the treaty which created the Board, refused to accept its decisions, and seceded. This violent measure was not taken by the Administration without uneasiness, for England might reasonably have resented it; but after some further delay the British government consented to negotiate again, and at last accepted a round sum of three million dollars in full discharge of the British claim. This

was a case in which England was the aggrieved party;
she behaved equally well in other cases where the
United States were aggrieved. Rufus King complained
that her admiralty courts in the West Indies and at
Halifax were a scandal; in deference to his remonstrances these courts were thoroughly reformed by Act
of Parliament. The vice-admiralty court at Nassau
condemned the American brigantine " Leopard," engaged in carrying Malaga wine from the United States
to the Spanish West Indies. The American minister
complained of the decision, and within three days the
King's Advocate reported in his favor.[1] The report
was itself founded on Sir William Scott's favorable decision in the case of the " Polly." Soon afterward the American minister complained that Captain
Pellew, of the " Cleopatra," and Admiral Parker had
not effectually restrained their subordinates on the
American station; both officers were promptly recalled. Although the Ministry had not yet consented
to make any arrangement on the practice of impressment, Rufus King felt much hope that they
might consent even to this reform; meanwhile Lord
Grenville checked the practice, and professed a strong
wish to find some expedient that should take its
place.

There was no reason to doubt the sincerity of the
British Foreign Office in wishing friendship. Its pol-
icy was well expressed in a despatch written from
Philadelphia by Robert Liston, the British minister,

[1] Rufus King to Madison, April 12, 1801; State Papers, ii. 490.

shortly before he left the United States to return
home : [1] —

" The advantages to be ultimately reaped from a per-
severance in the line of conduct which Great Britain has
adopted for the last four years appear to my mind to be
infallible and of infinite magnitude ; the profitable consequences of a state of hostility, small and uncertain.   I
have been pleasing my imagination with looking forward
to the distant spectacle of all the northern continent of
America covered with friendly though not subject States,
consuming our manufactures, speaking our language,
proud of their parent State, attached to her prosperity.
War must bring with it extensive damage to our navigation, the probable loss of Canada, and the *world* behind
it, the propagation of enmity and prejudices which it may
be impossible to eradicate.   The system of the American
government does not strike me, with the near view I have
of it, as being in so perilous a situation as is imagined in
Europe.   I am willing to avoid political prophecies, but
I confess I think it will get on well enough if the country
remains in peace ; and if they go to war, the fabric may
acquire strength.   God forbid that it should be to our
detriment, and to the triumph of our enemies ! "

[1] Liston to Grenville (private), May 7, 1800 ; MSS. British
Archives.

CHAPTER XV.

FEBRUARY 4, 1801, one month before the inauguration of President Jefferson, Pitt suddenly retired from office, and was succeeded by a weak ministry, in which Mr. Addington, afterward Lord Sidmouth, took the post vacated by Pitt. No event could have been happier for the prospects of President Jefferson, who might fairly count upon Addington's weakness to prevent his interference in American affairs.

Knowing himself to be universally regarded as the friend and admirer of France, Jefferson was the more anxious not to be classed by the British government among the enemies of England. Even before he was inaugurated, he took occasion to request Edward Thornton, the British *chargé*, —

" With great earnestness, to assure his Majesty's government that it should experience during his administration as cordial and sincere acts of friendship as had ever been received under that of his predecessors. " I am aware," said the President elect, " that I have been represented as hostile to Great Britain ; but this has been done only for electioneering purposes, and I hope henceforward such language will be used no longer. I can appeal to all my past conduct that in everything in which I have been engaged relatively to England, I have always been guided by a liberal policy. I wish to be at the head of affairs no longer than while I am influenced by such sentiments of equal liberality toward all nations. There is nothing to which I have a greater repugnance than to establish distinctions in favor of one nation against another."

The day after his inauguration he returned to the subject : —

" There is nothing I have more, or I may say so much, at heart as to adjust happily all differences between us, and to cultivate the most cordial harmony and good understanding. The English government is too just, I am persuaded, to regard newspaper trash, and the assertions contained in them that I am a creature of France and an enemy of Great Britain. For *republican* France I may have felt some interest ; but that is long over ; and there is assuredly nothing in the present government of that country which could naturally incline me to show the smallest undue partiality to it at the expense of Great Britain, or indeed of any other country." [1]

Thornton felt no great confidence in the new President's protests, and thought it possible that Jefferson had " on this, as he seems to have done on many late public occasions, taxed his imagination to supply the deficiency of his feelings." All Englishmen were attached to the Federalist and New England interest ; they could not understand that Virginia should be a safer friend than Massachusetts. Yet in truth

[1] Thornton to Grenville, March 7, 1801 ; MSS. British Archives.

Jefferson never was more serious than when he made these professions. The Southern republicans had nothing to gain from a quarrel with England; they neither wished for Canada, nor aspired to create shipping or manufactures : their chief antagonist was not England, but Spain. The only Power which could seriously injure them was Great Britain ; and the only injury they could inflict in return was by conquering Canada for the benefit of Northern influence, or by building up manufactures which they disliked, or by cutting off their own markets for tobacco and cotton. Nothing warranted a belief that men like Jefferson, Madison, and Gallatin would ever seek a quarrel with England.

The British Ministry soon laid aside any doubts they might have felt on the subject. Lord Grenville, who retired with Pitt, was succeeded as Foreign Secretary by Lord Hawkesbury, afterward better known as Lord Liverpool. The new Ministry negotiated for peace with Bonaparte. Oct. 1, 1801, the preliminaries were signed, and the world found itself again in a sort of repose, broken only by the bloody doings at St. Domingo and Guadeloupe. England returned, like France and Spain, to the rigor of the colonial system. The customs entries of New York, Boston, and Philadelphia rapidly diminished in number ; American shipping declined ; but Madison was relieved from the burden of belligerent disputes, which had been the chief anxiety of his predecessors in the State Department.

Yet peace did not put an end to all difficulties. Rufus King continued to negotiate in London in regard to the outstanding British debts, twice recognized by treaty, yet still unpaid by the United States ; in regard to the boundary of Maine and that of the extreme northwest territory at the source of the Mississippi ; and finally, in regard to impressments ; while Edward Thornton at Washington complained that, in spite of peace and the decline of American shipping, encouragement was still offered to the desertion of British seamen in every port of the United States, — in fact that this means was systematically used to prevent British shipping from entering American ports in competition with the shipping of America. When Madison alleged that the national government had no share in such unfriendly conduct, Thornton thrust under his eyes the law of Virginia, — a law enacted by President Jefferson's political friends in his political interests, — which forbade, under penalty of death, any magistrate of Virginia to be instrumental in surrendering deserters or criminals, even in cases where they were bound by treaty to do so. Madison could not deny that this legislation was contrary to a treaty right which the United States government was bound to enforce. He admitted that American shipmasters and consuls in British ports habitually asked the benefit of the British law, and received it ; but he could hold out only a remote hope that mutual legislation might solve the difficulty by applying the merchant-seamen laws of the two coun-

tries reciprocally. In conversation with Thornton
he lamented, with every appearance of sincerity and
candor, the deficiency of the existing laws, and did
not dispute that Great Britain could hardly be blamed
for refusing the surrender of seamen on her side ;
but when Thornton asked him to order the return of
a man who under aggravated circumstances had deserted from the British ship-of-war " Andromache "
in the port of Norfolk, and had been immediately
engaged on the United States revenue cutter there,
Madison replied in a note coldly reiterating the fact,
with which both parties were already acquainted,
that neither the law of nations nor the provisions of
any treaty enjoined the mutual restitution of seamen.
This recognized formula, under which governments
commonly express a refusal to act, was understood
by Thornton as equivalent to an avowal that the new
Administration, controlled by Virginians, would not
venture, even in the future emergency of a demand
for extradition under treaty, to risk the displeasure of
Virginia.[1] Desertion, therefore, received no discour-
agement from the United States government ; on the
contrary, deserters, known to be such, were received
at once into the national service, and their surrender
refused. Under such circumstances the British government was not likely to be more accommodating
than the American.

As the summer of 1802 approached, President

[1] Thornton to Hawkesbury, Oct. 25 and Nov. 26, 1802 : MSS.
British Archives.

Jefferson drew into closer and more confidential relations with Thornton. During the Federalist rule the two countries were never on more affectionate terms. At London Rufus King and Christopher Gore received courteous attention from Lord Hawkesbury. At Washington, Thornton's intimacy at the White House roused the jealousy and alarm of Pichon. As Bonaparte's projects against Louisiana disclosed themselves, and as Leclerc's first successes at St. Domingo opened the French path to New Orleans, Jefferson began to pay sudden and almost eager court to Thornton, who was a little embarrassed by the freedom with which the President denounced the First Consul. The preliminary articles of peace between France and England had been signed Oct. 1, 1801 ; but the treaty of Amiens, which made these articles definitive, was signed only March 25, 1802. Addington was naturally anxious that the peace should be maintained ; indeed, no one could doubt that the existence of his Ministry depended on maintaining it. Thornton had no instructions which warranted him in intriguing against the First Consul, or in making preparations for a new war ; and yet hardly was the treaty of Amiens made public, when President Jefferson began to talk as though England were still at war, and it were only a question of time when the United States must become her ally. The Louisiana question excited him. In April he wrote his letters to Dupont and Livingston. At about the same time he took Thornton into his confidence.

" I have had many occasions since it was first started,"
wrote Thornton,[1] " of conversing freely with Mr. Jefferson on this topic, which is indeed peculiarly interesting
to him, and his reflections on which he utters with perhaps
too little caution to persons who are not disposed to think
very favorably of any change of sentiments with respect
to France.   He not only regards the cession of Louisiana
and New Orleans as a certain cause of future war between
the two countries, but makes no scruple to say that if the
force of the United States should be unable to expel the
French from those settlements, they must have recourse
to the assistance of other Powers, meaning unquestionably
Great Britain.   With regard to France and the person
who is at the head of its government, whether in consequence of the projected cession of Louisiana or of the
little account which seems to be made of the United
States as well at Paris as by French officers in other parts
of the world, Mr. Jefferson speaks in very unqualified
terms of the usurpation of Bonaparte, of the arbitrary
nature and spirit of his government, of his love of flattery
and vain pomp, — features, according to Mr. Jefferson,
which indicate the frivolous character of his mind rather
than a condescension to the taste of the French people.
The presses in America devoted to the President's Administration make use of the same language ; and without pretending to say that this party is cured of its
bitterness against Great Britain, I can safely venture to
assure your Lordship that its predilection for France
scarcely exists even in name."

After the stoppage of the *entrepôt* at New Orleans,
when public opinion seemed intent on driving Jeffer-

[1] Thornton to Hawkesbury, July 3, 1802 ; MSS. British
Archives.

son into the war with France which he had predicted,
Thornton found himself and his government in favor
at Washington. The Republicans were even better
disposed than the Federalists. Jefferson was willing
to abolish between England and America the discrimi-
nating duties on shipping which the New England
Federalists had imposed, and which they still wished
to maintain for use in the disputed West Indian trade.
He told Thornton that he could no doubt carry the
repeal of these countervailing duties through Congress
over the heads of the opposition,[1] " but he wished it
to be adopted in consequence of their own conviction, rather than by a contrary conduct to afford
them the least ground for asserting that the Southern
States were carrying into execution their scheme of
ruin against the navigation and commerce of their
Eastern brethren." Jefferson was rapidly becoming
the friend and confidant of England. Thornton, naturally delighted with his own success, and with the
mortifications and anxieties of Yrujo and Pichon,
went so far as to urge his government to help the
views of the United States against Louisiana:[2] —

" I should hope, my Lord, that by having some share
in the delivery of this Island of New Orleans to the
United States, which it will be impossible to keep from
them whenever they choose to employ force, his Majesty's

[1] Thornton to Hawkesbury, Dec. 31, 1802 ; MSS. British
Archives.
[2] Thornton to Hawkesbury, Jan. 3, 1803 ; MSS. British
Archives.

government may hereafter attach still more this country to our interests, and derive all the advantage possible from the intercourse with that important part of the world. A very great change has gradually taken place in the opinions of all ranks in this government in favor of Great Britain, which has struck observers more likely to be impartial than myself. A sense of a common interest has a great share in the change; but the conduct of France in all her relations has not failed to produce its full effect; and I find men, formerly the most vehement in their politics, asserting in the most unqualified terms the necessity of a union among all the members of the civilized world to check her encroachments and to assure the general tranquillity."

A few days later the President nominated Monroe to act with Livingston and Pinckney in an attempt to purchase New Orleans. This step, which was openly avowed to be the alternative and perhaps the antecedent of war with France, brought Thornton into still more confidential relations with the Government. Finding that the Secretary of State was as cautious as the President was talkative, Thornton carried on an active intercourse with the latter. He first offered to detain the British government packet for Monroe's use; but it was found that a month or two of delay would be necessary. Then, without instructions from his Government, Thornton took a bolder step:[1] —

"This state of things has naturally excited a sentiment of common interest, and has encouraged me to enter with

[1] Thornton to Hawkesbury, Jan. 31, 1803; MSS. British Archives.

more freedom into the subject, as well with the President as with Mr. Madison, than I should otherwise have thought right, without being acquainted with the views of his Majesty's government. Under this impression, I ventured, immediately after the nomination and before the first arrival of Mr. Monroe, to inquire of the President whether it was his intention to let him pass over to England, and hold any conversation with his Majesty's ministers upon the general question of the free navigation of the Mississippi. The inquiry was somewhat premature, and I made it with some apology. Mr. Jefferson replied, however, unaffectedly, that at so early a stage of the business he had scarcely thought himself what it might be proper to do ; . . . that, on the whole, he thought it very probable that Mr. Monroe might cross the Channel. . . . Some time after Mr. Monroe's arrival, actuated by the same view, I mentioned to Mr. Jefferson that it would give me pleasure to furnish the former with an introduction to his Majesty's ambassador at Paris, as it would afford me the occasion of making Lord Whitworth acquainted with the nature of the object in dispute between this country, France, and Spain, and would give to Mr. Monroe, if he were disposed of himself, or were instructed by his Government to seek it, a more ready pretext for opening himself to his Lordship, and of keeping him apprised of the progress and turn of the negotiation. Mr. Jefferson seemed pleased with this offer, and said he was sure Mr. Monroe would accept it with great thankfulness."

Madison talked less freely than his chief, and contented himself with explaining to the British representative that the views of the Government in

sending Monroe to France were limited to the hope of
inducing the First Consul by money, or other means
of persuasion, to cede in Louisiana a place of deposit
over which the United States might have absolute
jurisdiction. He did not tell Thornton of the decision
made by the Cabinet, and the instructions given to
Monroe, April 18, 1803, to offer terms of alliance with
England in case the First Consul should make war;[1]
but the tone of cordiality in Government and people,
both in public and private, in New York, Boston, and
Philadelphia, as in the South and West, was gratify-
ing to British pride, and would have been still more
so had not the community somewhat too openly
avowed the intention of leaving England, if possible,
to fight alone. At the first news of the approaching
rupture between France and England, this wish began
to appear so plainly that Thornton was staggered by
it. The Americans took no trouble to conceal the
hope that England would have to fight their battles
for them.[2]

"The manifest advantage that such a state of things is
calculated to give to their negotiation with France, and
which is already sensibly felt in the altered tone and conduct of the French government, . . . will sufficiently account for their wishes and for this belief. But possessing
the same opinion of the encroachments of France, and of
the barrier which Great Britain alone places between her
and the United States, and actuated, as I really believe

[1] See p. 2.

[2] Thornton to Hawkesbury, May 30, 1803; MSS. British
Archives.

they are, by sincere wishes for our success, I am afraid
they begin to see more clearly that in a state of war we
are effectually fighting their battles, without the necessity of their active interference ; and they recur once
more to the flattering prospect of peace and a lucrative
neutrality."

In this state of doubt President Jefferson continued
his intimate relations with Thornton.

"He expressed himself very freely," wrote Thornton,
May 30, 1803, "on the contemptible and frivolous conduct, as he termed it, of a Government that could alter
its language so entirely on the prospect of an approaching
rupture with another nation, — which he acknowledged
instantly, on my mention of it, had been the case toward
Mr. Livingston."

Jefferson attributed Bonaparte's returning courtesy
to fear rather than to foresight. Thornton himself
began to feel the danger that Bonaparte, after all,
might outwit him. He revised his opinion about Louisiana. England, he saw, had the strongest motives
for wishing France to keep that province.

"The most desirable state of things," he wrote,
"seems to be that France should become mistress of
Louisiana, because her influence in the United States
would be by that event lost forever, and she could only
be dispossessed by a concert between Great Britain and
America in a common cause, which would produce an
indissoluble bond of union and amity between the two
countries."

This cordiality between England and the United
States lasted without interruption until midsummer.

Pichon complained, as has been shown, of the attentions paid to Thornton by the President.[1] "I remarked at table that he redoubled his courtesies and attentions toward the British *chargé*." The dinner was in the month of January; in the following June Pichon wrote that the President had begun to accept the idea of seeing the British at New Orleans:[2] —

'Mr. Jefferson told me a few days ago that he was engaged in letting that Power know that her presence there would be seen with regret; but I perceive that, little by little, people are familiarizing themselves with this eventuality, as their fears increase in regard to us. They are so convinced that England sees more and more her true interests in relation to the United States, and is resolved to conciliate them, that they have no doubt of her lending herself to some arrangement. What they fear most is that, as the price of this accommodation, she may require the United States to take an active part in the indispensable war; and this is what they ardently wish to avoid."

Until July 3, 1803, the relations between President Jefferson's government and that of Great Britain were so cordial as to raise a doubt whether the United States could avoid becoming an ally of England, and taking part in the war with France. Suddenly came the new convulsion of Europe.

[1] Pichon to Talleyrand, 8 Pluviôse, An xi. (Jan. 28, 1803); Archives des Aff. Étr., MSS.

[2] Pichon to Talleyrand, 14 Prairial, An xii. (June 3, 1803); Archives des Aff. Étr., MSS.

" It was on the third of this month," wrote Pichon
July 7, 1803, " the eve of the anniversary of Independence, that we received two pieces of news of the deepest
interest for this country, — that of the rupture between
France and England, proclaimed by the latter on May
16, and that of the cession of Louisiana and New Orleans,
made by us on April 30." [1]

The next day, when Pichon attended the usual
reception at the White House, he found himself received in a manner very different from that to which
he had been of late accustomed.

The two events, thus coming together, were sure
to affect seriously the attitude of the United States
toward England. Not only did Jefferson no longer
need British aid, but he found himself in a position
where he could afford with comparative freedom to
insist upon his own terms of neutrality. He had
always felt that Great Britain did not sufficiently
respect this neutrality ; he never failed to speak of
Jay's treaty in terms of vehement dislike; and he
freely avowed his intention of allowing all commercial
treaties to expire. The relation between these treaties and the rights of neutrality was simple. Jefferson wanted no treaties which would prevent him from
using commercial weapons against nations that violated American neutrality ; and therefore he reserved
to Congress the right to direct commerce in whatever
paths the Government might prefer.

[1] Pichon to Talleyrand, 18 Messidor, An xii. (July 7, 1803);
Archives des Aff. Étr., MSS.

"On the subject of treaties," he wrote,[1] "our system is to have none with any nation, as far as can be avoided. The treaty with England has therefore not been renewed, and all overtures for treaty with other nations have been declined. We believe that with nations, as with individuals, dealings may be carried on as advantageously, perhaps more so, while their continuance depends on a voluntary good treatment, as if fixed by a contract, which, when it becomes injurious to either, is made by forced constructions to mean what suits them, and becomes a cause of war instead of a bond of peace."

Such a system was best suited to the strongest nations, and to those which could control their dealings to most advantage. The Administration believed that the United States stood in this position.

The President and Secretary Madison were inclined to assert authority in their relations with foreign Powers. Even so early as the preceding February, before Monroe sailed for Europe, Madison told Pichon of this intention.[2] "He added," wrote Pichon to Talleyrand, "that if war should be renewed, as seemed probable, the United States would be disposed to take a higher tone than heretofore, that Europe had put their spirit of moderation to proofs that would be no longer endured." Immediately after hearing of the Louisiana cession, Pichon wrote that the same

---

[1] Jefferson to Mazzei, July 18, 1804; Works, iv. 552.

[2] Pichon to Talleyrand, 1 Ventôse, An xi. (Feb. 20, 1803); Archives des Aff. Étr., MSS.

spirit continued to animate the Government.[1] "It is certain that they propose to cause the neutrality of the United States to be more exactly respected by the belligerent Powers than in the last war. The Government has often shown its intentions in this respect, from the time when everything pointed to an infallible rupture between us and England." President Jefferson, while avowing a pacific policy, explained that his hopes of peace were founded on his power to affect the interests of the belligerents. At the same moment when Pichon wrote thus to Talleyrand, the President wrote to the Earl of Buchan:[2] —

"My hope of preserving peace for our country is not founded in the Quaker principle of non-resistance under every wrong, but in the belief that a just and friendly conduct on our part will procure justice and friendship from others. In the existing contest, each of the combatants will find an interest in our friendship."

He was confident that he could control France and England:[3] "I do not believe we shall have as much to swallow from them as our predecessors had."

The Louisiana question being settled, the field was clear for the United States to take high ground in behalf of neutral rights; and inevitably the first step must be taken against England. No one denied that thus far the administration of Addington had be-

[1] Pichon to Talleyrand, 18 Messidor, An xii. (July 7, 1803); Archives des Aff. Étr., MSS.

[2] Jefferson to Earl of Buchan, July 10, 1803; **Works,** iv. 493.

[3] Jefferson to General Gates, July 11, 1803; Works, iv. 494.

haved well toward the United States. Rufus King brought to America at the same time with news of the Louisiana treaty, or had sent shortly before, two conventions by which long-standing differences were settled. One of these conventions disposed of the old subject of British debts, — the British government accepting a round sum of six hundred thousand pounds on behalf of the creditors.[1] The other created two commissions for running the boundary line between Maine and Nova Scotia, and between the Lake of the Woods and the Mississippi River.[2] King went so far as to express the opinion that had he not been on the eve of his departure, he might have succeeded in making some arrangement about impressments ; and he assured Gallatin that the actual Administration in England was the most favorable that had existed or could exist for the interests of the United States; its only misfortune was its weakness.[3] The conduct of the British government in regard to Louisiana proved the truth of King's assertion. Not only did it offer no opposition to the sale, but it lent every possible assistance to the transfer ; and under its eye, with its consent, Alexander Baring made the financial arrangements which were to furnish Bonaparte with ten million American dollars to pay the preliminary expenses of an invasion of England.

[1] State Papers, ii. 382.   [2] State Papers, ii. 584.
[3] Gallatin to Jefferson, Aug. 18, 1803; Gallatin's Works, i. 140.

Nevertheless, if the United States government intended to take a high tone in regard to neutral rights, it must do so from the beginning of the war. Aware that success in regard to England, as in regard to Spain, depended on asserting at the outset, and maintaining with obstinacy, the principles intended to be established, the President and Secretary Madison lost no time in causing their attitude to be clearly understood. An opportunity of asserting this authoritative tone was given by the appearance of a new British minister at Washington; and thus it happened that at the time when the Secretary of State was preparing for his collision with the Marquis of Casa Yrujo and the Spanish empire, he took on his hands the more serious task of curbing the pretensions of Anthony Merry and the King of England.

CHAPTER XVI.

ONE of Addington's friendly acts was the appointment of Anthony Merry as British minister to the United States. For this selection Rufus King was directly responsible. Two names were mentioned to him by the Foreign Office as those of the persons entitled to claim the place; one was that of Merry, the other was that of Francis James Jackson.

"As I have had the opportunity of knowing both these gentlemen during my residence here," wrote Minister King to Secretary Madison,[1] "it was not without some regret that I heard of the intention to appoint Mr. Jackson in lieu of Mr. Merry. From this information I have been led to make further inquiry concerning their reputations, and the result has proved rather to increase than to lessen my solicitude. Mr. Jackson is said to be positive, vain, and intolerant. He is moreover filled with English prejudices in respect to all other countries, and as far as his opinions concerning the United States are known, seems more likely to disserve than to benefit a liberal intercourse between them and his own country. On the other hand, Mr. Merry appears to be a plain, unassuming, and amiable man, who having lived for

[1] King to Madison, April 10, 1802 ; MSS. State Department Archives.

many years in Spain is in almost every point of character the reverse of Mr. Jackson, who were he to go to
America would go for the sake of present employment
and with the hope of leaving it as soon as he could receive a similar appointment in Europe; while Mr. Merry
wishes for the mission with the view of obtaining what
he believes will prove to be an agreeable and permanent
residence."

In deference to Rufus King's wishes or for some
other reason Merry received the appointment. Doubtless he came to America in the hope of finding a
" permanent residence," as King remarked; but it
could hardly be agreeable, as he hoped. He was a
thorough Englishman, with a wife more English than
himself. He was not prepared for the isolation of
the so-called Federal City, and he did not expect
to arrive at a moment when the United States government, pleased with having curbed Bonaparte, was preparing to chasten Spain and to discipline England.

Landing at Norfolk from a ship of war Nov. 4, 1803,
Merry was obliged to hire a vessel to carry himself
and his belongings to Washington, where, after a
tempestuous voyage, he at last arrived, November 26.
Possibly Mr. and Mrs. Merry, like other travellers,
would have grumbled even though Washington had
supplied them with Aladdin's palace and Aladdin's
lamp to furnish it; but the truth was not to be denied
that the Federal City offered few conveniences, and
was better suited for members of Congress, who lived
without wives in boarding-houses, than for foreign

ministers, with complaining wives, who were required
to set up large establishments and to entertain on a
European scale.

"I cannot describe to you," wrote Merry privately,[1]
"the difficulty and expense which I have to encounter in
fixing myself in a habitation.   By dint of money I have
just secured two small houses on the common which is
meant to become in time the city of Washington.   They
are mere shells of houses, with bare walls and without
fixtures of any kind, even without a pump or well, all
which I must provide at my own cost.   Provisions of any
kind, especially vegetables, are frequently hardly to be
obtained at any price.   So miserable is our situation."

Had these been the worst trials that awaited the
new British minister, he might have been glad to
meet them; for when once surmounted, they favored
him by preventing social rivalry.   Unfortunately he
met more serious annoyances.   Until his arrival,
Yrujo was the only minister of full rank in the
United States; and Yrujo's intimate relations at the
White House had given him family privileges.   For
this reason the Spanish minister made no struggle
to maintain etiquette, but living mostly in Philadelphia disregarded the want of what he considered
good manners at Washington, according to which he
was placed on the same social footing with his own
secretary of legation.   Yet Yrujo, American in many
respects, belonged to the school of Spanish diplomacy which had for centuries studied points of honor.

[1] Merry to Hammond, Dec. 7, 1803; MSS. British Archives.

He might well have made with his own mouth the celebrated retort which one of his predecessors made to Philip II., who reproached him with sacrificing an interest to a ceremony: "How a ceremony? Your Majesty's self is but a ceremony!" Although Yrujo submitted to Jefferson, he quarrelled with Pichon on this point, for Pichon was only a secretary in charge of the French legation. In November, 1803, Yrujo's friendship for Jefferson was cooling, and he waited the arrival of Merry in the hope of finding a champion of diplomatic rights. Jefferson, on the other hand, waited Merry's arrival in order to establish, once for all, a new social code; and that there might be no misunderstanding, he drafted with his own hand the rules which were to control Executive society, — rules intended to correct a tendency toward monarchical habits introduced by President Washington.

In 1801 on coming into power Jefferson announced that he would admit not the smallest distinction that might separate him from the mass of his fellow-citizens. He dispensed with the habit of setting apart certain days and hours for receiving visits of business or curiosity, announcing that he would on any day and at any hour receive in a friendly and hospitable manner those who should call upon him.[1] He evidently wished to place the White House on the footing of easy and generous hospitality which

[1] Thornton to Hawkesbury, Dec. 9, 1801; MSS. British Archives.

was the pride of every Virginia gentleman. No man
should be turned away from its doors; its table,
liberal and excellent, should be filled with equal
guests, whose self-respect should be hurt by no arti-
ficial rules of precedence. Such hospitality cost both
time and money; but Washington was a petty village,
society was very small, and Jefferson was a poor
economist. He entertained freely and handsomely.

" Yesterday I dined with the President," wrote Senator
Plumer of New Hampshire, Dec. 25, 1802.[1] "His rule
is to have about ten members of Congress at a time.
We sat down to the table at four, rose at six, and
walked immediately into another room and drank coffee.
We had a very good dinner, with a profusion of fruits
and sweetmeats. The wine was the best I ever drank,
particularly the champagne, which was indeed delicious.
I wish his French politics were as good as his French
wines."

So long as this manner of life concerned only the
few Americans who were then residents or visitors
at Washington, Jefferson found no great difficulty
in mixing his company and disregarding precedence.
Guests accommodated themselves to the ways of the
house, took care of their own comfort, went to table
without special request, and sat wherever they found
a vacant chair; but foreigners could hardly be expected at first to understand what Jefferson called
the rule of pell-mell. Thornton and Pichon, being
only secretaries of legation, rather gained than lost

[1] Life of William Plumer, p. 245.

by it; but Yrujo resented it in secret; and all eyes
were turned to see how the new British minister
would conduct himself in the scramble.

Either before or soon after Merry's arrival the
President wrote the rules, which he called "Canons of Etiquette to be observed by the Executive;"[1]
and these canons ultimately received the approval of
the Cabinet. Foreign ministers, he said, were to pay
the first visit to the "ministers of the nation;" their
wives were to receive the first visit from the wives of
"national ministers." No grades among diplomatic
members were to give precedence; "all are perfectly
equal, whether foreign or domestic, titled or untitled,
in or out of office." Finally, "to maintain the principle of equality, or of *pêle-mêle*, and prevent the
growth of precedence out of courtesy, the members
of the Executive will practise at their own houses,
and recommend an adherence to, the ancient usage
of the country, — of gentlemen in mass giving precedence to the ladies in mass in passing from one apart-
ment where they are assembled into another." Such,
according to Rufus King, whose aid was invoked on
this occasion, was the usage in London.

Merry duly arrived in Washington, and was told by
Madison that the President would receive his letter
of credence Nov. 29, according to the usual formality.
At the appointed hour the British minister, in diplomatic uniform, as was required in the absence of any
hint to the contrary, called upon Madison, and was

[1] Jefferson's Works, ix. 454.

taken to the White House, where he was received by the President. Jefferson's manner of receiving guests was well known, although this was the first occasion on which he had given audience to a new foreign minister. Among several accounts of his appearance at such times, that of Senator Plumer was one of the best.

" In a few moments after our arrival," said the senator, writing two years before Merry's mishap,[1] "a tall, high-boned man came into the room. He was dressed, or rather undressed, in an old brown coat, red waistcoat, old corduroy small-clothes much soiled, woollen hose, and slippers without heels. I thought him a servant, when General Varnum surprised me by announcing that it was the President."

The " Evening Post," about a year later, described him as habitually appearing in public " dressed in long boots with tops turned down about the ankles like a Virginia buck ; overalls of corduroy faded, by frequent immersions in soap suds, from yellow to a dull white; a red single-breasted waistcoat; a light brown coat with brass buttons, both coat and waistcoat quite threadbare ; linen very considerably soiled ; hair uncombed and beard unshaven." In truth the Virginia republicans cared little for dress. " You know that the Virginians have some pride in appearing in simple habiliments," wrote Joseph Story in regard to Jefferson, " and are willing to rest their claim to attention upon their force of mind and sua-

[1] Life of William Plumer, p. 242.

vity of manners." Indeed, " Virginia carelessness "
was almost a proverb.[1]

On the occasion of Merry's reception, the President's chief offence in etiquette consisted in the
slippers without heels. No law of the United States
or treaty stipulation forbade Jefferson to receive
Merry in heelless slippers, or for that matter in bare
feet, if he thought proper to do so. Yet Virginia
gentlemen did not intentionally mortify their guests ;
and perhaps Madison would have done better to relieve the President of such a suspicion by notifying
Merry beforehand that he would not be expected
to wear full dress. In that case the British minister
might have complimented Jefferson by himself appearing in slippers without heels.

A card of invitation was next sent, asking Mr. and
Mrs. Merry to dine at the White House, December 2.
Such an invitation was in diplomatic usage equivalent
to a command, and Merry at once accepted it. The
new minister was then told that he must call on the
heads of departments. He remonstrated, saying that
Liston, his predecessor, had been required to make
the first visit only to the Secretary of State.; but he
was told, in effect, that what had been done under
the last Administration was no rule for the present
one. Merry acquiesced, and made his calls. These
pin-thrusts irritated him ; but he was more seriously
inconvenienced by the sudden withdrawal of diplomatic privileges by the Senate, although Vice-

[1] Life of Joseph Story, pp 151, 158.

President Burr took occasion to explain that the
Senate's action was quite unconnected with the
President's " canons of etiquette," and was in truth
due to some indiscretion of Yrujo in the House of
Representatives.

Meanwhile the President took an unusual step.
When two countries were at war, neutral governments commonly refrained from inviting the representative of one belligerent to meet the representative of
the other, unless on formal occasions where the entire
diplomatic body was invited, or in crowds where contact was not necessary. Still more rarely were such
incongruous guests invited to an entertainment supposed to be given in honor of either individual.   No
one knew this rule better than Jefferson, who had
been himself four years in diplomatic service at Paris,
besides being three years Secretary of State to President Washington at Philadelphia.   He knew that
the last person whom Merry would care to meet was
Pichon, the French *chargé;* yet he not only invited
Pichon, but pressed him to attend.   The Frenchman,
aware that Merry was to be mortified by the etiquette
of the dinner, and watching with delight the process
by which Jefferson, day after day, took a higher tone
toward England, wrote an account of the affair to
Talleyrand.[1]   He said : —

" I was invited to this dinner. I had learned from
the President what was the matter (*ce qui en était*),

[1] Pichon to Talleyrand, 15 Pluviôse, An xii. (Feb. 5, 1804) ;
Archives des Aff. Étr., MSS.

when I went to tell him that I was going for some days to Baltimore, where I was called by the affairs of the frigate 'La Poursuivante.' The President was so obliging as to urge my return in order to be present with Mme. Pichon at the dinner (*Le Président eut l'honnêteté de me presser de revenir pour être au diner*). I came back here, although business required a longer stay at Baltimore. Apart from the reason of respect due to the President, I had that of witnessing what might happen (*j'avais celle de connaître ce qui se passerait*)."

Pichon accordingly hurried back from Baltimore, especially at the President's request, in order to have the pleasure of seeing Jefferson humiliate his own guest in his own house.

Pichon was gratified by the result. At four o'clock on the afternoon of Dec. 2, 1803, this curious party assembled at the White House, — Mr. and Mrs. Merry, the Marquis Yrujo and his American wife, M. Pichon and his American wife, Mr. and Mrs. Madison, and some other persons whose names were not mentioned. When dinner was announced, the President offered his hand to Mrs. Madison and took her to table, placing her on his right. Mme. Yrujo took her seat on his left.

"Mrs. Merry was placed by Mr. Madison below the Spanish minister, who sat next to Mrs. Madison. With respect to me," continued the British minister in his account of the affair,[1] "I was proceeding to place myself, though without invitation, next to the wife of the

[1] Merry to Hawkesbury, Dec. 6, 1803; MSS. British Archives.

Spanish minister, when a member of the House of Representatives passed quickly by me and took the seat, without Mr. Jefferson's using any means to prevent it, or taking any care that I might be otherwise placed. . .

" I will beg leave to intrude a moment longer on your Lordship's time," continued Merry's report, " by adding to this narrative that among the persons (none of those who were of this country were the principal officers of the government except Mr. Madison) whom the President selected for a dinner which was understood to be given to me, was M. Pichon the French *chargé d'affaires*. I use the word *selected*, because it could not be considered as a diplomatic dinner, since he omitted to invite to it the Danish *chargé d'affaires*, who, with the Spanish minister, form the whole body."

Merry's report was brief ; but Yrujo, who also made an official report to his Government, after mentioning the neglect shown to Merry before dinner, added a remark that explained the situation more exactly : [1] —

" I observed immediately the impression that such a proceeding of the President must have on Mr. and Mrs. Merry ; and their resentment could not but be increased at seeing the manifest, and in my opinion studied, preference given by the President throughout to me and my wife over him and Mrs. Merry."

There the matter might have rested, had not Madison carried the new " canons " beyond the point of endurance. December 6, four days after the dinner at the White House, the British minister was to dine

[1] Yrujo to Cevallos, Feb. 7, 1804 ; MSS. Spanish Archives.

with the Secretary of State. Pichon and Yrujo were again present, and all the Cabinet with their wives. Yrujo's report described the scene that followed.

" I should observe," said he, " that until then my wife and I had enjoyed in the houses of Cabinet ministers the precedence of which we had been deprived in the President's house ; but on this day the Secretary of State too altered his custom, without informing us beforehand of his resolution, and took to table the wife of the Secretary of the Treasury. This unexpected conduct produced at first some confusion, during which the wife of the British minister was left without any one giving her his hand, until her husband advanced, with visible indignation, and himself took her to table."

Even Pichon, though pleased to see the British minister humbled, felt his diplomatic pride a little scandalized at this proceeding. He admitted that it was an innovation, and added, —

" There is no doubt that Mr. Madison in this instance wished to establish in his house the same formality as at the President's, in order to make Mr. Merry feel more keenly the scandal he had made ; but this incident increased it."

The scandal which Merry had made consisted in saying that he believed his treatment at the White House was a premeditated insult against his country. Madison's course took away any remaining doubt on the subject in his mind. Merry became bitter. He wrote home informally : [1] —

[1] Merry to Hammond, Dec. 7, 1803 ; MSS. British Archives.

" On this occasion, also, the *pas* and the preference in every respect was taken by, and given to, the wives of the Secretaries of the Departments (a set of beings as little without the manners as without the appearance of gentlewomen), the foreign ministers and their wives being left to take care of themselves. In short the latter are now placed here in a situation so degrading to the countries they represent, and so personally disagreeable to themselves, as to have become almost intolerable. The case yesterday was so marked and so irritating that I determined to hand Mrs. Merry myself to the table, and to place ourselves wherever we might conveniently find seats."

Merry then received an official explanation that Jefferson invariably gave precedence to the wives of his Cabinet ministers, and that he made no exceptions in favor of foreigners in his rule of *pêle-mêle*.[1] Merry notified Lord Hawkesbury to that effect. He did not fail to point out the signs which indicated to him that these proceedings were but part of a general plan intended to press on the British government. In truth, the whole issue lay in the question whether that intent influenced Jefferson's behavior.

A sort of civil war ensued in the little society of Washington, in which the women took prominent part, and Mrs. Merry gave back with interest the insults she considered herself to have received. The

[1] Madison to Monroe, 19 Jan., 1804. Madison MSS., State Department Archives. Merry to Hawkesbury, 30 Jan., 1801. MSS. British Archives.

first serious evil was an alliance between Merry and
Yrujo, the two men whom Jefferson had most interest in keeping apart.   Pichon wrote home a lively
account of the hostilities that followed.[1]

" M. Yrujo, who is vanity itself, blew the flame more
vigorously than ever. . . . He concerted reprisals with
Mr. Merry, and it was agreed that whenever they should
entertain the secretaries and their wives, they should take
none of them to table, but should give their hands to
their own wives.   This resolution was carried out at a
dinner given some days afterward by M. Yrujo.   Mr.
and Mrs. Merry were next invited by the Secretary of
the Navy.   Mrs. Merry refused; yet this minister, a
very well-bred man (*homme fort poli*), had so arranged
things as to give her his hand.   Apparently what had
taken place at Mr. Madison's was thought harsh (*dur*),
and it was wished to bring Mr. and Mrs. Merry back to
a reconciliation.   The Cabinet took up the question, as
reported in the newspaper of which I sent you an extract,
and it was resolved that hereafter the President should
give his hand to the lady who might happen to be nearest
him, and that there should be no precedence.   Mr. Merry
was invited to a tea by the Secretary of War and by the
Secretary of the Treasury.   To avoid all discussion he
wholly refused the first, and after accepting the second
he did not come.   Finally, New Year's Day gave another
occasion for scandal.   On this day, as on the Fourth
of July, it is the custom to call upon the President; and
even the ladies go there.   This year neither Mme. Yrujo
nor Mrs. Merry went, and the Marquis took care to

[1] Pichon to Talleyrand, 15 Pluviôse, An xii. (Feb. 5, 1804);
Archives des Aff. Étr., MSS.

answer every one who inquired after his wife's health,
that she was perfectly well. Since then Washington
society is turned upside down; all the women are to the
last degree exasperated against Mrs. Merry; the Federal
newspapers have taken up the matter, and increased the
irritation by sarcasms on the Administration and by making a burlesque of the facts, which the Government has
not thought proper to correct. The arrival of M. Bonaparte with his wife in the midst of all this explosion has
furnished Mr. Merry with new griefs. The President
asked M. and Mme. Bonaparte to dinner, and gave his
hand to Madame. There was, however, this difference
between the two cases, — the President had invited on
this day, besides myself and Mme. Pichon, only the
two Messrs. Smith and their wives, who are of Mme.
Bonaparte's family. But when Mr. Merry heard of it,
he remarked that Mme. Bonaparte had on this occasion
taken precedence of the wife of the Secretary of the
Navy. . . I am aware," continued the delighted Pichon,
" that with tact on the part of Mr. Jefferson he might
have avoided all these scandals."

The British minister wrote to Lord Hawkesbury
a brief account of his reception, closing with the
remark : [1] —

" Under these circumstances, my Lord, I have thought
it advisable to avoid all occasions where I and my wife
might be exposed to a repetition of the same want of
distinction toward us until I shall have received authority from you to acquiesce in it, by a signification of his
Majesty's pleasure to that effect."

[1] Merry to Hawkesbury, Dec. 31, 1803 ; MSS. British
Archives.

Accordingly, when the President invited the two ministers to dine at the White House without their wives, they replied that they could not accept the invitation until after receiving instructions from their Governments. Jefferson regarded this concerted answer as an insult.[1] He too lost his temper so far as to indulge in sharp comments, and thought the matter important enough to call for explanation. In a private letter to Monroe, dated Jan. 8, 1804, he wrote:[2] —

" Mr. Merry is with us, and we believe him to be personally as desirable a character as could have been sent us ; but he is unluckily associated with one of an opposite character in every point. She has already disturbed our harmony extremely. He began by claiming the first visit from the national ministers. He corrected himself in this ; but a pretension to take precedence at dinner, etc., over all others is persevered in. We have told him that the principle of society as well as of government with us is the equality of the individuals composing it; that no man here would come to a dinner where he was to be marked with inferiority to any other ; that we might as well attempt to force our principle of equality at St. James's as he his principle of precedence here. I had been in the habit when I invited female company (having no lady in my family) to ask one of the ladies of the four Secretaries to come and take care of my company,

[1] Pichon to Talleyrand, 27 Pluviôse, An xii. (Feb. 13, 1804) ; Archives des Aff. Étr., MSS.

[2] Jefferson to Monroe, Jan. 8, 1804 ; Monroe MSS., State Department Archives. Cf. Madison to Monroe, 16 Feb. 1804. Madison's Works, ii. 195–199.

and as she was to do the honors of the table I handed
her to dinner myself. That Mr. Merry might not construe this as giving them a precedence over Mrs. Merry
I have discontinued it, and here as in private houses the
pêle-mêle practice is adhered to. They have got Yrujo
to take a zealous part in the claim of precedence. It has
excited generally emotions of great contempt and indignation (in which the members of the Legislature participate sensibly) that the agents of foreign nations should
assume to dictate to us what shall be the laws of our
society. The consequence will be that Mr. and Mrs.
Merry will put themselves into coventry, and that he will
lose the best half of his usefulness to his nation, — that
derived from a perfectly familiar and private intercourse
with the Secretaries and myself. The latter, be assured,
is a virago, and in the short course of a few weeks has
established a degree of dislike among all classes which
one would have thought impossible in so short a time.
. . . With respect to Merry, he appears so reasonable
and good a man that I should be sorry to lose him as
long as there remains a possibility of reclaiming him
to the exercise of his own dispositions. If his wife per-
severes she must eat her soup at home, and we shall endeavor to draw him into society as if she did not exist."

Of all American hospitality none was so justly
famous as that of Virginia. In this State there was
probably not a white man, or even a negro slave, but
would have resented the charge that he was capable
of asking a stranger, a foreigner, a woman, under
his roof, with the knowledge that he was about to
inflict what the guest would feel as a humiliation.
Still less would he have selected his guest's only

enemy, and urged him to be present for the purpose
of witnessing the slight.   Reasons of state sometimes
gave occasion for such practices, but under the most
favorable conditions the tactics were unsafe.   Napoleon in the height of his power insulted queens, brow-
beat ambassadors, trampled on his ministers, and
made his wife and servants tremble ; but although
these manners could at his slightest hint be imitated
by a million soldiers, until Europe, from Cadiz to
Moscow, cowered under his multiplied brutality, the
insults and outrages recoiled upon him in the end.
Jefferson could not afford to adopt Napoleonic habits.
His soldiers were three thousand in number, and his
own training had not been that of a successful general; he had seven frigates, and was eager to lay them
up in a single dry-dock.   Peace was his passion.

To complicate this civil war in the little society of
Washington, Jerome Bonaparte appeared there, and
brought with him his young wife, Elizabeth Patterson,
of Baltimore.   Jerome married this beautiful girl
against the remonstrances of Pichon ; but after the
marriage took place, not only Pichon, but also Yrujo
and Jefferson, showed proper attention to the First
Consul's brother, who had selected for his wife a
niece of the Secretary of the Navy, and of so influential a senator as General Smith.   Yet nothing irritated Napoleon more than Jerome's marriage.   In
some respects it was even more objectionable to him
than that of Lucien, which gave rise to a family feud.
Pichon suspected what would be the First Consul's

feelings, and wrote letter after letter to clear himself
of blame. In doing so he could not but excite Napoleon's anger against American society, and especially
against the family of his new sister-in-law.

" It appears, Citizen Minister," wrote Pichon to Talleyrand,[1] " that General Smith, who in spite of the contrary
assurances he has given me, has always had this alliance
much at heart, has thrown his eyes on the mission to
Paris as a means of appeasing (*ramener*) the First
Consul. He has long since aimed at the diplomatic
career, for which he is little qualified ; this motive and
the near return of Mr. Livingston have decided his taste.
For some time there has been much question of this
nomination among the friends of General Smith. There
is also question of promoting, on the part of the First
Consul, for minister to this country, a selection which
should be connected with the other. It is thought that
the appointment of M. Jerome Bonaparte would be an
honorable mode of leaving the First Consul's brother
time to have his fault forgotten, and of preparing his
return to favor."

Such readiness among Jefferson's advisers to court
the favors of the young First Consul was sure not to
escape the eyes of the embittered Federalists. Pichon's account, although sharp in allusions to General
Smith's " vanity," was mild compared with the scorn
of the New Englanders. Apparently the new matrimonial alliance was taken seriously by prominent
Republican leaders. One of the Massachusetts sena-

[1] Pichon to Talleyrand, 30 Pluviôse, An xii. (Feb. 16, 1804);
Archives des Aff. Étr., MSS.

tors mentioned in his diary [1] a " curious conversation
between S. Smith, Breckenridge, Armstrong, and
Baldwin, about ' Smith's nephew, the First Consul's
brother.' Smith swells upon it to very extraordinary
dimensions." Pichon openly spoke of the whole
family connection, including both Robert and Samuel
Smith, and even Wilson Cary Nicholas, as possessed
with " an inconceivable infatuation " for the match;
" it was really the young man who was seduced."
Nothing that Pichon could say affected them. Senator J. Q. Adams remarked : " the Smiths are so elated
with their supposed elevation by this adventure, that
one step more would fit them for the discipline of
Dr. Willis," — the famous English expert in mental
diseases.[2]

The President and his friends might not know
enough of Napoleon's character to foresee the irritation which such reports would create in his mind,
but they were aware of the contrast between their
treatment of Jerome Bonaparte and their slights to
Anthony Merry. Had they felt any doubt upon the
subject, the free comments of the British minister
and his wife would have opened their eyes. In
truth, no doubt existed. Washington society was
in a manner ordered to proscribe the Merrys and
Yrujo, and pay court to Jerome and the Smiths.

Had this been all, the matter would have ended in
a personal quarrel between the two envoys and the

[1] Diary of J. Q. Adams (Jan. 7, 1804), i. 284.
[2] Ibid.

two Virginians, with which the public would have had no concern. Jefferson's " canons of etiquette " would in such a case have had no further importance than as an anecdote of his social habits. The seriousness of Jefferson's experiments in etiquette consisted in the belief that they were part of a political system which involved a sudden change of policy toward two great Powers. The " canons " were but the social expression of an altered feeling which found its political expression in acts marked by equal disregard of usage. The Spanish minister had already reason to know what he might expect; for six weeks before Merry's dinners John Randolph proclaimed in the House that West Florida belonged to the United States, and within the week that preceded Merry's reception, he brought in the Bill which authorized the President to annex Mobile. After such a proceeding, no diplomatist would have doubted what meaning to put upon the new code of Republican society. Merry's arrival, at the instant of this aggression upon Spain, was the signal for taking toward England a higher tone.

Merry could not fail to see what lay before him. From the President, notwithstanding heelless slippers and " canons of etiquette," the British minister heard none but friendly words. After the formal ceremony of delivering the letter of credence was over, —

" He desired me to sit down," wrote Merry,[1] " when we conversed for some time on general affairs. The

[1] Merry to Hawkesbury, Dec. 6, 1803; MSS. British Archives.

sentiments which he expressed respecting those of Europe appeared very properly to be by no means favorable to the spirit of ambition and aggrandizement of the present ruler in France, or to the personal character in any respect of the First Consul, and still less so to his conduct toward all nations."

From this subject the President passed to Spanish affairs and to the Spanish protest against the Louisiana cession, founded on Bonaparte's pledge never to alienate that province.

" This circumstance," continued Merry, " as well as the resistance altogether which Spain had unexpectedly brought forward in words, Mr. Jefferson considered as highly ridiculous, and as showing a very pitiful conduct on her part, since she did not appear to have taken any measures to support it either by preparation of defence on the spot, or by sending there a force to endeavor to prevent the occupation of the country by the troops of the United States. He concluded by saying that possession of it would, at all events, be taken."

If Merry did not contrive, after his dinner at the White House, to impart this conversation to his colleagues Yrujo and Pichon, he must have been a man remarkably free from malice. Meanwhile he had his own affairs to manage, and Madison was not so forbearing as the President. Merry's first despatch announced to his Government that Madison had already raised his tone. Without delay the matter of impressments was brought into prominence. The "pretended" blockade of Martinique and Guadeloupe was also strongly characterized.

" It is proper for me to notice," said Merry in his report of these remonstrances,[1] " that Mr. Madison gave great weight to them by renewing them on every occasion of my seeing him, and by his expressing that they were matters upon which this Government could not possibly be silent until a proper remedy for the evil should be applied by his Majesty's government. His observations were, however, made with great temper, and accompanied with the strongest assurances of the disposition of this Government to conciliate, and to concur in whatever means could be devised which should not be absolutely derogatory to their independence and interests, to establish principles and rules which should be satisfactory to both parties. . . . But, my Lord, while it is my duty to do justice to Mr. Madison's temperate and conciliatory language, I must not omit to observe that it indicated strongly a design on the part of this Government to avail themselves of the present conjuncture by persisting steadily in their demands of redress of their pretended grievances, in the hope of obtaining a greater respect to their flag, and of establishing a more convenient system of neutral navigation than the interests of the British empire have hitherto allowed his Majesty to concur in."

The British government was aware that its so-called right of impressment and its doctrine of blockade rested on force, and could not be maintained against superior force; but this consciousness rendered England only the more sensitive in regard to dangers that threatened her supremacy. Knowing that the United

[1] Merry to Hawkesbury, Dec. 6, 1803 ; MSS. British Archives.

States would be justified in declaring war at any moment, Great Britain looked uneasily for the first symptoms of retaliation.   When Madison took so earnest a tone, Merry might reasonably expect that his words would be followed by acts.

These shocks were not all that the new British minister was obliged to meet at the threshold of his residence in Washington.   At the moment when he was, as he thought, socially maltreated, and when he was told by Madison that America meant to insist on her neutral rights, he learned that the Government did not intend to ratify Rufus King's boundary convention.   The Senate held that the stipulations of its fifth article respecting the Mississippi might embarrass the new territory west of the river.   King knew of the Louisiana cession when he signed the treaty ; but the Senate had its own views on the subject, and under the lead of General Smith [1] preferred to follow them, as it had done in regard to the second article of the treaty with France, Sept. 30, 1800, and as it was about to do in regard to Pinckney's claims convention, Aug. 11, 1802, with Spain.   Merry was surprised to find that Madison, instead of explaining the grounds of the Senate's hesitation, or entering into discussion of the precise geographical difficulty, contented himself with a bald statement of the fact.   The British minister thought that this was not the most courteous way of dealing with a treaty negotiated after a full acquaintance with all the cir-

[1] Diary of J. Q. Adams (Oct. 31, 1803), i. 269.

cumstances, and he wrote to his Government to be on its guard : [1] —

" Notwithstanding Mr. Madison's assurances to the contrary, I have some reason to suspect that ideas of encroachment on his Majesty's just rights are entertained by some persons who have a voice in deciding upon the question of the ratification of this convention, not to say that I have much occasion to observe, from circumstances in general, that there exists here a strong impression of the consequence which this country is supposed to have acquired by the recent additions to the territory of the United States, as well as by the actual situation of affairs in Europe."

In view of the Mobile Act, introduced into Congress by Randolph on behalf of the government a week before this letter was written, Merry's suspicions could hardly be called unreasonable. A like stretch of authority applied to the northwest territory would have produced startling results.

Merry's suspicions that some assault was to be made upon England were strengthened when Madison, December 5, in pursuance of a call from the Senate, sent a list of impressments reported to the Department during the last year. According to this paper the whole number of impressments was forty-six, — three of which were made by France and her allies ; while of the forty-three made by Great Britain twenty-seven of the seamen were not American citizens. Of the entire number, twelve were

[1] Merry to Hawkesbury, Dec. 6, 1803; MSS. British Archives.

stated to have had American papers; and of the
twelve, nearly half were impressed on land within
British jurisdiction. The grievance, serious as it
was, had not as yet reached proportions greater than
before the Peace of Amiens. Merry drew the inference that Jefferson's administration meant to adopt
stronger measures than had hitherto been thought
necessary. He soon began to see the scope which
the new policy was to take.

Dec. 22, 1803, Madison opened in a formal conference the diplomatic scheme which was the outcome
of these preliminary movements.[1] Beginning with a
repetition of complaints in regard to impressments,
and dwelling upon the great irritation created by
such arbitrary acts, the secretary next remonstrated
against the extent given to the law of blockade by
British cruisers in the West Indies, and at length
announced that the frequent repetition of these grievances had rendered it necessary for the United States
to take immediate steps to find a remedy for them.
Instructions would therefore be shortly sent to Monroe at London to negotiate a new convention on these
subjects. The American government would wish
that its flag should give complete protection to whatever persons might be under it, excepting only military enemies of the belligerent. Further, it would
propose that the right of visiting ships at sea should
be restrained; that the right of blockade should be
more strictly defined, and American ships be allowed,

[1] Merry to Hawkesbury, Dec. 31, 1803; MSS. British Archives.

in consideration of the distance, to clear for blockaded ports on the chance of the blockade being removed before they arrived; and finally that the direct
trade between the West Indies and Europe should be
thrown open to American commerce without requiring
it to pass through a port of the United States.

In return Madison offered to the British government the unconditional surrender of deserters by sea
and land, together with certain precautions against
the smuggling of articles contraband of war.

Although Madison pressed the necessity of an immediate understanding on these points, he did so in
his usual temperate and conciliatory manner; while
Merry frankly avowed that he could give no hopes of
such propositions being listened to. He did this the
more decisively because Congress seemed about to
take the matter of impressments into its own hands,
and was already debating a Bill for the protection of
seamen by measures which tended to hostilities.
Madison disavowed responsibility for the legislation,
although he defended it in principle.[1] Merry contented himself for the time by saying that if the
United States government sought their remedy in
municipal law, the matter would immediately cease
to be a subject of negotiation.

Thus, in one short month, the two governments
were brought to what the British minister supposed to
be the verge of rupture. That any government should

---

[1] Merry to Hawkesbury, Jan. 20, 1804; Jan. 30, 1804; MSS.
British Archives.

take so well-considered a position without meaning to support it by acts, was not probable. Acts of some kind, more or less hostile in their nature, were certainly intended by the United States government in case Great Britain should persist in contempt for neutral rights ; the sudden change of tone at Washington left no doubt on this point. Edward Thornton, who had not yet been transferred to another post, wrote in consternation to the Foreign Office, fearing that blame might be attached to his own conduct while in charge of the legation : [1] —

" When I compare the complexion of Mr. Merry's correspondence with that of my own, particularly during the course of the last summer, before the intelligence of the Louisiana purchase reached this country, I can scarcely credit the testimony of my own senses in examining the turn which affairs have taken, and the manifest ill-will discovered toward us by the Government at the present moment. . . . I believe that the simple truth of the case is, after all, the circumstance . . . that a real change has taken place in the views of this Government, which may be dated from the first arrival of the intelligence relative to the Louisiana purchase, and which has since derived additional force and acrimony from the opinion that Great Britain cannot resist, under her present pressure, the new claims of the United States, and now, from the necessity they are under of recurring to the influence of France in order to support their demands against Spain. . . . The cession of Louisiana, notwithstanding that the circumstances under which it was made ought to

[1] Thornton to Hammond, Jan. 29, 1804 ; MSS. British Archives.

convince the vainest of men that he was not the sole
agent in the transaction, has elevated the President beyond imagination in his own opinion; and I have no
doubt that he thinks of securing himself at the next
election by having to boast of concessions and advantages
derived from us, similar to those he has gained from
France, — that is, great in appearance, and at a comparatively insignificant expense."

From such premises, the conclusion, so far as concerned England, was inevitable; and Thornton agreed
with Merry in affirming it without reserve : —

" Everything, as it relates to this government, now depends on our firmness.　If we yield an iota without a real
and perfect equivalent (not such imaginary equivalents as
Mr. Madison mentions to Mr. Merry), we are lost."

CHAPTER XVII.

WHATEVER objects the President and the Secretary of State may have expected to gain by their change of tone in the winter of 1803–1804 toward Spain and England, they must have been strangely free from human passions if they were unconscious of making at least two personal enemies upon whose ill-will they might count. If they were unaware of giving their victims cause for bitterness, — or if, as seemed more probable, they were indifferent to it, — the frequent chances of retaliation which the two ministers enjoyed soon showed that in diplomacy revenge was not only sweet but easy. Even the vehement Spanish hatred felt by Yrujo for Madison fell short of the patient Anglo-Saxon antipathy rooted in the minds of the British minister and his wife. When Yrujo, in March, 1804, burst into the State Department with the Mobile Act in his hand and denounced Madison to his face as party to an " infamous libel," he succeeded in greatly annoying the secretary without violating Jefferson's " canons of etiquette." Under the code of republican manners which the President and his secretary had introduced, they could not fairly object to anything which Yrujo might choose to say

or do. Absolute equality and " the rule of *pêle-mêle* "
reached their natural conclusion between such hosts
and guests in freedom of language and vehemence of
passion. What might have been Merry's feelings or
conduct had he met with more cordiality and courtesy
was uncertain ; but the mortifications of his first
month at Washington embittered his temper, and
left distinct marks of acrimony in the diplomacy
of America and England, until war wiped out the
memory of reciprocal annoyances. The Spaniard's
enmity was already a peril to Madison's ambition,
and one which became more threatening every day ;
but the Englishman's steady resentment was perhaps more mischievous, if less noisy. The first
effect of Jefferson's tactics was to ally the British
minister with Yrujo ; the second bound him to Senator Pickering and Representative Griswold ; the
third united his fortunes with those of Aaron Burr.
Merry entered the path of secret conspiracy ; he became the confidant of all the intriguers in Washington, and gave to their intrigues the support of his
official influence.

The Federalists worked mischievously to widen the
breach between the British minister and the President. They encouraged Merry's resentment. Late
in January, nearly two months after the first *pêle-
mêle*, Madison officially informed Merry for the first
time that the President meant to recognize no precedence between foreign ministers, but that all, even
including secretaries of legation in charge, were to be

treated with perfect equality, or what Madison termed
" a complete pell-mell," and would be received, even
at their first audience, with no more ceremony than
was practised toward any other individual.	Merry
replied that this notice should have been given to
him on his arrival, and that he could not acqui-
esce in it without instructions.	He then wrote to
his Government,[1] —

" I have now but too much reason to fear, what I did
not at first suspect, that the marked inattention toward
me of the present Administration of this country has
been a part of their unfriendly disposition toward his
Majesty and toward the nation which I have the
honor to represent."

At the same moment, in January and February,
1804, Pickering and Griswold were plotting their New
England confederacy.	Merry was taken by them into
the secret, and gave them aid.	The Senate, February
9, voted to strike out the fifth article of Rufus
King's boundary convention, and to approve the
other articles, which provided for fixing the disputed boundary-line of Maine, New Hampshire, and
Vermont.	Merry wrote to his Government that the
object of cancelling the fifth article was to deprive
Great Britain of her treaty-right to navigate the
Mississippi : [2] —

[1] Merry to Hawkesbury, Jan. 30, 1804 ; MSS. British
Archives.

[2] Merry to Hawkesbury, March 1, 1804 : MSS. British
Archives.

"It is hardly necessary for me to point out to your Lordship that the other articles of the convention are of great importance to the Eastern States of America, which are much interested in the immediate settlement of the eastern boundary. I am led to believe from the language of some of the members of this State [Massachusetts] that their anxiety on this head is so great that the rejection of those articles by his Majesty would, as having been occasioned by the exclusion on the part of this government of the fifth article, prove to be a great exciting cause to them to go forward rapidly in the steps which they have already commenced toward a separation from the Southern part of the Union. The members of the Senate have availed themselves of the opportunity of their being collected here to hold private meetings on this subject, and I learn from them that their plans and calculations respecting the event have been long seriously resolved. They think that whenever it shall take place it will happen suddenly, yet with quietness and the universal concurrence of the people. Although it does not appear to be their opinion that any external secret agency would accelerate the moment, they naturally look forward to Great Britain for support and assistance whenever the occasion shall arrive."

As the summer of 1804 came on, Merry's despatches grew more sombre. He reported that at Norfolk twelve British ships were detained at one time in consequence of the desertion of their seamen, several of whom had entered the United States service on the frigates which were under orders for Tripoli. Six British seamen having deserted at Charleston and re-enlisted in the same way, Merry remonstrated. He was told that the seamen, having voluntarily enlisted in the United States service, could not be restored, because the British government never restored American seamen who had voluntarily enlisted. Merry could only reply that the British government did not knowingly enlist deserters. On the other hand, Madison remonstrated in " high language," " accompanied even with some degree of menace," against the conduct of Captain Bradley of the frigate " Cambrian," one of the British squadron cruising off Sandy Hook, for taking a British seaman out of a British vessel within American jurisdiction. Merry added that in contrast to this strictness toward England the authorities had allowed the officers of the French frigate " La Poursuivante," at Baltimore, to send armed parties on shore at night for the purpose of seizing French seamen, one of whom they had actually taken by force from a Spanish vessel lying at the wharf.

" From this government having brought into such serious discussion objects which would certainly have passed unnoticed had they occurred in relation to the King's enemies, his Majesty's ministers may be led to suspect that such a resolution has been dictated by some hostile design," wrote Merry, with increasing solemnity ; " but it is proper for me to observe that . . . I cannot persuade myself that they will dare to provoke hostilities with his Majesty, at least before Mr. Jefferson's re-election to the Presidency shall have taken place." [1]

[1] Merry to Harrowby, July 18, 1804; MSS. British Archives.

Merry made a representation to Madison on impressments; but his arguments did not satisfy the secretary. "This specimen of Merry shows him to be a mere diplomatic pettifogger," wrote Madison privately to the President.[1]

Merry's temper was in this stage of ever-increasing irritability, when an event occurred which gave him, as it seemed, a chance to gratify his resentments. After the adjournment of Congress in March the British minister heard nothing from Pickering and Griswold. Early in June he wrote home that the democrats were carrying all the elections:[2] —

"In addition to this triumph of the reigning party, there have lately appeared in the prints of this country, which are generally made the instruments of the measures of all parties, publications of the discovery that has been made of secret meetings held at this place by some of the Federal members during the last sitting of Congress for the purpose of consulting upon the important point of the separation of the Eastern from the Southern States, which publications seem to have imposed a complete silence upon the Federal adherents."

A few weeks afterward, July 11, occurred the duel between Burr and Hamilton. Merry had no relations with Hamilton, and felt no peculiar interest in his fate; but he had become intimate with Burr at Washington, and watched his career with the curiosity which

[1] Madison to Jefferson, Aug. 28, 1804; Jefferson MSS.

[2] Merry to Hawkesbury, June 2, 1804; MSS. British Archives.

was the natural result of their common hatred of Jefferson. July 21 Burr fled from New York, and a few days afterward reached Philadelphia, where Merry was passing the summer. While there, Burr sent one of his friends — an Englishman named Williamson — to the British minister with a startling message, which Merry immediately transmitted to his Government: [1] —

"I have just received an offer from Mr. Burr, the actual Vice-President of the United States (which situation he is about to resign), to lend his assistance to his Majesty's government in any manner in which they may think fit to employ him, particularly in endeavoring to effect a separation of the western part of the United States from that which lies between the Atlantic and the mountains, in its whole extent. His proposition on this and other subjects will be fully detailed to your Lordship by Colonel Williamson, who has been the bearer of them to me, and who will embark for England in a few days. It is therefore only necessary for me to add that if after what is generally known of the profligacy of Mr. Burr's character, his Majesty's minister should think proper to listen to his offer, his present situation in this country, where he is now cast off as much by the democratic as by the Federal party, and where he still preserves connections with some people of influence, added to his great ambition and spirit of revenge against the present Administration, may possibly induce him to exert the talents and activity which he possesses with fidelity to his employers."

[1] Merry to Harrowby, Aug. 6, 1804 ; MSS. British Archives.

Meanwhile a change of ministry occurred in England. Pitt returned to power, representing a state of feeling toward America very different from that which prevailed under the mild rule of Addington. Subordinates were quick to feel such changes in the temper of their superiors. Every British officer knew that henceforth he had behind him an energetic government, which required vigorous action in maintaining what it claimed as British rights. Merry felt the new impulse like the rest; but Pitt's return acted most seriously on the naval service. After the renewal of the war in May, 1803, a small British squadron cruised off Sandy Hook, keeping a sharp look-out for French frigates in New York Harbor, and searching every merchant-vessel for enemy's property. During the summer of 1804 this annoyance became steadily greater, until the port of New York was almost blockaded, and every vessel that sailed out or in was liable not only to be stopped and searched, but to lose some part of its crew by impressment. The British ministry did indeed instantly recall Captain Bradley of the "Cambrian" for violating American jurisdiction, and gave strict orders for the lenient exercise of belligerent rights; but all the more it showed the intention of insisting upon the submission of America to such rules as England should prescribe. The President, already in trouble with Spain, began to feel the double peril; but Congress pressed him forward, and even while busy with the trial of Judge Chase it found time for two measures which greatly disturbed the British envoy.

The first of these measures was an "Act for the more effectual preservation of peace in the ports and harbors of the United States." Under this law any United States marshal, on the warrant of any United States judge, was bound to board any British or other foreign ship-of-war lying in American waters, and seize every person charged with having violated the peace. If the marshal should be resisted, or if surrender was not made, he must call in the military power, and compel surrender by force of arms. If death should ensue, he should be held blameless; but the resisting party should be punished as for felonious homicide. Further, the President was authorized to interdict at will the ports of the United States to all or any armed vessels of a foreign nation; and to arrest and indict any foreign officer who should come within the jurisdiction after committing on the high seas "any trespass or tort, or any spoliation, on board any vessel of the United States, or any unlawful interruption or vexation of trading-vessels actually coming to or going from the United States."

Such laws were commonly understood in diplomacy as removing the subject in question from the field of negotiation, preliminary to reprisals and war. The Act was passed with little debate in the last hours of the session, in the midst of the confusion which followed the acquittal of Judge Chase.

Merry immediately called on the Secretary of State, and asked him for some assurance that might serve to quiet the apprehensions which his Government would feel on reading the Act.[1] Madison could give none, except that the President would probably not exercise for the present his discretionary powers. As for the words, " any trespass or tort," Madison frankly avowed " he could not but confess they were meant to imply the impressment of any individual whatsoever from on board an American vessel, the exercise of which pretended right on the part of his Majesty's officers was a matter, he said, which the sense of the people at large would never allow the government of this country to acquiesce in."

To this announcement Merry replied in substance that the right was one which would certainly never be abandoned by his Government ; and there the matter rested at the close of Jefferson's first term. Madison assured the British minister that the authority granted to the President by Congress over foreign ships of war in American waters would not at present be enforced. He went even a step further toward conciliation. The Legislature of Virginia was induced quietly to modify the Act which had hitherto offered so much encouragement to the desertion of British seamen.[2]

The second threatening measure was a Resolution of the Senate, March 2, 1805, calling upon the Secre-

[1] Merry to Harrowby, March 4, 1805; MSS. British Archives.
[2] Merry to Harrowby, March 29, 1805; MSS. British Archives.

tary of State for such Acts of the British Parliament
as imposed heavier duties on the exportation of merchandise to the United States than on similar goods
exported to the nations of Europe. Such an export duty upon merchandise for the United States
and the West Indies had in fact been imposed by
Parliament some two years before ; and this Resolution foreshadowed some commercial retaliation
by Congress.

While sending to his Government these warnings
to expect from Jefferson's second administration a
degree of hostility more active than from the first,
Merry suggested means of giving the United States
occupation that should induce them to leave England
alone. A new element of conspiracy disclosed itself
to the British minister.

Under the Louisiana treaty of cession, the United
States government had promised that " the inhabitants of the ceded territory shall be incorporated in
the Union of the United States, and admitted as soon
as possible, according to the principles of the Federal
Constitution, to the enjoyment of all the rights, advantages, and immunities of citizens of the United
States." This pledge had been broken. The usual
display of casuistry had been made to prove that the
infraction of treaty was no infraction at all ; but
the more outspoken Republicans avowed, as has been
already shown, that the people of Louisiana could not
be trusted, or in the commoner phrase that they were
unfit for self-government, and must be treated as a

conquered race until they learned to consider themselves American citizens.

The people of New Orleans finding themselves in a position of dependence, which, owing chiefly to their hatred of Governor Claiborne, seemed more irritating than their old Spanish servitude, sent three representatives to Washington to urge upon Congress the duty of executing the treaty. Messieurs Sauvé, Derbigny, and Destréhan accordingly appeared at Washington, and in December, 1804, presented a remonstrance so strong that Government was greatly embarrassed to deal with it.[1] Any reply that should repudiate either the treaty obligation or the principles of American liberty and self-government was out of the question; any reply that should affirm either the one or the other was fatal to the system established by Congress in Louisiana. John Randolph, on whose shoulders the duty fell, made a report on the subject. "It is only under the torture," said he, "that this article of the treaty of Paris can be made to speak the language ascribed to it by the memorialists;" but after explaining in his own way what the article did not mean, he surprised his audience by admitting in effect that the law of the last session was repugnant to the Constitution, and that the people of Louisiana had a right to self-government.[2] Senator Giles said

[1] Remonstrance of the People of Louisiana, Dec. 31, 1804; Annals of Congress, 1804–1805, Appendix, p. 1597.

[2] Report of Committee, Jan. 25, 1805; Annals of Congress, 1804–1805, p. 1014.

in private that Randolph's report was "a perfect transcript of Randolph's own character; it began by setting the claims of the Louisianians at defiance, and concluded with a proposal to give them more than they asked."[1]

Under these influences the three delegates from the creole society succeeded in getting, not what they asked, but a general admission that the people of Louisiana had political rights, which Congress recognized by an Act, approved March 2, 1805, to the extent of allowing them to elect a General Assembly of twenty-five representatives, and of promising them admission into the Union whenever their free inhabitants should reach the number of sixty thousand. Considering that the people of Louisiana were supposed to be entitled to " *all* the rights, advantages, and immunities of citizens," Messieurs Sauvé, Derbigny, and Destréhan thought the concession too small, and expressed themselves strongly on the subject. Naturally the British minister, as well as other ill-affected persons at Washington, listened eagerly to the discontent which promised to breed hostility to the Union.

" The deputies above mentioned," wrote Merry to his Government,[2] " who while they had any hopes of obtaining the redress of their grievances had carefully avoided giving any umbrage or jealousy to the Government by visiting or holding any intercourse with the

[1] Diary of J. Q. Adams (Feb. 1, 1805), i. 342.

[2] Merry to Harrowby, (No. 14), March 29, 1805; MSS. British Archives.

agents of foreign Powers at this place, when they found that their fate was decided, although the law had not as yet passed, no longer abstained from communicating with those agents, nor from expressing very publicly the great dissatisfaction which the law would occasion among their constituents, — going even so far as to say that it would not be tolerated, and that they would be obliged to seek redress from some other quarter; while they observed that the opportunity they had had of obtaining a correct knowledge of the state of things in this country, and of witnessing the proceedings of Congress, afforded them no confidence in the stability of the Union, and furnished them with such strong motives to be dissatisfied with the form and mode of government as to make them regret extremely the connection which they had been forced into with it. These sentiments they continued to express till the moment of their departure from hence, which took place the day after the close of the session."

Another man watched the attitude of the three delegates with extreme interest. Aaron Burr, March 4, 1805, ceased to hold the office of Vice-president. Since the previous August he had awaited the report of his friend Colonel Williamson, who entered into conferences with members of the British ministry, hoping to gain their support for Burr's plan of creating a Western Confederacy in the Valley of the Ohio. No sooner was Burr out of office than he went to Merry with new communications, which Merry hastened to send to his Government in a despatch marked "Most secret" in triplicate.[1]

[1] Merry to Harrowby, (No. 15), most secret, March 29, 1805.

" Mr. Burr (with whom I know that the deputies became very intimate during their residence here) has mentioned to me that the inhabitants of Louisiana seem determined to render themselves independent of the United States, and that the execution of their design is only delayed by the difficulty of obtaining previously an assurance of protection and assistance from some foreign Power, and of concerting and connecting their independence with that of the inhabitants of the western parts of the United States, who must always have a command over them by the rivers which communicate with the Mississippi. It is clear that Mr. Burr (although he has not as yet confided to me the exact nature and extent of his plan) means to endeavor to be the instrument of effecting such a connection."

For this purpose Burr asked the aid of the British government, and defined the nature of the assistance he should need, — a British squadron at the mouth of the Mississippi, and a loan of half a million dollars.

" I have only to add that if a strict confidence could be placed in him, he certainly possesses, perhaps in a much greater degree than any other individual in this country, all the talents, energy, intrepidity, and firmness which are required for such an enterprise."

Pending an answer to this proposal, Burr was to visit New Orleans and make himself the head of creole disaffection.

Merry was launched into the full tide of conspiracy. At the close of Jefferson's first term he saw reason to hope that he might soon repay with interest the debt of personal and political annoyance which he owed.

While Yrujo was actively engaged in bringing upon
Madison the anger of Spain and France, Merry
endeavored to draw his Government into a system
of open and secret reprisals upon the President.

That the new French minister was little better disposed than Merry and Yrujo has been already shown;
but his causes for ill-will were of a different and less
personal nature. Before Turreau's arrival at Washington in November, 1804, Pichon in one of his last
despatches declared that Jefferson had already alienated every foreign Power whose enmity could be
dangerous to the United States.

"The state of foreign relations offers a perspective
which must put Mr. Jefferson's character to proof,"
Pichon wrote to Talleyrand in September, 1804.[1] "The
United States find themselves compromised and at odds
with France, England, and Spain at the same time. This
state of things is in great part due to the indecision of
the President, and to the policy which leads him to sacrifice everything for the sake of his popularity."

The complaint was common to all French ministers
in the United States, and meant little more than that
all Presidents and policies displeased them by stopping short of war on England, which was the object
of French diplomacy ; but this letter also showed that
in Pichon's eyes the President had no friends. When
Turreau arrived, a few weeks afterward, he quickly
intimated that the President need expect from him

[1] Pichon to Talleyrand, 16 Fructidor, An xii. (Sept. 3, 1804);
Archives des Aff. Étr., MSS.

not even such sentimental sympathy as had been so kindly given by Pichon.

At the same moment it was noticed that Jefferson changed his style of dress. "He has improved much in the article of dress," wrote Senator Plumer in December, 1804 ;[1] "he has laid aside the old slippers, red waistcoat, and soiled corduroy small-clothes, and was dressed all in black, with clean linen and powdered hair." Apparently the President had profited by the criticisms of the British minister, and was willing to avoid similar comments from the new French envoy ; but he supposed that the Frenchman would show equal civility, and assume an equally republican style. He was mistaken. November 23, undisturbed by Merry's experience, Turreau presented himself at his first audience in full regimentals, and with so much gold lace that Jefferson was half inclined to resent it as an impertinence.[2] Turreau next refused to meet Merry at dinner. He followed up these demonstrations by embracing the cause of Yrujo, and ridiculing Madison to his face. He began by warning his Government that "these people have been thoroughly spoiled ; it is time to put them back into their place."[3]

Turreau became intimate with the deputies from Louisiana, and notified Talleyrand that a separation of

[1] Life of Plumer, p. 326.

[2] Diary of J. Q. Adams (Nov. 23, 1804), i. 316.

[3] Turreau to Talleyrand, 27 Janvier, 1805 ; Archives des Aff. Étr., MSS.

the western country from the Union was universally
expected. Already, within three months of his arrival,
he put his finger on the men who were to accomplish
it.[1] Destréhan, he said, was a man of high merit;
" but being only moderately ambitious, and head of a
numerous family, — having acquired, too, a great personal esteem, — he is not likely to become the principal mover in innovations which are always dangerous
without a combination of evidently favorable chances.
It is still less likely that he will ever be the instrument of strangers who should seek to excite troubles
for their personal advantage." As for Sauvé, much
inferior to his colleague in abilities, he would be
guided by Destréhan's influence. Derbigny was different. " Young still, with wit, ready expression,
and French manners, I believe him to be greedy of
fortune and fame; I suspect that every *rôle* will suit
him, in order to acquire the one or the other; but
there are men of more importance whom circumstances are taking to Louisiana."

Then Turreau, for the information of Talleyrand,
drew a portrait of the military commander of Upper
Louisiana, who had his headquarters at St. Louis, and
whose influence on future events was to be watched.

" General Wilkinson is forty-eight years of age. He
has an amiable exterior. Though said to be well-informed
in civil and political matters, his military capacity is
small. Ambitious and easily dazzled, fond of show and

[1] Turreau to Talleyrand, 9 Mars, 1805 ; Archives des Aff. Étr.,
MSS.

appearances, he complains rather indiscreetly, and especially after dinner, of the form of his government, which leaves officers few chances of fortune, advancement, and glory, and which does not pay its military chiefs enough to support a proper style. He listened with pleasure, or rather with enthusiasm, to the details which I gave him in regard to the organization, the dress, and the force of the French army. My uniform, the order with which I am decorated, are objects of envy to him; and he seems to hold to the American service only because he can do no better. General Wilkinson is the most intimate friend, or rather the most devoted creature, of Colonel Burr."

Talleyrand had become acquainted with Burr in the United States, and needed no warnings against him; but Turreau showed himself well-informed:

" Mr. Burr's career is generally looked upon as finished; but he is far from sharing that opinion, and I believe he would rather sacrifice the interests of his country than renounce celebrity and fortune. Although Louisiana is still only a Territory, it has obtained the right of sending a delegate to Congress. Louisiana is therefore to become the theatre of Mr. Burr's new intrigues; he is going there under the ægis of General Wilkinson."

Perhaps Turreau received this information from Derbigny, which might account for his estimate of the young man. Certainly Derbigny knew all that Turreau reported, for in an affidavit [1] two years afterward he admitted his knowledge.

[1] Affidavit of Peter Derbigny, Aug. 27, 1807. Clark's Proofs against Wilkinson; Note 18. App. p. 38.

" In the winter of 1804–1805," Derbigny made oath, " being then at Washington City in the capacity of a deputy from the inhabitants of Louisiana to Congress, jointly with Messrs. Destréhan and Sauvé, he was introduced to Colonel Burr, then Vice-president of the United States, by General Wilkinson, who strongly recommended to this deponent, and as he believes to his colleagues, to cultivate the acquaintance of Colonel Burr, — whom he used to call ' the first gentleman in America,' telling them that he was a man of the most eminent talents both as a politician and as a military character ; and . . . General Wilkinson told him several times that Colonel Burr, so soon as his Vice-presidency would be at an end, would go to Louisiana, where he had certain projects, adding that he was such a man as to succeed in anything he would undertake, and inviting this deponent to give him all the information in his power respecting that country ; which mysterious hints appeared to this deponent very extraordinary, though he could not then understand them."

What Derbigny in 1807 professed not to have understood, seemed in 1804 clear to Turreau and Merry as well as to others. Turreau closed his catalogue by the significant remark : " I am not the only person who thinks that the assemblage of such men in a country already discontented is enough to give rise to serious troubles there." The treasonable plans of Burr and Wilkinson were a matter of common notoriety, and roused anxious comment even in the mind of John Randolph, who was nursing at home the mortification of Judge Chase's acquittal.[1] Randolph complained of "the easy cre-dulity of Mr. Jefferson's temper," which made the President a fit material for intriguers to work upon. Certainly at the close of his first administration Jefferson seemed surrounded by enemies. The New England Federalists, the Louisiana creoles, Burr and his crew of adventurers in every part of the Union, joined hands with the ministers of England and Spain to make a hostile circle round the President; while the minister of France looked on without a wish to save the government whose friendship Bona-parte had sought to obtain at the cost of the most valuable province and the most splendid traditions of the French people.

[1] Adams's Randolph, p. 157.

CHAPTER XVIII.

AFTER aiding to negotiate the Louisiana treaty at Paris, in April and May, 1803, Monroe, as the story has already told, being forbidden by Bonaparte to pursue his journey to Madrid, followed his alternative instructions, to take the post which Rufus King was vacating in London. King left England in the middle of May, 1803; Monroe arrived in London July 18, when the war between England and France was already two months old.

The mild Addington ministry was still in power, and nothing had yet happened to excite Monroe's alarm in regard to British policy in the United States. On the contrary, the ministry aided the Louisiana purchase with readiness that might reasonably have surprised an American minister, while the friendliest spirit was shown by Lord Hawkesbury in all matters of detail. Except the standing dispute about impressments, every old point of collision had been successfully removed by King, whose two conventions, — the one for discharging British debts recognized by treaty, the other for settling the boundaries of New England and of the northwest territory, — seemed to free the countries for the first time from the annoying inheritance of disputes entailed by the definitive treaty which closed the Revolutionary War in 1783. The calm which seemed to prevail throughout England in regard to her relations with America contrasted sharply with the excitement shown by the English people in all their allusions to the Corsican demon, as they thought him, whose regiments, gathering at Boulogne, they might expect to see at any moment encamped at Hastings, where no hostile camp-fire had burned since the night, seven hundred years before, when the body of an English king, hedged about with the dead bodies of a whole English aristocracy, lay stiff and stark on the bloody hillside, victims of another French adventurer. England was intent on her own imminent dangers; and under the strain which the renewal of her painful efforts brought with it, she was glad to leave America alone.

Yet calm as the atmosphere appeared to be, signs of future storm were not wholly wanting. Had Monroe been naturally anxious, he might, without seeking far, have found cause for anxiety serious enough to take away all appetite for Spanish travel, and to hold him close to his post until some one should consent to relieve him from an ungrateful and unpromising duty. The American minister at London in 1804 could hope to gain nothing either for his country or for himself, and he stood always on the verge of disaster; but when he was required to take a "high tone" in the face of a nation almost insane with anxiety, he challenged more chances of mortification than any but a desperate politician would have cared to risk.

Monroe had at first nothing to do but to watch the course of public opinion in England. During the autumn of 1803, while President Jefferson and Secretary Madison at Washington received Merry with a changed policy, and all through the winter, while Washington was torn by " canons of etiquette" and by contests of strength between Jefferson, Madison, Casa Yrujo, and Merry, the United States minister in London was left at peace to study the political problems which bore on his own fortunes and on those of his friends at home, as well as on the interests of the Union.

Beneath the calm of general society mutterings of discontent from powerful interests could be heard, — occasional outbursts of jealousy, revivals of old and virulent passions, inveterate prejudices, which made as yet but little noise in the Press or in Parliament, but which rankled in the breasts of individuals. One of the earlier symptoms of trouble came in a familiar shape. For twenty years, whenever a question had arisen of hostility to American trade or of prejudice against American character, the first of Englishmen to stimulate it, and the loudest to proclaim the dangers of Great Britain, had been John Baker Holroyd, Earl of Sheffield, whose memory might have been lost under the weight of his pamphlets had it not been embalmed in the autobiography of Gibbon. Lord Sheffield felt such devotion to the

British navigation laws as could be likened only to
the idolatry which a savage felt toward his fetich;
one might almost have supposed that to him the
State, the Church, and the liberties of England, the
privileges of her nobility, and even the person of her
sovereign, were sacred chiefly because they guaranteed
the safety of her maritime system. This fanaticism
of an honest mind led to results so extravagant as to
become at times ridiculous. The existence of the
United States was a protest against Lord Sheffield's
political religion; and therefore in his eyes the United
States were no better than a nation of criminals,
capable of betraying their God for pieces of silver.
The independence of America had shattered the navigation system of England into fragments; but Lord
Sheffield clung the more desperately to his broken
idol. Among the portions which had been saved were
the West Indian colonies. If at that day the navigation laws had one object more important than another,
it was to foster the prosperity of these islands, in
order that their sugar and molasses, coffee and rum,
might give freight to British shippers and employment to British seamen; but to Lord Sheffield the
islands were only a degree less obnoxious than the
revolted United States, for they were American at
heart, complaining because they were forbidden to
trade freely with New York and Boston, and even
asserting that when the navigation laws were strictly
enforced their slaves died of starvation and disease.
Lord Sheffield seriously thought them ungrateful to

murmur, and held it their duty to perish in silence rather than ask a relaxation of the law.

The rupture of the Peace of Amiens, in May, 1803, set Lord Sheffield again at work; and unfortunately the material lay ready to his hand. The whole subject of his discourse related to a single fact; but this fact was full of alarm to the English people. The extraordinary decrease of British tonnage in the American trade, the corresponding increase of American shipping, and the loud exultation of the Yankees over the British shipmasters were proofs of the danger which menaced England, whose existence depended on maritime strength. In the month of February, 1804, Lord Sheffield published a pamphlet,[1] which dwelt on these calamities as due to the wanton relaxation of the navigation laws and the senseless clamor of the colonies. He was answered in a pamphlet[2] written by one of the colonial agents; and the answer was convincing, so far as Lord Sheffield's argument was concerned, but his array of statistics remained to disturb the British mind.

Monroe might therefore count on having, some day, to meet whatever mischief the shipping interest of Great Britain could cause. No argument was needed to prove that the navy would support with zeal whatever demands should be made by the mercantile

[1] Strictures, etc., on the Navigation and Colonial System of Great Britain. London, 1804.

[2] Claims of the British West Indian Colonists. By G. W. Jordan. London, 1804.

marine. There remained the immense influence of the West Indian colonies to consider; and if this should be brought into active sympathy with the ship-owners and the royal marine against American trade, no minister in England — not even Pitt himself at the height of his power — would be strong enough to resist the combination.

The staple product of the West Indian islands was sugar, and owing to several causes the profits of the planters had until 1798 been large. The insurrection of the Haytian negroes in 1792 annihilated for the time the supply of sugar from St. Domingo; prices rose in consequence, and a great increase in the number of sugar plantations naturally followed. Several of the Dutch and French islands fell into the hands of England, and adventurers flocked to them, eager to invest British capital in new sugar-fields. Under this impulse the supply again increased. Cuba, Porto Rico, Guadeloupe, and at last St. Domingo itself under Toussaint's rule poured sugar into the market. American ships carried French and Spanish sugar to Europe until it became a drug. The high price lasted till 1798; in that year Pitt even imposed a heavy additional duty upon it as a sure source of revenue. In 1799 the effect of over-production first became apparent. During the next few years the price of sugar fell, until great suffering began to pre-vail in the islands, and the planters wrote piteous letters of distress to England. Their agents wrote back that the English market was flooded with colonial produce : " Send no more sugar home ; give it away rather ! " was their advice, — and the colonists, without the means of purchasing even the necessaries of life, supplicated government to let them send their sugar to the United States, to be exchanged for American produce.[1]

This the government dared not do, for the shipping interest must in such a case be sacrificed. Debarred from this outlet for their produce, the colonists looked about them for some other resource ; and since they were not allowed to act independently of the ship-masters, they saw no other course than to join hands with the shipping interest, and to invoke the aid of the navigation laws. The glut of the European market was caused by American neutrals, who were allowed to carry French and Spanish sugars from the West Indies to Europe. If this neutral trade could be stopped, the supply of French and Spanish sugar would be left to rot in Cuba and Guadeloupe, while British colonial produce would enjoy a monopoly throughout Europe.

Even before the Peace of Amiens this policy gained many adherents, and the Peace tended to strengthen their influence. The Addington ministry was not only weak in character, but timid in policy ; and by a natural reaction it threw restless and ambitious younger statesmen into an attitude of protest. A new departure was felt to be necessary ; and the nervous energy of England, strained almost to in-

[1] Lowe's Enquiry, 4th edition, 1808.

sanity by the anxieties of ten years' desperate danger, exhausted itself in the cry for one great commanding spirit, who should meet Bonaparte with his own weapons on his own field.

This cry produced George Canning. Of him and his qualities much will be said hereafter, when his rise to power shall have made him a more prominent figure ; here need be noticed only the forces which sought assertion through him, and the nature of the passions which he was peculiarly qualified to express. At all times nations have been most imperilled by the violence of disappointed or terrified interests ; but the danger was never so great as when these interests joined to a greed for selfish gain the cry for an unscrupulous chief. Every American schoolboy once knew by heart the famous outburst of Canning, which began, " Away with the cant of ' measures, not men ' ! " but of the millions of persons who read or heard this favorite extract few understood its meaning to American interests and feelings. This celebrated speech, made Dec. 8, 1802, at a time when Addington's cautious ministry still held office, was intended to dwarf Addington and elevate Pitt, — to ridicule caution and extol violence. " Sir," cried Canning, " to meet, to check, to resist, to stand up against Bonaparte, we want arms of the same kind. I vote for the large military establishments with all my heart ; but for the purpose of coping with Bonaparte, one great, commanding spirit is worth them all."

" Arms of the same kind " were, speaking generally, irresponsible violence and disregard of morality. The great, commanding spirit of the moment was Mr. Pitt ; but between the lines of this speech, by the light of its author's whole career, the secret was easily read that in his opinion the man of the future who could best meet Bonaparte on his own ground with his own weapons was not William Pitt, but George Canning.

After many months of warfare against Addington, Canning was gratified. In May, 1804, Addington retired from office, carrying into the House of Lords the new title of Lord Sidmouth, while Pitt returned to power. No one of note returned with him. His old colleague, Lord Grenville, refused to join his Administration, and Charles James Fox was personally excluded by King George. To fill the Foreign Office Pitt could find no better man than Lord Harrowby, — a personage of very second-rate importance in politics. With a Cabinet so weak as to command little respect, and reactionary as was required to suit the King's growing prejudices, Pitt was obliged to disguise his feebleness by the vigor of his measures. While creating, by expenditure of money, a new coalition against Napoleon, he was unable to disregard the great moneyed and social interests which were clamoring for a spirited policy against neutrals and especially against America. In private he avowed his determination to re-establish the old system, and his regret that he should ever have been,

most reluctantly, induced to relax the maritime rights
of Britain.[1]

That Monroe should have been the last person in
London to know the secret thoughts of Pitt was not
surprising The Board of Trade commonly exerted
more influence than the Foreign Office over the relations of England with the United States ; and George
Rose, Vice-President of the Board of Trade, Pitt's devoted friend and a Tory after Lord Sheffield's heart,
would never have chosen Monroe as a confidant of
schemes under discussion in his department.   Lord
Harrowby was but the mouthpiece of other men.
From him Monroe could expect to hear only what
had already been decided.   Nevertheless a little study
of the mercantile interests of the city, and a careful
inquiry into the private opinions of men like Rose
and Canning, might have thrown some light on the
future, and would naturally have roused anxiety in
the mind of Monroe.

Pitt's return to power, with the intention of chan-
ging the American policy which had been pursued
since the negotiation of Jay's treaty, happened very
nearly to coincide with the arrival at the Foreign
Office of Merry's most alarming despatches, announcing that Madison required the total abandonment of
impressments, the restriction of blockades and the

---

[1] Anti-Jacobin Review, August, 1807, p. 368; Introduction to
Reports, etc., on Navigation, p. 22; Atcheson's American Encroachments, London, 1808, p. lxxvii; Baring's Inquiry, London,
1808, p. **73**.

right of search, and complete freedom in the colonial
trade, as the conditions on which the friendship of
the United States could be preserved. The announcement of President Jefferson's high tone was accompanied by the British minister's account of his own
social mortifications by the President and the Secretary of State ; of the Senate's refusal to approve the
fifth article of Rufus King's boundary convention,
in order to attack the British right of navigating the
Mississippi ; and by drafts of bills pending in Congress, under which any British admiral, even though
it were Nelson himself, who should ever have taken a
seaman out of an American vessel, was to be arrested
in the streets of the first American port where he
might go ashore, and to suffer indefinite imprison-
ment among thieves and felons in the calaboose.

May 30, 1804, Monroe had his first interview with
Lord Harrowby. In such cases the new secretary,
about to receive a foreign minister, commonly sent
for the late correspondence, in order to learn something about the subjects on which he was to have an
opinion. Beyond a doubt Lord Harrowby had on his
table the despatches of Merry, written between November and April, which he probably finished reading at
about the moment when Monroe was announced at
the door.

Under such circumstances, Monroe reported to his
Government that Lord Harrowby's manners were de-
signedly unfriendly ; his reception was rough, his comments on the Senate's habit of mutilating treaties

were harsh, his conduct throughout the interview
was calculated to wound and to irritate.[1] After this
unpromising experience, two months were allowed to
pass without further demonstration on either side.
Then Lord Harrowby called Monroe's attention to the
twelfth article of Jay's treaty, which regulated the
commercial relations between the British West Indies
and the United States, and which had expired by
limitation. He suggested its renewal, according to
its old terms, until two years after the next general
peace.   To this offer Monroe replied, with the utmost
frankness, " that the President wished to postpone
this matter until he could include impressment and
neutral rights in the treaty ; that we must begin *de
novo ;* that America was a young and thriving country ; that in 1794 she had had little experience, since
then she understood her interests better ; and that a
new treaty should omit certain things from that of
1794, and include others.   The most urgent part was
that which respected our seamen." [2]

An approaching contact of opposite forces always
interests men's imagination. On one side, Pitt and
Lord Harrowby stood meditating the details of measures, which they had decided in principle, for taking
from the United States most of the commercial advantages hitherto enjoyed by them ; on the other side
stood Monroe and Jefferson, equally confident, telling
the Englishmen that very much greater advantages

[1] Monroe to Madison, June 3, 1804; State Papers, iii. 92.
[2] Monroe to Madison, Aug. 7, 1804; State Papers, iii. 94.

must be conceded. That one or the other of these forces must very soon give way was evident; and if ever an American minister in London needed to be on the alert, with every faculty strained to its utmost, the autumn of 1804 was such a moment. Monroe, aware of his danger, gave full warning to the President. Even as early as June 3, after his first interview with Lord Harrowby, he wrote that a change of policy was imminent. "My most earnest advice is to look to the possibility of such a change."[1]

Lord Harrowby also gave every reasonable warning. His reply to Monroe's demands for further negotiation was simple, — nothing need be expected from him. He refused to do any business at all, on the plea of other occupations incident to the formation of a new ministry.[2] Monroe sent him the draft of the comprehensive treaty which Madison had forwarded, but Lord Harrowby declined for the present to discuss it. Then Monroe came to the conclusion that his presence in London was no longer necessary; and accordingly, Oct. 8, 1804, he started for Paris and Madrid. Until July 23, 1805, the legation at London was left in charge of a secretary.

A month after his departure, Lord Harrowby wrote a letter of instructions[3] to Merry in reply to the series of despatches received from Washington.

---

[1] Monroe to Madison, June 3, 1804; State Papers, iii. 92.

[2] Monroe to Madison, Sept. 8, 1804; MSS. State Department Archives.

[3] Harrowby to Merry, Nov. 7, 1804; MSS. British Archives.

" His Majesty's government," he said, " have perceived with considerable concern, from some of your most recent despatches, the increasing acrimony which appears to pervade the representations that have been made to you by the American Secretary of State on the subject of the impressment of seamen from on board of American ships. The pretension advanced by Mr. Madison that the American flag should protect every individual sailing under it on board of a merchant-ship is too extravagant to require any serious refutation. In the exercise of the right, which has been asserted by his Majesty and his predecessors for ages, of reclaiming from a foreign service the subjects of Great Britain, whether they are found on the high seas or in the ports of his own dominions, irregularities must undoubtedly frequently occur; but the utmost solicitude has been uniformly manifested by his Majesty's government to prevent them as far as may be possible, and to repress them whenever they have actually taken place."

Intending to pursue the same course in the future, the Government would without delay give the strictest orders to its naval officers " to observe the utmost lenity in visiting ships on the high seas, and to abstain from impressments in the ports of the United States."

In regard to commercial questions, Lord Harrowby offered to consider the treaty of 1794 as in force until some new arrangement could be formed. Until the decision of the President should be known, it was "intended to propose to Parliament to lodge the power of regulating the commerce with America in the King in Council, in the same manner as before the treaty of 1794." The offer of considering the treaty as in force " must be regarded as a boon to America; and it was made merely under the persuasion that if accepted it would be accepted with a view to maintain a friendly relation between the two countries, and to avoid in the interval everything which could lead to interrupt it. If this system is followed in America, it will be followed here in every respect with an anxious desire for the continuance of harmony and cordiality."

The same conditional and semi-threatening disposition toward good-will ran through the rest of these instructions. In regard to the boundary convention, his Majesty's government would at all times be ready to reopen the whole subject; " but they can never acquiesce in the precedent which in this as well as in a former instance the American government has endeavored to establish, of agreeing to ratify such parts of a convention as they may select, and of rejecting other stipulations of it, formally agreed upon by a minister invested with full powers for the purpose."

Finally, Merry was to " avoid, as far as possible, any language which might be conceived to be of a menacing or hostile tendency, or which might be construed into an indication of a desire on the part of his Majesty's government to decline any discussion of the several points now pending between the two countries." Lord Harrowby clearly wished to encourage discussion to the utmost. He left the

" canons of etiquette " unnoticed, and offered not even a hint at any change of policy meditated by his Government.

So matters remained in England during the last months of President Jefferson's first term. On both sides new movements were intended ; but while those of the United States government were foreseen and announced in advance by Merry, those of the British ministry were hidden under a veil of secrecy, which might perhaps have been no more penetrable to Monroe had he remained in London to watch them than they were to him in his retreat at Aranjuez.

To the world at large nothing in the relations of the United States with England, France, or Spain seemed alarming. The world knew little of what was taking place. Only men who stood between these forces could understand their movements and predict the moment of collision ; but if these men, like Merry, Turreau, and Yrujo, had been asked March 3, 1805, to point out the brightest part of Jefferson's political horizon, they would probably have agreed with one voice that everything in Europe threatened disaster, and that the only glimpse of blue sky was to be seen on the shores of Africa. The greatest triumph to be then hoped from Jefferson's peace policy was the brilliant close of his only war.

During the year 1804 the little American fleet in the Mediterranean made famous some names which within ten years were to become more famous still.

With the "Constitution," the only heavy frigate on
the station after the loss of the "Philadelphia," and
with half-a-dozen small brigs and schooners, Preble
worked manfully at his task of annoying the Pacha of
Tripoli.   Three years' experience showed that a mere
blockade answered no other purpose than to protect
in part American commerce.   It had not shaken the
Pacha in the demand of black-mail as his condition of
peace.   Bainbridge, still held a prisoner in the town,
believed that Jefferson must choose between paying
what the Pacha asked, or sending eight or ten thousand men to attack him in his castle.   Black-mail was
the life of the small pirate rulers, and they could not
abandon it without making a precedent fatal to themselves, and inviting insurrection from their subjects.
Preble could only strike the coast with fear; and during the summer of 1804 he began a series of dashing
assaults with the "Constitution," helped by four new
craft, — the "Argus" and "Syren," fine sixteen-gun
brigs; the "Nautilus" and "Vixen," fourteen-gun
schooners; the "Enterprise," of twelve guns, and a
captured Tripolitan brig of sixteen guns, re-named the
"Scourge," — all supported by eight small gunboats
borrowed from the King of Naples who was also at
war with Tripoli.   Thus commanding a force of about
one hundred and fifty guns, and more than a thousand men, August 3, carrying his flag-ship into the
harbor, Preble engaged the Tripolitan batteries at
very short range for two hours.   Fortunately, the
Mussulmans could not or did not depress their guns

enough to injure the frigate, and after throwing many broadsides into the batteries and town, Preble retired without losing a man. His gunboat flotilla was equally daring, but not so lucky. One division was commanded by Lieutenant Somers, the other by Stephen Decatur. They attacked the Tripolitan gunboats and captured three, besides sinking more; but James Decatur was killed. A few days afterward, August 7, the attack was repeated, and some five hundred 24-lb. shot were thrown into the batteries and town. August 24 a third bombardment took place within the month; and although Preble knew that Barron was near at hand with a strong reinforcement, August 29 he carried his flotilla a fourth time into the harbor, and again threw several hundred solid shot into the town. A fifth bombardment, the heaviest of all, took place early in September. In these affairs, so poor was the Tripolitan gunnery or courage that the Americans suffered almost no loss beyond that of a few spars. The only serious disaster, besides the death of James Decatur, was never explained. Preble, wishing to try the effect of a fireship, on the night of September 4 sent one of his best officers, Lieutenant Somers, into the harbor with the ketch "Intrepid" filled with powder, bombs, and shell. The "Argus," "Vixen," and "Nautilus" escorted Somers to shoal water, and waited for him to rejoin them in his boats. They saw the batteries fire upon him; then they heard a sudden and premature explosion. All night the three cruisers waited anxiously outside, but Somers never returned. He and his men vanished ; no vestige or tidings of them could ever be found.

Considering Preble's narrow means, the economy of the Department, and the condition of his small vessels, nothing in American naval history was more creditable than the vigor of his blockade in the summer of 1804 ; but he could not confidently assert that any number of such attacks would force the Pacha to make peace. A week after the loss of Somers in the " Intrepid " Commodore Samuel Barron arrived, bringing with him nearly the whole available navy of the United States, and relieved Preble from the command. Preble returned home, and was rewarded for his services by a gold medal from Congress. Two years afterward he died of consumption.

Barron had with him such a force as the United States never before or since sent in hostile array across the ocean, — two forty-fours, the " Constitution " and the " President ; " two thirty-eight gun frigates, the " Constellation " and the " Congress ; " the " Essex," of thirty-two guns ; the new brigs, " Hornet " of eighteen, and the " Syren " and " Argus " of sixteen ; the twelve-gun schooners " Vixen," " Nautilus," and " Enterprise ; " ten new, well-built American gunboats ; and two bomb-vessels. With the exception of the frigates " Chesapeake " and " United States," hardly a sea-going vessel was left at home. Commanded by young officers like John Rodgers and Stephen Decatur, Chauncey, Stewart, and Isaac Hull, such a squadron reflected credit on Robert Smith's administration of the navy.

Nevertheless the Pacha did not yield, and Barron was obliged by the season to abandon hope of making his strength immediately felt. Six months later the commodore, owing to ill-health, yielded the command to John Rodgers, while the Pacha was still uninjured by the squadron. As the summer of 1805 approached, fear of Rodgers's impending attack possibly helped to turn the Pacha's mind toward concession; but his pacific temper was also much affected by events on land, in which appeared so striking a combination of qualities, — enterprise and daring so romantic and even Quixotic that for at least half a century every boy in America listened to the story with the same delight with which he read the Arabian Nights.

A Connecticut Yankee, William Eaton, was the hero of the adventure. Born in 1764, Eaton had led a checkered career. At nineteen he was a sergeant in the Revolutionary army. After the peace he persisted, against harassing difficulties, in obtaining what was then thought a classical education; in his twenty-seventh year he took a degree at Dartmouth. He next opened a school in Windsor, Vermont, and was chosen clerk to the Vermont legislature. Senator Bradley, in 1792, procured for him a captain's commission in the United States army. His career in the service was varied by insubordination, disobedience to orders, charges, counter-charges, a court-martial, and a sentence of suspension not confirmed by the Secretary of War. In 1797 he was sent as consul to Tunis, where he remained until the outbreak of the war with Tripoli in 1801. Tunis was the nearest neighbor to Tripoli, about four hundred miles away; and the consul held a position of much delicacy and importance. In the year 1801 an elder brother of the reigning Pacha of Tripoli resided in Tunis, and to him Eaton turned in the hope of using his services. This man, Hamet Caramelli, the rightful Pacha of Tripoli, had been driven into exile some eight or nine years before by a rebellion which placed his younger brother Yusuf on the throne. Eaton conceived the idea of restoring Hamet, and by this act of strength impressing all the Mahometan Powers with terror of the United States. In pursuit of this plan he spent more than twenty thousand dollars, embroiled himself with the Bey of Tunis, quarrelled with the naval commanders, and in 1803 returned to America to lay his case before the President and Congress.

Although no one could be surprised that the President and his Cabinet hesitated to put themselves without reserve in the hands of an adventurer, Eaton's anger was extreme at finding the Government earnest for peace rather than war. Himself a Connecticut Federalist, a close friend of Timothy Pickering, he expressed his feelings in his private letters with the bitterness as well as with the humor of his class.[1]

[1] Life of General William Eaton, Brookfield, 1813, p. 262.

" I waited on the President and the Attorney-General. One of them was civil, and the other grave. . . . I endeavored to enforce conviction on the mind of Mr. Lincoln of the necessity of meeting the aggressions of Barbary by retaliation. He waived the subject, and amused me with predictions of a political millennium which was about to happen in the United States. The millennium was to usher in upon us as the irresistible consequence of the goodness of heart, integrity of mind, and correctness of disposition of Mr. Jefferson. All nations, even pirates and savages, were to be moved by the influence of his persuasive virtue and masterly skill in diplomacy."

Eaton's interviews probably took place at the moment when the Louisiana treaty confirmed the Cabinet in its peace policy and in reliance on diplomacy. In March, 1804, Eaton succeeded in returning to the Mediterranean as naval agent, but without special powers for the purpose he had in mind.

" The President becomes reserved; the Secretary of War ' believes we had better pay tribute,' — he said this to me in his own office. Gallatin, like a cowardly Jew, shrinks behind the counter. Mr. Madison ' leaves everything to the Secretary of the Navy Department.' And I am ordered on the expedition by Secretary Smith, — who, by the by, is as much of a gentleman and a soldier as his relation with the Administration will suffer, — without any special instructions to regulate my conduct."

With no other authority to act as a military officer than a vague recommendation from the President as a man who was likely to be extremely useful to Barron, Eaton returned with Barron's large squadron.

He felt himself ill-treated, for he was irritable and
self-asserting by nature, and was haunted by a fixed
idea too unreasonable for the President to adopt; but
he chose to act without authority rather than not act
at all, for he was born an adventurer, and difficulties
which seemed to cooler heads insurmountable were
nothing in his eyes.   Sept. 5, 1804, he arrived at
Malta, and thence sailed to Alexandria; for in the
meanwhile Hamet had been driven to take refuge in
Egypt, and Eaton on reaching Cairo, Dec. 8, 1804,
found that the object of his search was shut up in
Minyeh on the Nile with some rebellious Mamelukes,
besieged by the viceroy's troops.   After infinite exertions and at no little personal danger, Eaton brought
Hamet to Alexandria, where they collected some five
hundred men, of whom one hundred were Christians
recruited on the spot.   Eaton made a convention
with Hamet, arranged a plan of joint operations with
Barron, and then at about the time when President
Jefferson was delivering his second Inaugural Address,
the navy agent led his little army into the desert with
the courage of Alexander the Great, to conquer an
African kingdom.

So motley a horde of Americans, Greeks, Tripolitans,
and Arab camel-drivers had never before been seen
on the soil of Egypt.   Without discipline, cohesion, or
sources of supply, even without water for days, their
march of five hundred miles was a sort of miracle.
Eaton's indomitable obstinacy barely escaped ending
in his massacre by the Arabs, or by their desertion in

a mass with Hamet at their head ; yet in about six weeks they succeeded, April 17, 1805, in reaching Bomba, where to Eaton's consternation and despair he found no American ships.[1]

" Nothing could prevail on our Arabs to believe that any had been there. They abused us as impostors and infidels, and said we had drawn them into that situation with treacherous views. All began now to think of the means of individual safety ; and the Arabs came to a resolution to separate from us the next morning. I recommended an attempt to get into Derne. This was thought impracticable. I went off with my Christians, and kept up fires upon a high mountain in our rear all night. At eight the next morning, at the instant when our camp was about breaking up, the Pacha's casnadar, Zaid, who had ascended the mountain for a last look-out, discovered *a sail!* It was the ' Argus ;' Captain Hull had seen our smokes, and stood in. Language is too poor to paint the joy and exultation which this messenger of life excited in every breast."

Drawing supplies from the brig the little army rested a few days ; and then, April 25, moved against Derne, where they found the town held by a garrison of eight hundred men who had thrown up earthworks and loopholed the terraces and houses for musketry. Eaton sent to the governor a flag of truce, which was sent back with the Eastern message, — " My head, or yours ! " Three cruisers, the " Nautilus," " Argus," and " Hornet," acted in concert with Eaton, and a vigorous combined attack, April 27, drove the governor

[1] Life of Eaton, p. 328.

and his garrison from the town. Eaton received a
ball through the left wrist, but could not afford to be
disabled, for on the news of his arrival a large force
was sent from Tripoli to dislodge him; and he was
obliged to fight another little battle, May 13, which
would have been a massacre had not the ships' guns
held the Tripolitans in awe. Skirmishing continued
another month without further results. Eaton had
not the force to advance upon Tripoli, which was
nearly seven hundred miles to the westward, and
Hamet found no such popular support at Derne as
he had hoped.

What influence Eaton's success at Derne had on
the Pacha at Tripoli was never perfectly understood;
but the Pacha knew that Rodgers was making ready
for an assault, beside which the hottest of Preble's
bombardments would seem gentle; Eaton at Derne
with Hamet was an incessant and indefinite threat;
his own subjects were suffering, and might at any
moment break into violence; a change of ruler was
so common a matter, as Yusuf had reason to re-
member, that in the alternative of losing his throne
and head in one way or the other, he decided that
peace was less hazardous than war. Immediately
upon hearing that his troops had failed to retake
Derne, he entered into negotiations with Tobias Lear,
the American Consul-General at Algiers, who had
come to Tripoli for the purpose; and on this occasion the Pacha negotiated with all the rapidity that
could be wished. June 3, 1805, he submitted to the

disgrace of making peace without being expressly
paid for it, and Lear on his side consented to ran-
som the crew of the "Philadelphia" for sixty thousand dollars.

When Eaton learned what Lear had done, his anger
was great and not unreasonable. That Lear should
have made a treaty which sacrificed Eaton's Mahometan allies, and paid sixty thousand dollars for the
imprisoned seamen at a moment when Eaton held
Derne, and could, as he thought, with two hundred
marines on shore and an immense fleet at sea drive
the Pacha out of his dominions within six weeks,
was astonishing. Lear's only excuse was the fear of
causing a massacre of the "Philadelphia's" crew, —
a reason which Eaton thought unfounded and insuffi-
cient, and which was certainly, from a military point
of view, inadmissible. The treaty left the Mahometan allies at Derne to be massacred, and threw Hamet
on Eaton's hands. Deposited at Syracuse with a suite
of thirty persons without means of support, Caramelli
became a suppliant for alms to the United States
Congress. Eaton declared the treaty disgraceful, and
thenceforth his grievances against the government
took an acute form. The settlement of his accounts
was slow and difficult. He returned to America and
received great attentions, which made him none the
less loud in complaint, until at last he died in 1811 a
victim to drink and to craving for excitement. Eaton
was beyond question a man of extraordinary energies
and genius ; he had even the rare courage to dis-

please his own Federalist friends in 1807, because of
defending Jefferson who had done nothing for him,
but who at a critical moment represented in his eyes
the Union.

Meanwhile peace with Tripoli was obtained without
tribute, but at the cost of sixty thousand dollars, and
at the expense of Eaton and his desperate band of
followers at Derne. Hamet Caramelli received at last
a small sum of money from Congress, and through
American influence was some years afterward made
governor of Derne. Thus after four years of unceas-
ing effort the episode of the Tripolitan war came to
a triumphant end. Its chief result was to improve
the navy and give it a firmer hold on popular sympathy. If the once famous battles of Truxton and
the older seamen were ignored by the Republicans,
Preble and Rodgers, Decatur and Hull, became brilliant names ; the midnight death of Somers was told
in every farmhouse ; the hand-to-hand struggles of
Decatur against thrice his numbers inflamed the
imagination of school-boys who had never heard that
Jefferson and his party once declaimed against a
navy. Even the blindest could see that one more
step would bring the people to the point so much
dreaded by Jefferson, of wishing to match their forty-
fours against some enemy better worthy of their
powers than the pirates of Tripoli.

There was strong reason to think that this wish
might soon be gratified; for on the same day when
Lear, in the " Essex," appeared off Tripoli and began

his negotiation for peace, Monroe's travelling-carriage
rumbled through the gates of Madrid and began its
dusty journey across the plains of Castile, bearing an
angry and disappointed diplomatist from one humiliation to another.

INDEX TO VOLS. I. AND II.

END OF VOL. II.